★ ★ ★

PRAISES FOR

CREATIVITY FOR ENTERTAINERS

"Bruce "Charlie" Johnson understands the business of comedy entertainment. Better yet, he knows how to share his knowledge in a wonderfully effective manner." **– DUANE LAFLIN,** Past President International Fellowship of Christian Magicians

"When Bruce "Charlie" Johnson takes on a subject you know it will be well researched, clearly written, and filled with fascinating anecdotes to keep it interesting." **– NORM BARNHART,** Clowning Around Magazine

"Bruce "Charlie" Johnson, with his vast knowledge of the history of clowning, knows hundreds of routines and dozens of fun and zany ways to perform those routines. This book is an indispensable guide to all things pertaining to variety entertainment." **– DEBBIE O'CARROLL,** Territorial Vice-President for Massachusetts International Brotherhood of Magicians

CREATIVITY FOR
ENTERTAINERS
VOLUME 4

COMEDY
TECHNIQUES
FOR VARIETY ARTISTS

Written & Illustrated by

BRUCE JOHNSON A.K.A **CHARLIE** THE JUGGLING **CLOWN**

Printed in the United States of America
Illustrated by Bruce Johnson

ISBN (Paperback): 979-8-9862772-0-2
ISBN (Hardcover): 979-8-9862772-1-9

First Edition

10 9 8 7 6 5 4 3 2 1

Ohana is a Hawaiian word for family. It means more than just the family that we are born into. It also means the family of friends that we choose.

I DEDICATE THIS BOOK TO TWO FATHERS OF MY OHANA.

Bruce L. Johnson is the father of the family that I was fortunate to be born into.

Dr. Richard Snowberg is the father of the Clown Camp family, a group of peers and friends that I have been honored to be a part of since 1986.

★ ★ ★

TABLE OF CONTENTS

SEE ★ FOR EXERCISES

★ ★ ★

FOREWORD

BRUCE JOHNSON IS passionate, kind, honest, and meticulous
in life; these values also apply to his research and writing.
As an author, Bruce has an intrinsic ability to present the ped-
agogy and history of the clown, variety arts, and circus in the
most extraordinary, understandable detail. This ability is directly
related to the fact Bruce has been a part of the very history he has
researched for over forty years. As a result, he views historical
content as both a dedicated historian and a talented performing
artist; the reader benefits immensely from Bruce walking the
walk, albeit humbly, in his mismatched clown shoes.

Keeping in touch with his creative spirit, Bruce is one of the
longest-running staff members with Clown Camp, the clown and
variety arts training program founded by Dr. Richard Snowberg
in 1981. Over 5,000 people have attended the program. Clown
Camp participants have celebrated Bruce's exemplary work in
the classroom and on stage for many years.

I have grown as a performing artist through Bruce's books and thoughtful guidance. Reading any of his books is, without a doubt, time well spent for your performance and audience. So, find a comfy space and allow this book to help you embrace the past, the present, and the future of your craft.

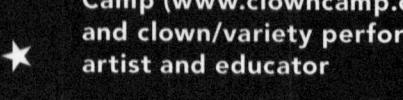

★ **KENNY AHERN**

★ Managing Director, Clown
Camp (www.clowncamp.org)
and clown/variety performing
★ artist and educator

★   ★   ★

INTRODUCTION

BROTHER LOOSE & DIMM

SOME PEOPLE FEEL that being accused of not having a sense of humor is an insult. Everyone wants to be thought of as a funny person.

There are many reasons why comedy is an asset to a variety artist.

Randy Pryor kept telling his juggling students, "Flash is Cash. Yucks are Bucks." I have discovered that being able to provide comedy opens more opportunities for me. I was hired to provide a comedy magic act during a concert by a group of barber shop quartets and choruses. I have also been scheduled many times to perform a comedy juggling act during a show performed by magicians who performed very little comedy. I have represented the United States in international clown performances. Often those shows would include one serious magic or juggling act. We judge things by contrast. The presence of a comedy act during a serious show enhances the dramatic effect of the other acts. A serious act during a comedy show enhances the humor of the other acts. If you perform a solo show, I think it is more effective if you include contrasting serious and comedy routines.

Comedy helps form connections. A psychological study showed that if a couple laughed together during their first date, they were more likely to go on a second date. I know that my wife's favorite friends are all ones that are able to make her laugh, and who she can make laugh. Including humor in your act helps you connect with your audience, and helps unite your audience.

Many variety artists use their skills as a teaching tool. This is particularly true in library and school shows that may require an educational component. Some entertainers use their skills to teach safety, character development, or spiritual lessons. Humor can be a very effective teaching tool, especially if the humor is closely related to the lesson.

I was a first-grade teacher one year in the Bible Study Fellowship Children's Program. The topic that year was the life and work of Moses. Early in the year, we studied the ten plagues in Egypt that led to the Exodus. We needed to review that information periodically. My teaching partner prepared a True/False quiz. One of the questions was "The plague of ladybugs." All of the kids laughed at that because they knew that ladybugs are harmless. We told them that it was the plague of locusts, another bug whose name began with the letter L. When we reviewed the material again a few weeks later, none of the students could remember all ten of the plagues, but every one remembered the locusts. It was the only one that every one remembered because they all remembered the lady bug joke which reminded them of the other insect starting with the letter "L."

International Clown Hall of Fame Inductee Bert Williams said, "I do not believe there is any such thing as innate humor. It has to be developed by hard work and study, just as every other human quality..."

No matter how much experience you have creating comedy, you can increase your ability to add humor to your life and art by studying how it has been created and performed, and by practice yourself. That is the purpose of this book.

It is a course in adding more comedy to a variety arts act for entertaining a family audience. It is not a book on performing standup comedy. I have limited experience with that performance style. Also, standup comedy is the subject of many books.

According to Steve Allen, "There is no one right way to make people laugh."

My intention is not to force you to do it the way that I do it. I hope to give you options that help you explore and discover the way that is right for you. I also hope that I help you avoid taking the wrong paths.

I have seen many performers whose humor falls flat or actually alienates their audience. I was fortunate that my first instructors steered me away from some common mistakes.

I have included some of my own routines in this book. That is to demonstrate that this is practical material that you can use. It is not just theory that I have copied from somewhere else.

Evaluate everything that I have written, and then decide if it is relevant to your own performances. No instructor or author is perfect. This book is a greatly expanded version of *Comedy Techniques for Entertainers*, a book that I wrote in 1986. I have learned a lot about creating and performing comedy since then. I have learned that there were some errors in that original version, and have corrected them here.

I have tried to verify everything. If I read something, I tested it with my own experiences. If I thought I had learned something from my experiences and observations, I did research to see if others had observed the same thing.

I have tried to explain where I have learned something, and provide samples of it being used. I have learned a lot by reading comic strips, listening to classic radio comedy, and watching movies and television programs. Media, in particular internet platforms, have made them currently accessible. That means you can study these examples yourself. Unfortunately, I have not always been able to identify the original broadcast dates of radio and television programs.

By studying entertainment history, we can learn what those who went before us learned by trial and error without having to make the same mistakes ourselves. Understanding comedy will strengthen your efforts and reveal new options.

This book is the result of a lifetime of study and practice. My mother said that comedy shows were always my favorite television programs. I loved variety arts growing up.

I didn't just want to observe it. I wanted to know how it was created. My family would frequently visit Knott's Berry Farm when I was growing up. Tony Kemeny performed a puppet show in a gypsy wagon at the park. On hot days, he would leave the back door ajar to provide a little ventilation. While the rest of my family sat in benches in front of the stage watching the show, I snuck around back to peek through the opening and watched how Tony performed the show. I was particularly fascinated by how he switched puppets.

I loved watching "The Magic Land of Allakkazam" on television. It was sponsored by Kellogg's. I learned my first magic tricks in second grade when directions for some tricks were printed on the back of Kellogg's cereal boxes to promote the TV show. A year later, I got my first magic kit. I have studied magic ever since then.

I also loved animation, especially that produced by the Walt Disney Studios. About the same time that I started studying magic, my parents gave me *Walt Disney The Art of Animation* by Bob Thomas. That sparked my interest in studying animation history. I have read everything that I could find on that subject. I wanted to know more than just how the image of movement was created. I wanted to know how the characters were developed and the humor was written.

I became a Cub Scout when I was eight-years-old. That year I appeared as a clown for the first time when my Den performed a circus style barber skit. I continued to perform skits at Cub Scout events, and later at Boy Scout meetings and campfires. I didn't realize it at the time, but many of the skits that I was learning were based on traditional clown acts. When I was in Junior High, I began writing my own original skits for scout events. Looking back, they weren't great, but they were the beginning.

I have heard many people talk about the importance of lifelong learning. However, my father taught it to me by his example. At the age of 80, he decided to pursue magic as a hobby. He told me that he wanted something to do in the evening besides watch TV. So, he practiced magic every evening. He eventually did two public performances of magic.

A few years after he began studying magic, my father attended a class that I taught on origami at California Clown Campin'. He became interested in origami. During the last week of his life, he was my roommate when I was on the Clown Camp staff. Every evening, while I prepared my visual aids for my next day of classes, he folded paper. The next day he presented those models to Clown Camp participants and to employees of the university that hosts Clown Camp. He thanked the employees for the work they were doing in support of the clowns. When he passed away two days after Clown Camp ended, I received a sympathy card signed by many of the university employees.

Following my father's example, I am continuing my education. In the past year I have been learning to play a musical instrument called a kalimba and to spin poi balls. I have started playing with how to use those new skills in my performances. I have continued to write new comedy material, either for my own use or for others.

I have continued to study comedy and showmanship. In the past month, I have read two books that are relevant. One is *Clown: The Physical Comedian*, by Joe Dieffenbacher. Joe's descriptions of lessons learned crystalized for me some concepts that I had observed in my own performances but never expressed. His book is a great companion to this one. I focus a lot on verbal humor while Joe avoids verbal humor. He concentrates on communicating using your body. His students create sounds but don't utilize actual words. Combing both approaches will give you a great variety of tools to use in connecting with and entertaining your audience.

The other book I read in the past month is *The Haunted Mansion: Imagineering a Disney Classic* by Jason Surrell. The book details the tension between people who thought Disneyland's Haunted Mansion should be scary and people who thought it should be humorous. It was combining both approaches that made it one of the most popular amusement park attractions around the world. It has been included in every location where a Disney Magic Kingdom has been built. Surrell describes how in each new location they had to get to know their audience and personalize the attraction instead of merely duplicating what they had already created. This book also emphasized the importance of telling a story in entertainment. I have not included information from that book in this text, but it amplifies some of the things that I have written.

Just writing comedy is not enough. I know that I am not the best judge of my own material. It is important to perform some of your material to see how the audience responds. Fanny Brice said, "Your audience gives you everything you need. There is no director who can direct you like an audience."

Be sure that you pay attention to your audience. One of the other performers in a variety show was portraying a mafia type character. He spoke in a husky whisper. Audience members kept yelling for him to speak up because they couldn't understand anything that he said. When he came off stage, he whispered to me, "They don't understand. This is how my character speaks."

No, he didn't understand. The audience was telling him that he made the wrong choice and that voice was not working. Nobody responded to his jokes because they didn't know what they were. His act was a waste of the audience's time.

It is important to remember that as an entertainer, you are there to meet the needs of the audience, not the other way around.

Joe E. Brown said, "The best comedy is that which the audience itself helps to build. The experienced comedian is always on the lookout for the hints and suggestions that come to him through audience reaction."

I have gotten many ideas from a comment made by an audience member during a performance. In one of my juggling bits, after I have juggled three balls, I hold up a sign asking if the audience would like to see my juggle with four. Then I juggle with two balls and a large number four cut out of plywood. After the laughter, I do a short four-ball juggling routine. One day a man yelled, "Can you juggle with five?" I couldn't do it then. However, the next day I cut a number five out of plywood. I kept it in my prop trunk for years. I didn't get to use it often. However, when somebody challenged me to juggle with five, I got tremendous laughter by being able to pull that number out.

I have also learned a lot of comedy lines from audience members. When somebody yells out a funny line, I lead the audience in applauding them. I always have a pad of paper and a pen in a pocket of my costume. I get a laugh when I pull it out to write down that person's comment. What the audience doesn't realize is that I am writing it down so I don't forget it. Then I use it myself when I have the next opportunity.

When you insert a new comedy routine or line into a normal performance, put it between two existing routines that you know are sure fire. The first routine warms up the audience so they are ready to respond positively. If the response to your new routine is not as good as you wish, the next routine will win back the audience. Most of the people will forget the routine that fell flat.

Of course, if you get great response the first time you perform an idea you know that it is a good idea. If the response is not what you wish, don't give up too soon. When I introduce a new routine, I am nervous so I don't perform it as smoothly as possible. If it falls flat, I don't know if it was because my presentation was flawed or if the idea itself was flawed. It can take several performances to decide. Sometimes when I believe in an idea, I will occasionally try different presentations over the years. Eventually, I figure out a way that works. Then what was a flawed idea becomes part of my permanent repertoire.

When most authors talk about writing comedy, they are referring to verbal routines. However, many of the same techniques can be applied to nonverbal variety acts.

Here is a description of one of my nonverbal juggling routines. I will refer back to it in describing applications of the comedy techniques.

Naughty Ball & Clay Ball

I BEGIN JUGGLING WITH a yellow ball and two red balls. I toss the yellow ball wide to my left so that I miss it. It bounces away from me. I retrieve it and begin juggling again. After a few throws, I toss it wide to my left again so I miss it a second time. Depending upon the circumstances, I sometimes step on the bouncing ball. That makes it bounce back high enough that I can catch it. Otherwise, I simply chase the ball and grab it. Then I shake my finger at the ball admonishing it for not behaving.

I begin juggling again. I toss the yellow ball wide to my left a third time. However, now at the last second, I extend my left arm straight out so I catch the ball. I continue juggling. When the yellow ball is in my right hand again, I throw it wide to my left. I extend my left arm to catch it at the last moment, and continue juggling.

When the yellow ball is in my right hand, I throw it a little higher than normal. I let it fall and hit the floor in front of me. When it bounces high enough, I resume juggling. I throw the yellow ball a little bit higher again, let it bounce, and resume juggling. I throw one of the red balls a lot higher, and let it fall to the floor. It bounces higher than before, and when it comes back down, I continue juggling. I throw the next red ball extremely high, and let it fall to the floor. It hits with a splat and does not bounce. I follow its expected path up into the air with my eyes.

I remain looking upward until somebody calls my attention to the ball on the ground. Then I pick it up. I decide to test it out. I throw it down hard. Once again, it just splats against the ground. I pick it up, put it in my prop case, and get another red ball. When I test it out by throwing it down, it bounces high into the air. I catch it.

I begin juggling again. After a few throws, I toss all three balls higher than normal. I let them all fall to the floor and bounce. When the first ball peaks and comes back down, I catch it and make the next throw. I catch each ball in sequence and throw it again so that I am back into a normal cascade juggling pattern.

I let all three balls bounce a second time, and return to a normal cascade pattern.

Suddenly the yellow ball flies wide to my left. Again, I catch it at the last possible moment and continue juggling. I do a second wide throw with the yellow ball, catch it, and continue juggling. The yellow ball flies wide to the right a third time. I catch it again. However, instead of tossing it so that I continue with a normal three ball pattern, I move my left hand behind me hiding the yellow ball. I am now juggling the two red balls with just my right hand. Each ball moves up and down in a straight line while by right hand moves back and forth alternately catching and tossing the balls. I can't figure out what has happened to the yellow ball. I start scratching my head with my left hand. I notice that the yellow ball is in that hand.

I try to return the yellow ball to the juggling pattern. However, I don't let go of it. I raise my left hand up and down in unison with the rise and fall of the red ball that is in the center. I continue this a few times. Jugglers call this a 2-1 Fake.

Then I pause briefly with the left hand. I move the ball over so it is above the red ball that is closest to the center of the body. I lift and lower my hand so the yellow ball stays a few inches above the red ball. It creates the illusion that a short piece of string is connecting the two balls. Jugglers call this a Yo-Yo.

I finally toss the yellow ball into the air and begin a three-ball cascade pattern. Suddenly I toss the yellow ball so it goes higher than normal arching over the other two balls. I toss it back in a high arch. The yellow ball is following a rainbow shaped path while the other two balls follow an infinity sign path. I repeat that long enough for the audience to understand what is happening. Frequently, the audience will react in some way to this trick.

Then I begin performing a trick called a Triangle. In this trick, the red balls follow the normal infinity sign path, while the yellow ball follows a path that forms a triangular shape in the air.

Finally, I perform the Triangle continuously with all three balls. This looks very complicated. I act as if I am becoming confused by the actions of the balls. I catch all three balls, and then strike a pose. The audience always breaks into applause at this point.

When I was performing a juggling act in a circus, I would continue with another juggling routine. When I was performing my solo variety show, I would often follow this routine with a magic routine.

THE EXERCISES

THE DISCUSSION OF comedy techniques is not the most important part of this book. The exercises are more important. The only real way to learn to create comedy is to actually work at creating it.

Creativity is like a muscle. The more that you exercise it the stronger it becomes. Attempt each exercise, even if you don't think you will use the results in your own performances. That attempt will increase your ability to write comedy which improves the material that you might potentially perform.

I encourage you to start a notebook for recording your responses to the exercises. Having that on paper is better than entering it into a digital device. Flipping actual pages of paper provides glimpses of a variety of ideas increasing the chance that serendipity will lead you to new discoveries.

An idea quota is the minimum number of ideas you are going to try to generate. It is useful because it keeps you engaged. Creativity can be thought of as a flow of ideas. In general, you have a sudden burst of inspiration. Then the flow gets clogged. The rate of new ideas slows and they don't seem to be as good as your first ideas. If you continue working the clog eventually gets cleared and new ideas flow. Often those later ideas are your best ones.

Don't be discouraged if all of your responses to the exercises are not great ones. I have used ten as the idea quota for many of the exercises. Creativity experts talk about the Ten Percent Rule. That is an estimate that only about ten percent of your ideas will be useable. So, if you write ten jokes, on average one of them will be a good one. To me that is freeing. I know that every joke or idea does not have to be good. If I write enough jokes some of them will be useable.

Actually, if my goal is to create a five-minute routine, I write as much as possible. I often end up with a ten-minute routine. Then I edit it myself. I start performing it before audiences, and edit it further. Finally, I distill it down to a five-minute routine that is only the best material that I can write. I think of it as the Goldilocks principle. Having something to compare it to helps me determine what is just right.

I was graduated by California State University – Long Beach with a BA in Technical Theater. Herb Camburn taught many of my classes. When he gave out an assignment, it was the minimum requirement. Herb did not grade us on how much we knew, but by how much we learned. He expected his students to set their own requirements based on their experience. If you had no experience with a process or project, you could do what he had assigned. If you had more experience, he expected you to do something more difficult to challenge yourself. He said if we depended upon his assignments to challenge us, our development would stop when the class ended. However, if we learned to continue challenging ourselves, our development as theater artists could continue throughout our lifetime.

So, these exercises are the minimum requirement. If you have more experience, go beyond that. For example, if you have written Knock Knock jokes before and discover that you quickly reach the idea quota that I set, then set a new quota to challenge yourself to accomplish more.

Don't think of these as just exercises. Approach them as potential inspiration for something that you might perform. As it is presented, an exercise may not have an obvious application. However, it might start a train of thought that will lead you to something else that you can apply.

The exercises are varied. In some you will write individual jokes. In others you will write a brief routine. In others you will play an improvisation game as part of a group. If you don't belong to a variety arts organization, you can still play the games. I have introduced improvisation as a party game at an event where the guests were not entertainers. They have a lot of fun, and I get to exercise my ability to create material.

You can also form an informal group studying this book. The group would meet occasionally to share their responses to the exercises. That way you can encourage each other. The ideas of others may inspire you to create further new ideas. It also provides you with an audience to test the effectiveness of your ideas.

Be generous with your ideas. When you have an idea that doesn't fit your style, suggest it to somebody who might be able to use it.

People that I have suggested ideas to have reciprocated by suggesting to me ideas that they thought I might be able to use.

Also, other people often see something in my idea that I didn't realize was there. My idea inspired them to create a different idea. When they told me what they had done, that inspired me to create another different idea. By sharing ideas, we created two or more ideas that neither one of us would have created by working alone.

As my career evolves, the requirements for ideas that I can use changes. In the early 1990's, I met Dottie Goldfarb. She was a professional violinist who wanted to become a clown. She didn't know how to make her violin playing funny. So, I helped her develop some musical clown routines. I had the pleasure of seeing her perform them successfully. She has since passed away. I recently started learning to play a musical instrument called a kalimba. Now I will be able to use some of the ideas that I developed for her in my own performances. I will perform them in her memory.

★   ★   ★

FAVORITE COMIC STRIPS

FILM DIRECTOR FREDERICO Fellini said, "I learned the essence of comedy from comic strips."

My father used to refer to the comic pages in our local newspaper as my higher education. Throughout this book you will find examples of things that I learned by reading comic strips. Now you will start that process yourself.

☞ Collect 25 individual comic panels or strips that you like. Don't just collect 25 examples. Choose ones that you think are really funny. You will be working with those strips in other exercises in this book.

There is another reason for reading comic strips every day. Humor works as a mental warm up. The majority of jokes start with one meaning of a word and then switch meanings. For example, "Which animals took the most luggage on Noah's Ark? The elephants because they took their trunks".

That joke starts by defining "trunk" as a piece of luggage, and then switches to defining it as a part of an elephant's anatomy. Switching definitions like that forces you to be more mentally flexible which helps you to be more creative.

Compilations of comic strips, often celebrating an anniversary of the strip's debut, are great resources. They provide you with a treasure trove of comedy to study. Often those books include comments by the artist detailing how they work and the type of humor that they employ. I have learned a lot by collecting and reading those books.

DEFINITION OF A JOKE

MELVIN HELITZER DEFINES a joke as "anything that makes PEOPLE laugh. "

That is an important definition to remember when talking about comedy techniques. Certain techniques, which are used frequently by comedians, have been identified. People do tend to laugh at these techniques, which is why they are used so often. However, using those techniques does not guarantee laughter.

Also, every joke does not use one of these techniques. When I began clowning, I was working my way through college as an assistant janitor at a church. So, I decided to become a clown janitor. My oldest sister became a clown at the same time. She decided that she wanted to be a sailor clown. For our first parade appearance, we decided that I would carry a mop and bucket. When I set my bucket down, she would go fishing in it and catch a rubber boot. In order to have something to do, I began mopping the street. I quickly discovered that I had to move to the side of the street so every audience member could see what she was doing. About half way through the parade, I accidentally mopped off someone's shoe. They started to laugh. So, a little further down the route, I mopped off someone's shoe on purpose. They laughed. I experimented with that, and discovered that people would almost always laugh when I cleaned off their feet. I began to always carry a feather duster with me.

Now over forty-five years later, I know that if somebody does not laugh, I can often break the ice by dusting off their feet. I have never been able to figure out why people think it is funny. However, since it makes people laugh, it is a joke.

I recently heard from a woman that I met in 1974. She was in a junior majorette group that appeared in many of the same parades in which I appeared. She wrote, "I remember you fondly because you brightened my childhood by dusting off my shoes."

Patty Wooten is a nurse who turned to clowning following traumatic events in her life. She felt that she needed some source of fun. She attended a continuing education clown course at San Diego State University. Nursing homes were some of the first places where she performed. As she experienced the effects of laughter in her life, and witnessed what it did for the nursing home residents, she became interested in the study of humor. She became involved in the Association of Applied Therapeutic Humor. Patty began networking with those who were conducting research into the links between humor and physical health and between humor and mental health. She eventually served as the AATH President and was honored with their Lifetime Achievement Award. She taught nurses how to use humor in their profession, both as a personal coping tool to counter the stress of their job and as a way to aid their patients in their recovery. She taught clowns the benefit of humor and how they could become part of a team caring for hospital patients and nursing home residents.

Patty taught a three-way test for the effectiveness of humor. She said it must be the appropriate material at the appropriate time for the appropriate audience. I had the pleasure of attending many different educational programs taught by Patty. When she was talking to an audience of nurses, her jokes contained many more references to body functions than when she was speaking to a lay audience. She warned the nurses that some jokes they would tell each other in order to relieve stress might be resented if relatives of a patient overheard them.

When Patty first started clowning, she created her Nancy Nurse character. It was an exaggerated nurse with oversized medical equipment. She started performing as Nancy Nurse for other nurses. They thought it was hilarious because they could identify with her. They suggested that she visit patients as Nancy Nurse. However, Patty discovered that patients were overwhelmed by this character. It was not appropriate for them. So, she created a second character she named Nurse Kindheart. She was a gentle character who spoke with a British accent. She was the compassionate nurse everyone wished they had.

According to Patty Wooten, there are three types of humor: groping, coping, and hoping.

Groping Humor, sometimes referred to as Gallows Humor, is protective humor. It provides comic balance. You laugh in spite of the situation. It gives you emotional distance so you are not overwhelmed. It is a declaration that the situation may be terrible, but it will not defeat you. Patty said, "To joke about the situation is sometimes the only power that you have."

A way Patty explained the use of Groping Humor is to close one eye and hold your hand up about six inches from your face. Look straight ahead. How much can you see? Now move your hand so it is an arm's length from your face. Now how much can you see while looking straight ahead? Think of your hand as the problem that you have encountered. When you are emotionally close to it, that is about all that you can see. When you are more emotionally distant, you can see more around the problem. The problem hasn't changed. However, your perspective has changed so it is not as overwhelming. That is what humor accomplishes.

An example she gave of Groping Humor was a home surrounded by water following Hurricane Katrina. A sign on the front of the house said, "For Sale Waterfront Property."

Coping Humor is aggressive humor. It provides comic relief. You are laughing at the situation. It allows you to express hostility and release tension. One performance theory is that you identify an "enemy" that you have in common with your audience, and then use your humor to attack that.

Patty would ask nurses, "Do you know the difference between the PLO and an HMO? You can negotiate with the PLO." (PLO stands for Palestinian Liberation Organization, a terrorist group. HMO stands for Health Management Organization, an insurance group issuing restrictions health care workers must follow in order to qualify for payment.)

Hoping Humor, the third type, is often gentle humor. It provides comic vision. You have accepted the situation. Instead of attacking an enemy, you bring people together through shared experiences.

Just getting a laugh is not enough. Melvin Helitzer said, "Humor is successful only when it entertains the public." That is a higher standard that many performers fail to understand.

★ ★ ★

EXERCISE

Favorite Comic Strips Part 2

☞ Look at each comic strip that you have collected. Why do you think that it is funny? Write down your response to each cartoon.

ALL LAUGHTER IS NOT EQUAL

However, ALL LAUGHTER is not equal or even desirable.

Dr. Raymond A. Moody, Jr. studied humor trying to document its healing power. He learned that laughter is not always associated with health. He discovered that a single, distinctive type of aberrant laugher is associated with three neurological disorders: pseudobulbar palsy, amyotrophic lateral sclerosis (Lou Gehrig's disease), and multiple sclerosis. Unusual laughter are also symptoms of Wilson's disease, epilepsy, pre-senile dementia, Klein-Levin syndrome, drug abuse, and some types of toxic poisoning. Dr. Moody said that one of the effects of sleep deprivation is laughing excessively at things you would not otherwise find funny. He also discovered that inappropriate or excessive laughter is a symptom of several psychological disorders.

Dr. Moody discovered that there are some cases where humor, and laughter, may be harmful. Patients with narcolepsy, a sleep disorder, find that sometimes laughter can trigger cataplexy, a condition where sudden loss of muscle tone causes them to collapse and not be able to move although they remain aware of their surroundings.

Tietze's Syndrome is an inflammation of the cartilage connecting the ribs to the breastbone. Laughter causes intense pain in Tietze's Syndrome patients that can scare them into believing they are having a heart attack.

There are also some psychological conditions that create Laughter Resistance.

However, humor, the psychological response, and laughter, the physical response, have great benefits for the majority of people.

Patty Wooten described different types of laughter.

1. Tee hee is a pressure releasing laugh. It is often a sign of embarrassment.
2. Ha, ha, huh is polite humor. You don't find it funny, but you feel that you need to fill the silence. You may be trying to encourage the person telling the joke. You might be trying to cover up that you have been offended.
3. Hee, hee is a reaction to being surprised.
4. Ho, ho is deep heart felt laughter. It is something that triggers your sense of mirth.

Famous comedians have repeatedly stated that the quality of the laugh is important. They said you can get a big laugh and alienate your audience at the same time.

During one of the Laugh-Makers Variety Arts Conferences, I helped produce five different family variety shows. There was a different show, open to the public, each night of the conference. It seemed like every magician and clown in those shows used a prop called a Breakaway Wand. It is a magic wand that looks normal, but when you hand it to an audience volunteer it breaks into several segments and hangs limply. The performer takes the wand back, and restores it to its rigid condition. They hand it to the volunteer and it falls apart a second time. During the conference, all of their volunteers were children.

While the Breakaway Wand kept getting laughter during the week, I noticed that the amount of laughter started declining each time it was used. Also, after the second show, the conference directors began getting complaints from parents about children consistently being the target of that practical joke. On the last night, a magician chose an older child who had been to all of the previous shows. This boy had been able to figure out how the wand worked. When the magician handed it to the boy, it broke. The boy immediately restored the wand, and handed it back to the magician. That meant that the wand broke in the magician's hand. The audience erupted in cheers. One of their representatives had defended them by turning the tables on the magician.

It is important to remember that a volunteer is a proxy for the rest of the audience. Audience members will feel they have been treated the way you have treated the volunteer. If one of your jokes is at the expense of an audience volunteer, you may get a laugh at that moment. But the rest of the audience may resent you because they feel like you have attacked them. If you treat the audience volunteer with respect and make them look good, the rest of the audience will like you.

Effective humor helps you connect with others. However, humor can have the opposite effect if someone is offended by your material. It may create a wall that you may not be able to overcome. I attended a worship service on Mother's Day where the pastor decided to start his sermon with jokes about women. His attempted humor put women down. I could tell that he completely lost the attention of the congregation. I saw everyone fidgeting and checking their watches throughout the sermon. Afterwards, I asked a woman what she thought of a statement he had made in the middle of the sermon. She said, "I don't know. I stopped listening after he told his jokes."

According to Patty Wooten, there are four topics that are most likely to offend people: religion, sex, politics, and race.

Her advice was that if you sense you offended your audience, you should acknowledge that by saying, "I'm sorry, I didn't mean to offend you. I was trying to lighten things up for you."

Then Patty suggests that you back off and analyze the interaction. Was it inappropriate material because it involved one of the four offensive areas? Was it appropriate material but delivered at the wrong time?

What is offensive is often determined by culture. Some Western observers have described clowning in Southeast Asia as being obscene. James R. Brandon, in *Theatre in Southeast Asia*, wrote, "It is considered bad taste in Southeast Asia to demonstrate sexual familiarity publicly through kissing, stroking, or other physical contact. On the other hand, references to physical organs and bodily functions are not considered offensive on the stage as they are in the West. In short, sexual conduct as shown in the drama of Southeast Asia is neither stricter nor looser than in the West, it is just different in certain ways."

On one of my trips to perform in Asia, our local contact told us not to make a gesture commonly used in America because in his country it had an obscene meaning. The gesture did not have that meaning in the USA.

Each entertainer must decide where they are going to draw the line for what is appropriate. Decency was one of Jack Benny's main qualities. While he was in England on vacation, a young woman swam across the English Channel. To cut down on drag, she didn't wear a swimsuit. Instead, her body was covered with grease to protect her from the cold. After he returned from vacation, Jack's writers came up with a line claiming that he had gone to England in order to grease her up. Jack laughed at the joke, and agreed that it was very funny. Then he edited it out of the script because he thought the young woman might be embarrassed by it.

I attended a Conference on Humor and Creativity, sponsored by the Humor Project. One of the speakers talked about the development of the sense of humor. He said a baby first responds to a smile with a smile. Then they laugh at a surprise. For example, playing peek-a-boo. Next, they enjoy forbidden subject humor. Then they enjoy word play. Finally, they begin to understand and enjoy irony and satire.

People lose their sense of humor in the reverse order that it is developed. First, they lose the ability to understand irony and satire. Then they no longer enjoy word play, leaving forbidden subject humor. That is why there are so many stereotypically dirty old men and women. When they lose that ability, they respond to surprise. Finally, their only response is a smile.

When entertainers perform at a nursing home for the first time, they are often disappointed by the apparent lack of response. However, if you understand the development of the sense of humor, you know that those who smile are responding in the best way that they can. People get excited when a baby smiles. A smile from a senior citizen is just as valuable. Medical science has confirmed that there are many mental and physical benefits from humor and laughter. When you entertain at a nursing home, you are making a contribution to their quality of life.

★ ★ ★

IDENTIFYING YOUR SENSE OF HUMOR

☞ Now study the list of what you like about your collection of comic strips. Are there any patterns or trends? Do several of the strips have something besides their creator in common?

☞ This is one way of identifying your sense of humor. The jokes that you like the most tend to be ones that resonate with some aspect of your personality. That may be the type of joke that you will be most successful at creating.

☞ Also, knowing what you think is funny will help you in performance. If you think something is funny, you will have greater confidence in presenting it.

Set Up & Surprise

Surprise is an often talked about element of humor. The majority of jokes can be described by saying, "You cause the audience to expect one thing, and then surprise them by doing something else. "

For example, "Can you tell me how long cows should be milked? The same as short ones."

The way the question is worded, people expect the answer to reflect the length of time required to milk a cow. Instead, they are surprised that the answer refers to the height of the cow.

Setting up a gag can then be defined as causing the audience to think and expect what you want them to. The surprise called the punchline, or sometimes simply the punch. Some American clowns call it the blow off.

There are many rules of three in comedy writing and performing. One of them is set up, set up, punch. According to this formula, you introduce what you want them to think, and then reinforce that thought. Finally, you reveal the surprise.

Here are two examples of one application of this rule of three.

(SET UP)
TEACHER: What's the opposite of misery?
STUDENT: Joy.

(SET UP)
TEACHER: That's right, What's the opposite of sorrow?
STUDENT: Happiness.

(PUNCH)
TEACHER: Right. What's the opposite of woe?
STUDENT: Giddy Up!

(SET UP)
TEACHER: What's the plural of man?
STUDENT: Men.

(SET UP)
TEACHER: What's the plural of woman?
STUDENT: Women.

(PUNCH)
TEACHER: What's the plural of child?
STUDENT: Twins

Set Up, Set Up, Punch is often used in verbal comedy. By studying comic strips, I discovered an important variation for variety artists, it is a visual set up, a verbal set up, and punch.

An example is the April 10, 1986 Dennis the Menace comic panel by Hank Ketcham. The drawing is a classroom where the teacher is pointing to pictures of farm animals drawn on a chalk board. She asks, "And what else did MacDonald have on his farm?"

Dennis answers, "French Fries!"

In the way Ketcham presented the cartoon, the drawings on the chalk board immediately cause you to start thinking in terms of animals. The teacher's question reminds you of the song "Old McDonald had a Farm" where a different animal is mentioned in each verse. Then Ketcham surprises you by changing the definition of MacDonald from a farmer to a chain of burger restaurants.

Here is how I applied that principle to a traditional clown gag. When I performed this in a circus, I would enter carrying a covered wicker basket on a tray. The lid was ajar and the end of a flute was sticking out of the basket. Sometimes I would hear audience members predict, "He's going to be a snake charmer."

I would set the basket down on an elephant tub or the ring curb. Then I would turn the tray up revealing that it was actually a sign. The sign said, "Danger Baby Rattler."

I would set the sign down so it was still visible. Then I opened the basket. I would pause cautiously, and then quickly grab the end of the flute. I would put the end of the flute in my mouth, and start blowing a note. A toy baby's rattle would float up out of the basket.

Danger
Baby
Ratteler

The appearance of the props was my visual set up. The words on the sign where my verbal set up. I noticed something interesting. We tend to see what we expect to see. Sometimes I would hear young kids ask a parent what the sign said. They would read, "Danger Baby Rattlesnake." That is not what was on the sign, but the visual set up was so strong that was what they thought it said. That increased the surprise when the toy rattle appeared.

Being able to see and understand your set up and punch is vital in visual comedy. If you announce that you are going to produce a dove, and then produce a piece of Dove candy, you have to use a candy bar that is large enough for the audience to see and easily identify.

Sets of three colored juggling balls frequently come with one ball in each of the primary colors. That means that none of the balls stands out from the others so there isn't one that attracts audience attention. In my Naughty Ball juggling routine, I substitute a second red ball for the blue one. Now the yellow ball stands out from the others. Read the description of the routine again and see how that helps the audience understand that one ball is acting differently from the others. I also wear blue clothes when performing the routine so the balls stand out more when they are in front of my chest.

When working on a clown gag, ask yourself, how can I visually make the audience think what I want? How can I reinforce that image with a sign or patter? How can I reveal the surprise?

You need to make sure that the audience understands your set up. Magicians tend to refer to magic with scarves as "silk" magic. When I first started performing a routine where four scarves turned into a banner depicting the front of a Tide detergent box. I used a sign announcing "Silks that become Tide." I overheard people reading the sign out loud saying, "slicks that become Tide." I realized that children weren't familiar with the word silks. So, I broke the habit of using that word in reference to that type of magic. Instead, I say, "scarves."

When I changed the wording of the sign, I also spelled become as "bekum." Having two misspelled words fits my character and doesn't call attention to the word tied being spelled as Tide.

☛ Look at how you set up your gags. Does your audience understand the set up? How can you strengthen the set up? How can you increase the impression you want to make? How can you make it less likely that audience members will guess the surprise?

★　★　★

ANALYZING CARTOON SET UPS

☛ Analyze your comic strip collection. What is the set up in each one? Is there a visual set up? How are words used to set up the joke? Did the artist use a rule of three? How is the surprise revealed?

TIMING

IMING IS A frequently mentioned element of comedy.

One aspect of timing involves setting up your gag. You give the audience enough time to think about what you want them to, but not enough time to guess what the surprise will be. In the cow example, you pause after the question to allow the audience to ponder the length of time needed to milk a cow, then you spring the punch line. Without the pause, the audience wouldn't think about the meaning of "long" and there would not be any surprise.

That is the function of a Straightman. The Straightman often repeats what the comic says to provide that pause. It is the Straightman's responsibility to determine how long the pause should be. Solo performers sometimes use a prop to provide the pause. Phyllis Diller carried a cigarette in a long holder. After she set up a joke, she would stop to tap off the ash, and then deliver the punch line.

Another aspect of timing involves laughter. You must pause after your joke to allow the audience time to laugh. If you start talking while they are still laughing, they will stop to listen to you. The audience doesn't want to miss anything.

The same is true with applause. A pause for applause does not mean just being silent. Often it means not moving. If you move, the audience thinks you are going to do something else so they stop laughing and applauding to pay attention to what you are doing next. This is particularly important if you are playing a character that is not speaking.

If you interrupt the laughter of your audience often enough, they won't start laughing after a joke. In effect, you've taught them not to laugh.

An opposite approach to timing was sometimes used on Jack Benny's radio program. Milt Josefsberg said Jack's writers referred to it as "Jack Jumps In".

On the October 13, 1946 episode of the "Jack Benny Show", Dennis Day said, "He's mad because I am alluring."

Jack responded, "It's silly for a man to say he's alluring."

Phil Harris asked, "What's wrong with that? My doctor said I'm alluring to strawberries."

"THAT'S ALLERGIC!" Jack shouted immediately before the audience had time to laugh.

According to Josefsberg, they knew that Jack could not speak while the audience was laughing because that would squelch their response. If he waited until the laughter peaked to correct Phil, it would be anticlimactic. So, the only possibility was to rush his correction before the audience began laughing. The added benefit was that it made Jack's character seem very eager to correct Phil whenever he had a chance. Also, by correcting Phil's mistake the entire audience understood the joke immediately. If individual audience members had to figure out what Phil meant, the start of laughter would have been staggered. Some people might have stopped laughing before others began.

Some comedians use a prop to help with timing laughing. Doing nothing while you wait for laughter can be uncomfortable. So, they gave themselves something to do. George Burns would puff on his cigar while the audience laughed. Would the use of a prop assist you in your timing? What would you use?

Another important use of timing creates the illusion that your character is real. The 1934 Disney cartoon titled "Playful Pluto" is a classic example. The cartoon was directed by Burt Gillett. In a sequence animated by Norm Ferguson, Pluto, the pup, gets tangled up with a piece of fly paper. For example, the paper is stuck to his right paw. He holds the paper down with his left paw, which allows him to pull his right paw free. However, now the paper is stuck to his left paw. During the entire sequence, Pluto keeps pausing. The pauses show that the dog is thinking about what to do next. The cartoon is considered a breakthrough in animation because for the first time a cartoon character appeared to have a thought process that made them seem real instead of just a drawing.

Lee "Juggles" Mullally was the Assistant Director at Clown Camp for many years. He was great at working with audience members on stage. Sometimes they did something truly unexpected. For example, one time he fanned out a deck of cards face up to show a woman that they were all different. She blurted out, "If I take one of those cards you will see which one it is."

In those situations, Lee would pause, look at the audience with a dead pan expression, and wait while they laughed. He told me that he let them think of their own punchline. Sometimes they laughed because they thought of something that would not fit his character, but he got their reaction without saying it. Then he would turn back to his audience volunteer with his response. Sometimes he had a joke, but more often he just took them seriously. With the woman who objected to the cards being face up, he said, "Oh, I guess maybe I should turn them over then."

Sometimes a pause is used to create emphasis and focus audience attention. In one version of my Scarves that Bekum Tide routine, I display four separate eighteen-inch scarves. I gather them up and squeeze them together. Suddenly, they transform into a thirty-six-inch scarf that has the Tide detergent logo painted on it. While performing the routine, I gather the individual scarves together. I do the move that switches the larger scarf for them. The fabric still looks like I am holding the separate scarves bundled together. I pause. I can tell that the audience attention sharpens then. Then I unfurl the Tide banner so it is visible for the first time. Then I pause again while the audience perceives what has happened. Those pauses act like a camera shutter freezing those images in the minds of the audience. It is kind of like the squares in a comic strip.

I use a silent script to help with my timing. That is what my character is thinking. During my Scarves that Bekum Tide routine, after I have gathered the scarves together, I think, "Now watch this. It is going to be amazing." Thinking that motivates the pause before I reveal that the scarves have been transformed. Also, although I don't actually say anything, I am having a conversation with the audience. Your expressions and body language communicate your thoughts.

When an act does not seem to be going over well with an audience, it is common to begin rushing to get that unpleasant experience over with quickly. Some people call that Rushitis. It is the worst thing that you can do because it ruins your timing. The rest of your jokes will fall flat because the audience does not have time to understand the set ups. I experienced that early in my circus career. We had an act that was not getting the response that it should. The other clowns began rushing to get it over with. The audience response tapered off more. The clowns began rushing even more. I tried to slow down the pace, but wasn't successful. Eventually, the act was taken out of the show.

If your audience is not responding as well as you hope, take a deep breath, and then purposely slow down a little. Look for an individual who is responding to you. Focus on them. Laugher is contagious. Soon people around them will begin laughing. Then identify a person in another section of the audience who is responding well. Focus on them briefly. Continue building up response in this way.

Another cause of rushing is a burst of adrenaline when you begin your performance. Randy Pryor taught his juggling students to place a stop sign in their act. That was something that caused them to pause and catch their breath. I used the Clay Ball gag. When the ball didn't bounce, I would look up into the air trying to find the ball. The audience always laughed at that point. I took a couple of slow deep breathes while they laughed. I thought to myself, "It's okay. They like me. Everything is going to be alright. Take it easy." That calmed me down and allowed me to control my timing. Your sense of time can become distorted while on stage. It seemed like the Clay Ball gag provided me with a long break, but watching video recordings of my shows convinced me that the pause was actually very short.

Sometimes it takes courage to wait for the audience. In my sorcerer's apprentice act, the magician has not shown up although his props have been set. The emcee asks me to watch the magician's props, while they search for the magician. As the emcee is leaving, I pick up a scarf from the magician's table. The emcee notices that, and says, "Charlie, put that back. I said watch, don't touch." I return the scarf to the table. Then I stand there motionless staring at the scarf. Sometimes it takes the audience a while to realize that I have taken the emcee literally and am actually watching the scarf. I don't move until I hear the audience laughing. Then I turn just my head to react to the audience. The rest of my body is motionless. While I am looking at the audience, the scarf flies from the table to my hand. That always causes a gasp from the audience. I look back at the table to see what has happened, and am surprised to see that the scarf is gone. Then I realize that it is back in my hand. That leads into my next magic effect.

In one of my card effects, I display four cards that each have a picture of a snowman. Then I reveal that the pictures have all changed to a snowman that has melted a third of the way. Next, I reveal that the pictures are now a snowman that has melted two thirds of the way. Finally, I display all four cards as blank. I can immediately make the picture of the complete snowman reappear. However, I have learned that it is best to pause. If they have enough time, an audience member will sometimes ask me to make the snowman come back. When I succeed in meeting their challenge, I get a greater audience response than when I am the one to decide to bring the snowman back.

☛ How can you improve the timing of your performances? Where should you add a pause? What can you do while pausing after the set up? What pose can you strike after the punchline to allow the audience to understand and either laugh or applaud? How can you use pauses to create the impression that you are thinking about what is happening? How can you use a stop sign in the beginning of your performance?

EXERCISE

SERIES OF FOUR

THIS JOKE FORMAT consists of four items. Johnny Hart frequently used this format in his "B.C." comic strip. In one strip, Willy walks into a cave with a "cave drawings" sign over the doorway. There are four drawings on the wall. Each drawing has a caption under it.

In this example, the first drawing is a clockface with the small hand at 12 and the large hand at 3. The caption is "Twelve Fifteen." The second drawing is a clockface with the small hand at 3 and the large hand at 8. The caption is "Three Twenty." The third drawing is a clockface with the small hand at 10 and the large hand at 4. The caption is "Ten Four." The fourth drawing is a silly drawing of a man's face. The caption is "Roger."

This is another example of set up, set up, punch. The relationship between the first and second drawing and the relationship between the second and third drawing are the set ups. The surprising relationship between the third and fourth drawing is the punchline. In the above example, the first two relationships are time of day. The last relationship is CB slang. (Citizen Band Radio was used by long distance drivers prior to cell phones. When talking on a CB radio, 10-4 meant "OK" and Roger meant "Received and Understood.")

This is also an example of combining visual set ups with verbal set ups.

Here is an example that I created.

☞ Now write your own ending to

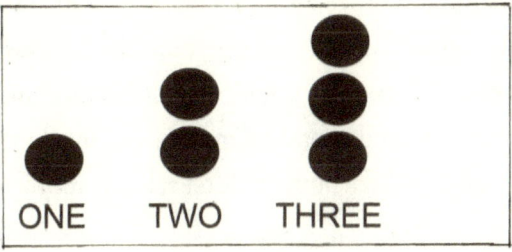

COMMENTS

The best choice depends upon your audience. Here is a joke that I would use for an audience of circus fans.

They would think it was hilarious. Members of the general public wouldn't understand it because they would not know the story behind it. Before his name became associated with the circus, P. T. Barnum owned and operated the famous American Museum in New York. The popularity of his museum created a problem. People would spend so much time inside that it soon filled to capacity, and Barnum couldn't sell any more admissions. His solution was to put up a sign directing people to the egress. When they followed the sign to see this exhibit, they discovered it directed them out an exit behind the museum. (Egress means exit.) If they wanted to reenter, they had to go around to the front and pay again. For circus fans, the reference would double the humor. They would laugh at the joke while also remembering the humor of the Barnum story.

Anytime you are writing material for a specific audience, using phrases and references that they use will increase the appeal and effectiveness of your humor. Anytime one joke brings to mind another joke, you create cumulative humor that increase your audience's enjoyment.

★ ★ ★

SLOW THINKER

THIS IS A special application of timing. The effect is a character whose thought process is so slow that it takes a while for things to register in their mind.

Buster Keaton said he learned to do this as a child touring with his parents in vaudeville. He said he discovered that when his father hit him in the rear with a broom, he got more laughter if he waited five seconds before reacting to the pain. He theorized that the audience thought that it took that long for the pain to travel up his nerves to his brain.

Stan Laurel was another film comedian who used this technique. Watch how long it takes for him to register pain in his movies. This is a technique that I have used very successfully in some of my own performances.

Another manifestation of the slow thinker is the double take. The character sees something, but looks away before it registers in their brain. They suddenly look back to see if what they think they saw was really there. Rose Marie was a master of the take, and would sometimes do a triple take.

A way to control the timing on a Double Take is to use a silent script. In this case, you look at something. After you turn away, you think, "What was that?" Then you turn back. You can also react to what you have seen. You might think, "That was disgusting." Then you turn to see if it really was as disgusting as you thought. How you react to something is the source of the greatest humor.

You can build upon a Double Take by having the object moved before you look back at it. Then you doubt whether you actually saw it.

★ ★ ★

EXERCISE

FIFTY USES

THIS IS A common creativity exercise. I was assigned it many times in a variety of classes in high school and college.

☛ Choose a common object and make a list of fifty unusual uses for that object. Don't use the obvious. For example, if your object is a drinking glass unusual uses might be, "repair a broken high heel, " listen to the couple arguing in the next apartment," and "throw it at your spouse while you argue about your eavesdropping.".

☛ Time limit: If you have never done this exercise before, allow yourself a week. You should be able to complete it in that time. If you have done it before, use a shorter deadline. I have done it many times so I will sometimes complete this exercise in just one evening. The shortest time that it took was two hours.

☛ When you are finished, circle your five favorite ideas. Then read the comments.

COMMENTS

Look at the placement of your five favorite responses. For most people, they will be clumped at the beginning and end of the list, with very few in the center. In creativity, you have a rush of initial ideas. Then you struggle to come up with any additional ideas. The ideas in the center of the list tend to be things you write just to meet the goal. However, during this time, your subconscious is still at work without you being aware of it. Eventually, those ideas come to the surface. Don't give up too soon on generating ideas.

REPETITION

REPETITION CAN BE funny in itself, be boring, or be used to set up another gag.

One Rule of Three is Action, Repetition, Variation. You have to do something twice so the audience identifies the pattern. Then you surprise them by breaking the pattern. Reread the description of my Naughty Ball/Clay Ball routine to see how I have used it.

Another Rule of Three is Repetitions, Variation, and Reversal. The fifth episode (November 12, 1951) of "I Love Lucy" is titled the "Quiz Show". Lucy goes on a game show. She is asked to sing "My Bonnie Lies Over The Ocean". When she sings the word "ocean," the emcee squirts her with a seltzer bottle.

She demands to know why he did that. He explains, "According to our rules, every time you mention water, I will squirt you. Do you see?"

"Yes, I see."

"Sea," he yells, and squirts her again.

Confronting him, Lucy says, "Listen, I have a notion…"

"An ocean," he shouts as he squirts her again.

He explains that if she refuses to go through with the song, she loses the game and the prize money. She sings the song, getting squirted several more times, (Repetitions)

Following the song, Lucy grabs a spare bottle from the table to squirt the Emcee, but it is rigged to shoot backwards so she squirts herself. (Variation)

Later the quiz show's cast is relaxing backstage, and the Emcee is mixing drinks. He picks up a seltzer bottle, but it is the rigged one, so he squirts himself. (Reversal).

Some actions become funnier the more times they are done. In one of my routines, I juggle three clubs. I drop one of the clubs and stop holding a club in each hand. I gesture for somebody in the audience to pick up the dropped club for me. When they give it back to me, I open my hand to grasp it. The club that had been in that hand falls to the ground. Now I once more have a club in each hand. I gesture for the audience member to pick up the club that is now lying on the ground. Each time they hand a club to me, I drop one to take it. The laughter grows with each repetition.

Repetition for its own sake must be carefully used so that it doesn't become boring. Usually with a series of repetitions, each one becomes more stylized and faster. In the beginning you must be slow and clear enough for everyone to be able to see what is happening. Once they know, you can speed up and eliminate details. In my juggling club routine, I drop the club faster and faster. The first few times, I have to gesture for my volunteer to pick up the club that I just dropped. As they understand their part, I can eliminate that.

There is a lot of advice on the number of times you should repeat something. Some people say never more than three times, and others say never more than seven. The truth is it depends upon the gag and the audience. Ideally you should stop just as the audience reaction peaks. If they react less than they did to the previous repeat, you did it once too many times. Only through experience do you begin to sense where that point is.

Repeating sounds can be effective. One popular 1951 recording by Stan Freberg consisted of only two words, "John—Marcia", repeated with varying inflections

Repetition of phrases is also effective. These catch phrases can be an expression of the character's personality or reveal their relationship with another character. Here are some examples:

Red Skelton, as The Mean Liddle Kid, would say, "If I do it, I will get a spanking. I Dood It."

On the Fibber McGee and Molly radio program, Molly would tell Fibber, "Taint Funny McGee."

On the same program, the Old Timer would tell Fibber, "That's pretty good sonny, but that aint the way I heard it. The way that I heard it, one feller says to the other feller, "say," he said,..."

On the Honeymooners TV show, when Ralph Kramden got frustrated with Alice, he would say, "One of these days, Alice, Pow! Right to the moon!" Then when she was proven right, he would say contritely, "Alice, you're the greatest!"

In the Laurel and Hardy films, Oliver would tell Stanley, "This is another fine mess that you have gotten me into."

The phrases can be parodied by other characters. A switch on the phrase might make a good punch line. There is also a cumulative effect with the phrases. They bring to mind the humor of their previous uses which is added to the humor of that moment.

Sometimes these catch phrases become popular with the general public which extends the reach of the comedy. "The Court Jester", a 1955 film starring Danny Kaye, repeated one bit of dialogue many times. It was:

"Get it?"
"Got it."
"Good!"

After the movie came out, that became a popular catch phrase that was repeated many times, especially by college students, in a variety of situations.

Catch phrases can become an eagerly anticipated part of certain genres. In the British Pantomime, a specific type of holiday show, the clown would traditionally announce that they were going to do something. The kids in the audience would chant, "Oh, no you can't!"

The clown would respond, "Oh, yes, I can!"

The children would repeat, "Oh, no you can't!" This exchange was repeated several more times before the clown eventually performed the feat.

The Pantomime is the origin of the bit, but it isn't limited to it. When I have appeared in children's shows in the United Kingdom, I witnessed clowns performing it. As soon as children recognized the opportunity, they would gleefully shout out their line. They had been conditioned to expect it and to consider it funny. It was a great way to get them involved. It was a cliché, but very effective.

Children like repetition in a story, and will join in reciting the phrase. My first granddaughter loved a Gingerbread Man book. When she was a toddler, she asked me to read it to her many times. The title character kept saying, "Run as fast as you can. You can't catch me. I'm the Gingerbread Man." Every time that I came to that part of the story, she would say it along with me. She would also chant it at random times during the day.

David Mitchell used repetition in a magic trick he invented based on the story of the Three Little Pigs. He would instruct the audience to shout "Dum De Dum Dum" every time that he said "The Big Bad Wolf." That became a competition with the audience. Early in the routine, he would try to sneak in the phrase and continue with the story before the audience could respond. Later he would do something like say, "The Big Bad Guy."

Some of the audience members would say "Dum De Dum Dum!"

He would admonish them, "uh, uh, I didn't say the Big Bad Wolf." Then he would act chagrined when the audience responded to the name.

Music can also be repeated. On Edgar Bergen's radio program, the same tune was played just before Mortimer Snerd appeared. It was part of the set up. The audience always laughed in anticipation of Mortimer's stupidity.

Repetition usually leads to something else. It often serves as a set up. With my dropped club routine, I repeat it enough times that sometimes an audience member finds their own solution.

I had one little girl pull a club out of my hand so it was empty. She set that club carefully on the ground, stuck the one she had picked up in my hand, and marched off triumphantly. I have had people stick the end of the club handle in my mouth. If they don't find their own solution, when I sense that audience laughter is peaking, I stick one club into their other hand instead of dropping it. Now they are holding one club in each hand. I place the third club crosswise so it is sitting on the other two clubs. I put my hat on their head. Then I take their place in the audience as if I am expecting them to start juggling.

☛ How can you use repetition? Once the audience understands what is happening, how can you speed it up or make it stylized so it doesn't become boring?

☛ How can you use repetition as a set up? What do you want the audience to expect? How can you reinforce that expectation? What would you change to surprise them?

☛ How can you apply one of the rules of three? How can you use Action, Repetition, Variation? How can you use Repetition, Variation, Reversal?

☛ How might you use repetition of sounds or phrases? What catch phrase would reveal your character's personality? What phrase would reveal your relationship with another character?

★ ★ ★

MULTIPLE DEFINITIONS

A LOT OF JOKES depend upon words that have more than one meaning. The comedian makes the audience think of one meaning, and then suddenly switches to another meaning.

When I toured with the Funs-A-Poppin' Circus, my duties included performing a show owned goat act. Billy, the goat, had a bell hanging from his collar. According to the script provided by the show, the act concluded with Ed Russell, the Ringmaster, asking me, "Charlie, why does Billy have a bell around his neck?" I grabbed Billy's horns, and shook my head no. Ed responded, 'Oh, because his horns don't work."

☛ Here is a list of words with more than one meaning: Write as many definitions as you can for each one.

★ diamond
★ drive
★ bar
★ right and/or rite
★ page
★ answer
★ cross
★ fly
★ draw
★ grace
★ float
★ ace
★ bark
★ duck
★ hand

☛ Write a story or line which switches meaning for each word in the list.

COMMENTS

The January 31, 1985 "Donald Duck" comic strip shows Donald at his desk. He says, "In order to do a job well, one must be committed to the job. What's lacking here is a sense of commitment. " Donald storms into Scrooge's office, demanding, "Uncle Scrooge, I've got it. I need to be committed! "

The last panel shows Uncle Scrooge greeting two men wearing white jackets and carrying a net. He says, "He's in my office."

The same day, as part of a storyline about friends who were getting a divorce, the strip "Adam" by Brian Basset used the same two meanings. Adam says, "Sometimes I wonder what makes a successful marriage?" His wife replies, ' 'Easy Knowing what commitment means, cause if you ever leave me, I'll have you committed!"

It is impossible that Brian Basset and the Disney staff copied each other. It is an example of simultaneous creativity. That is two or more people working independently coming up with the same idea. There is just so much raw material, and more than one person will probably rearrange it in the same way.

When you create material, don't be concerned that it has to be original. Just be concerned that it fits your style. Don't become upset when somebody else is doing material you created. They may have created it first. Don't be too quick or adamant in claiming to be the originator of a piece of material.

DELAYED ANTICIPATED ACTION

SOMETIMES REPETITION IS used to cause the audience to expect and anticipate an action which is then delayed.

According to James Agee, "the delay of the ultra-obvious can be just as funny as the ultimate surprise."

Actually, the delay adds an element of surprise. The audience knows what will happen, but not when.

Dimitri does this in his Train Porter act. Each time he opens a suitcase finding a musical instrument, he squeals in delight. Finally, he opens a suitcase and just looks at the audience without making a sound. The audience laughs, he squeals in delight, and the audience laughs again.

If something is obviously going to happen, you can't disappoint the audience. Part of the appeal is that audience members congratulate themselves on being smart enough to predict what will happen. Buster Keaton made a film called "High Sign" In

1921. In the film, he approached a banana peel, stepped over it, looked at the audience, and gave the high sign. He thought that slipping on a banana peel was too much of a cliché. Audience reaction to the scene at previews was negative because he made himself superior to them. Keaton said, "They don't like it when a comic is smarter than the audience. The audience wants his comic to be human, not clever. "

Keaton went back and shot the scene over so that he stepped over the first banana peel and then slipped on a second one that he hadn't seen.

Remember, you are doing everything for the audience's pleasure. You can't disappoint them by not giving them what they are eagerly anticipating.

A famous Delayed Anticipated Action joke was used often on "The Jack Benny Show" on radio. Mel Blanc played a railroad station public addresser announcing departing trains. One was leaving for Anaheim, Azusa, and Cucamonga." In subsequent episodes they began increasing a pause between "Cuca" and "Monga." The joke was repeated on the three or four shows each season where Jack and his cast was travelling by train. According to Milt Josefsberg, "We once set a record by having Mel's voice boom out, 'Train leaving on Track Five for Anaheim, Azusa, and Cuc –' And then we did a full five minutes of routines with other members of the cast before Mel finished that name and over the loudspeaker came the final syllables 'amonga,' getting a scream and applause from the audience who anticipated its coming but didn't know exactly when it would come."

Here is how this applies directly to a variety arts performance. I saw a magician pull out the nut can that is sold in joke shops. He shook the can so it rattled, and offered it to several of the audience members. Nobody took it because they knew it contained a spring snake. Then he opened the can, shook out a few peanuts, which he ate, and put the can away. It did get a little laughter, but it was not a warm laugh. I sensed that people resented him making them feel foolish.

So, I began performing my version with a delay. I started by performing the magician's gag about there actually being peanuts in the joke shop can. A little bit later I pulled out the can to enjoy some more peanuts. When I opened the can, two spring snakes shot out startling me. (I had switched cans.) This got a nice laugh from the audience.

Gags where a villain gets caught in his own trap must use delayed anticipated action. The villain has to be shown setting the trap, forgetting about it, almost getting caught several times, and then falling into it.

Delayed anticipated action is especially true with a pie. If you introduce a cream pie, the audience knows somebody will be hit by it. However, if you bring out a pie and immediately hit somebody, there is a little laughter, but not much, because there isn't any surprise. To be effective, you have to delay it. So, often the person with the pie is trying to sneak up on their victim. When the victim turns in their direction, they quickly hide the pie. That happens a few times. Each time it does, there is laughter. Somebody has to eventually get the pie in their face. The greatest laughter comes if there is a reversal. For example, the person with the pie trips and falls so they land face first in the pie.

☛ What does your audience anticipate? How can you increase that sense of anticipation? How can you surprise the audience by delaying that? What motivates the delay? How can you use reversal to surprise the audience by how the anticipated action happens?

★ ★ ★

SIMILAR SOUNDS

WHEN MY WIFE and I appear as Santa and Mrs. Claus, I say, "I was wondering if I should take my wagon or sleigh today. So, I turned to Mrs. Claus, and asked, "Do you see any snow, honey?" She replied.

"No, but I see the rain, dear."

Many jokes are based on similar sounding words or phrases.

☛ Write as many similar sounding words or phrases as possible for each of these words:

★ Caesar
★ right
★ spring
★ fowl
★ bore

* ★ maker
* ★ wurst
* ★ read
* ★ liquor
* ★ hoarse
* ★ bear
* ★ look

☞ Write at least ten jokes using two similar sounding words from your list above.

RUNNING GAG

A RUNNING GAG IS a situation, formula joke, or punchline being repeated.

Many Disney films included Running Gags. In "Splash" (1984), a scientist is trying to prove Madison is a Mermaid by getting her wet so her legs will transform back into a tail. He repeatedly misses, getting an innocent bystander soaked. The innocent bystander is always the same lady. Each time her husband's reaction becomes bigger and broader. The audience comes to eagerly anticipate each accident. This "oh—no—not—again" technique can be quite effective.

I grew up watching "Captain Kangaroo". Bob Keeshan, the star and creator of the show, used running gags extensively. Two of them involved puppet characters. Mr. Moose always pulled a practical joke on the Captain which caused ping pong balls to fall on his head. Bunny Rabbit always managed to steal carrots from the Captain.

Keeshan said that his use of Running Gags gave children a sense of confidence. They knew what was going to happen even though the adult did not. Their prediction coming true confirmed their intelligence.

Perhaps the most famous Running Gag in history was Fibber McGee's Hall Closet on the "Fibber McGee and Molly" radio program. A cacophony of falling objects was heard every time Fibber opened the closet door. When a ringing bell singled the cascade's conclusion, Fibber would comment, "I've got to clean out that closet one of these days."

The gag was not used in every program. The audience would have become tired of it done that frequently. It was performed for the first time on March 5, 1940. It actually occurred twice in that program. Over the years it was done often enough that the audience was aware that it might occur at any time. Listening to the recordings of the program, you can hear the studio audience begin laughing in anticipation when they realized that Fibber is going to open the closet. Then the laughter swelled when they realized that they were correct. The gag was used 127 times with the last occurrence on February 15, 1956.

It was used with variations. On the May 20, 1941 episode, Fibber is amazed that nothing falls out when Molly opens the closet door. On January 6, 1948, a burglar demanded that Fibber reveal where the silver is kept. Fibber directs him to the closet, and the thief is trapped by the deluge of falling objects when he opens the door. On several episodes, another character opens the closet looking for he way out of the house. It was such a famous gag that it was included in "The Sound Effects Man", a song in tribute to Foley Artists that was performed on the show three times.

Those examples from television and radio may not seem applicable to being a variety artist because they involve more than one show. However, many people involved in Vacation Bible School or Bible Camps do repeat shows. It is common for a Vacation Bible School to involve five daily performances during a week.

Sometimes performers do more than one show in a day. I was hired by the Emerald Downs Race Track to do four shows in one day on the children's area stage. I knew that many children would attend every show, so I made each different. One of the ways that I did that was by using Running Gags. For example, the second routine in each show was a torn and restored paper effect. However, each one was different. At the first show, I tore up a sheet of blank typing paper. When I restored it, there was a picture of a horse and "Welcome to Emerald Downs" as a headline. (That was my set up.) During the second show, I produced a sheet of paper with a picture of a turtle on it. I ripped that up and restored it with a picture of a horse. During the third show, I held up a strip of paper that said "Emerald Downs" but the second word was upside down. I tore that up, folded it together, and when I unfolded it a packet of paper fell to the floor of the stage. The unfolded paper had Emerald Downs printed correctly. Everyone thought the dropped paper was the torn pieces. I picked it up and opened it revealing that it was a complete paper strip with images of several horses running across it. During the fourth show, I had a child pick a card from an Animal Rummy Deck. They picked a horse. (I used a magic method called a Force to make sure that they selected the card I wanted.) There was a large envelope marked prediction hanging from the front of my magic table. When I pulled the prediction out of the envelope, it was a picture of a dog. I tore it up. When I restored it, it had a picture that matched the horse on the selected card.

It is possible to use a Running Gag during a single show. Jim Kleefeld included a running gag in an act that he performed during a 1990 Laugh-Makers Variety Arts Conference public show. He was going to perform the Arrow through the Head effect. The first arrow that he picked up, broke into pieces. A little later in the act, he picked up a box which fell apart spilling some confetti on the floor. He picked up a broom to sweep it up, and the broom handle fell apart. The number of breakaway props that he used in a short period was amazing.

> ☞ How can you add a running gag to your entertainment? If you do multiple shows for the same audience, what gag can you repeat in each show? How would you vary the repetitions? How can you use a running gag during the same performance or act?

★　★　★

FAVORITE JOKES

THE FIRST EXERCISE was creating a collection of comic strips that appeal to you.

☛ Now you will do the same thing with verbal jokes. Create a list of your twenty-five favorite verbal jokes. They can be riddles, knock knock jokes, stories, or other types.

☛ Over time, continue to add to your list.

CALL BACK

WHILE A RUNNING gag is something that is repeated several times, a Call Back is a reference or reminder of something that happened earlier in a performance.

I attended a Victor Borge concert in Long Beach, CA. After the show began, a couple entered and were seated. Victor asked them, "Where are you from?"

"Anaheim." (A thirty-minute drive from Long Beach.)

"Oh, that's nice. I'm from Denmark, and I got here on time."

Victor continued his performance. At one point, he made a reference to something that happened early in the show. He looked at the late arrivals, and said, "Oh, that was before you arrived." Then he explained what had happened earlier. He resumed his concert. A while later, he made another reference to something that had happened near the beginning of the show. He looked at the same couple, and said, "Oh, that was before you arrived. Ask the people sitting next to you. Maybe they can explain." Near the end of the show, he made another reference to something else that had happened early in the show. He looked at the couple, and said, "That was before you came in. If you couldn't arrive on time then the heck with you."

Call Backs are frequently thought of as occurring during one performance. However, they can occur over a longer period of time if the audience is the same. Clown Camp is a week-long educational program. It includes Staff on Stage performances every morning and evening. Those shows are very well attended. One year, Don and Dee Burda were performing a Staff on Stage show on Tuesday morning. Don put six candy sticks in a box that he called his growing machine. He announced that they would grow to a giant size in 24 hours. Dee interrupted him to say that would take too long. He repeated that it would take 24 hours. After a little discussion, Don agreed to use an accelerator. He pointed a noise maker at the box. Then he produced six eight-foot-tall candy sticks from the box.

I was scheduled to perform my Staff on Stage show on Wednesday morning. That meant that I would be performing 24 hours later. I quickly looked at a clock on the wall. The time was 8:14. During my show, at 8:14, I pulled an eight-foot-long candy stick out of my small prop box. Don jumped up from his seat in the audience, and shouted, "That must have been one that my accelerator missed. See, I said it would take 24 hours." Then while the audience roared with laughter, Don marched down the aisle. He kept quietly commenting to people on the ends of the rows about how pleased he was that his growing machine worked. I handed the candy stick to him, and people continued to laugh as he proudly paraded back up the aisle with his candy stick. That Call Back was possible because I knew how that magic trick worked and Don agreed to loan me one of his props.

Using a Call Back can provide unity to an act or show. The opening routine of my shows is often a plate spinning routine. Then about halfway through the show, I juggle clubs. My closing routine is spinning a plate on a mouth stick while I juggle clubs.

I also use the same music for the opening and closing of my show.

I sometimes refer to this type of Call Back as bookending the show. It creates a feeling of completeness. You don't have to tell the audience that your show is ending. They can sense it and are ready to give you additional applause in recognition of everything that you have done.

☞ How can you use a Call Back? How can you build upon something that happened earlier in your show by referring to it? How can you use a Call Back to bookend your show?

☞ If you are doing one of a series of shows for the same audience, how can you use a Call Back to an earlier show? How can you use a Call Back to pay tribute to another entertainer?

★ ★ ★

MORE MULTIPLE MEANINGS

IN THE EARLIER multiple meaning exercise, you used a list that I provided to write jokes based on words with multiple meanings.

☛ Now you will repeat the exercise, but with your own word list. Make a list of at least ten words with more than one meaning. Write as many definitions as you can for each word on your list. Then write at least ten jokes based on words from your list. That does not have to be one joke for each word. You can use the same word in more than one joke to meet your quota.

Synchronization

Aᴄᴄᴏʀᴅɪɴɢ ᴛᴏ Hᴇɴʀɪ Bergson, comedy is "something mechanical encrusted upon the living. "

When the movements of two or more characters are synchronized, they can appear mechanical instead of spontaneous. This unnaturalness can generate laughter. For example, when a group of clowns line up front to back as closely together as possible and then exit with their legs moving in exact synchronization.

George "Gigi" Percelly and Steve Pedley performed in ice shows as two identical looking Auguste clowns named Biddy and Baddy. Much of their humor was based on synchronized movement. They danced side by side performing identical choreography. Many of their skating moves were either identical or mirrored. At one point they were gliding backwards towards each other at high speed. Then at the exact same moment, they veered to their right a few feet and then straightened out again so they barely passed each other.

I sometimes used synchronized movement when I appeared in a parade with a group of clowns. I would walk directly toward another clown. We would stop before we hit each other. Then we simultaneously stepped sideways two-feet towards the north. We paused, and stepped two-feet sideways towards the south. Then we removed our hats, bowed, and gestured in the same direction for the other person to pass first. Finally, we grabbed hands, danced a waltz for a few revolutions. We stopped the dance facing the opposite direction from where we started. Then we each turned around and continued walking.

Sometimes the movement can be motivated by identical thoughts. In an episode of "Frazer", Frazer, Niles, and Martin have all three taken Eddie, Martin's dog, to the veterinarian to be fixed. They are sitting on a couch in the waiting room. When the vet's assistant takes Eddie into the operating room, there is a brief pause, and then all three men cross their legs at the exact same moment. It would not be as funny without the synchronization.

While synchronization is often thought of as identical or mirrored actions, it can also be opposite actions. A Whiteface clown is to the right of an Auguste clown. Initially both clowns are looking straight ahead. The Auguste turns their head to the right and stares at the Whiteface. The Whiteface becomes aware of the Auguste looking at them. They turn their head to the left to confront the Auguste. At the same time the Auguste turns their head forward. By the time the Whiteface is looking at them, they are no longer looking at him. The Whiteface turns their head back forward. At the same time, the Auguste turns their head to the right to stare at the Whiteface again. Their heads continue turning back and forth at the same time so that the Auguste frequently stares at the Whiteface, but the Whiteface doesn't catch them doing it. The conclusion is frequently for the Whiteface to catch them which leads to the next stage of their conflict. (I have seen ventriloquists do a similar routine with their puppets.)

I use this principle when I perform "Dead and Alive". The premise is that my partner has knocked me out. They are trying to get me straightened out so that I can be carried away. They finally get me straight laying in front of them. They stand up and look at the audience. When they do that, I raise my legs and torso so my body forms a V supported by my buttocks. Kids in the audience shout out that I am not straight. My partner looks down at me as I flatten out so I appear normal. They look up at the audience again, and at the same time I raise my legs and torso. The kids yell again. When my partner looks down, I flatten out again at the exact same time. My partner looks up, and I form a V shape again simultaneously as if strings are connected from my extremities to their forehead. This time when they look down, I remain holding position so they catch me. They yell at me, and I straighten out. Then they prepare to carry me out.

Synchronization can be verbal. In "Fight in the Market', the October 16, 1949 radio episode of "The Phil Harris – Alice Faye Show", Phil is being sued for ten thousand dollars by a man he got into a fight with at the market. Alice moans, "Oh, I don't see any way out of this."

Frankie says, "Oh, don't be a pessimist. Cheer up. Be happy. Why don't you sing, Alice?"

She replies, "I don't feel like singing."

Phil says, "I do."

In unison, Alice and Frankie exclaim, "Nobody asked you!"

That is greeted with laughter from the studio audience. After the laughter dies down, Phil sings a song.

Synchronized movement can also be used to isolate a character who is not part of the synchronization.

In "Buck Privates", a 1941 film starring Bud Abbott and Lou Costello, the two enlist in the army. Lou plays Herbie Brown. When they are being drilled in marching, Herbie initially turns the wrong way. The drill sergeant has a difficult time trying to figure out what orders to give in order to get Herbie back with the rest of the men. He finally gets Herbie back into the middle of the group, but facing the wrong direction. He holds onto Herbie so he can't turn. Then he orders the group to "about face." After everyone is facing the same direction, Herbie tells the sergeant, "We certainly had trouble with them, didn't we?"

★ ★ ★

SYNCHRONIZED MOVEMENT

OFTEN MOVEMENT IS done according to a count which indicates how long it takes to conclude that movement. The rate of counting remains constant. The number of counts for each movement may vary. That is particularly useful in Synchronized Movement. In this exercise, you will need to work with a partner.

Stand facing your partner. You will be performing the mirror image of each other. For example, you will use your right hand to do everything that your partner does with their left hand.

Start with one movement, for example, raising one arm from hanging at your side to directly overhead. Decide how many numbers you will count while moving your arm. The higher the number the slower you will move. If you select number six, you will slowly move your arm while counting to six. Make your movement smooth at the same rate so that you are half way when you have counted three. (Some people refer to this as counting the beats.) Choose a second movement and count. For example, you might decide to raise the other arm overhead, but use a lower number which means you will move your arm faster. If you choose to do it to a three count, your arm will move twice as fast as it had when you did it for a six count. When you finish each movement, you start over again at "one" to count the beats of the next movement.

Continue adding movements until you have a sequence that lasts about a minute. Don't just move your arms. Move other body parts as well. The final movement should be one that makes a noise. For example, it might be clapping your hands or snapping your fingers.

Now, practice the entire sequence while you both count the beats out loud together.

Next you will do the sequence while counting silently. Traditionally, a choreographer will set the counting rate by saying, "five, six, seven, eight." Then everyone starts moving at the same time. Face your partner. One of you sets the rate of beats by counting from five to eight out loud. Then you both begin moving at the same time while you silently count the beats.

Now, turn so that you are facing away from each other. One of you counts out loud from five to eight to establish the rate of beats. Then you both silently count the beats as you move. The sound caused by the final movement will indicate how close you were to ending at the same time. If you both make the sound at the same time, your movements were pretty well synchronized. If the sounds come far apart, your movements were not in sync.

☞ Try doing this exercise while music is playing. The beat of the song will help keep your count rate steady.

COMMENTS

This is how the movement was synchronized in the Dead & Alive routine. When I rose up forming the V, I stayed in that position for eight counts. When my partner looked away from me, he counted eight beats. Then I quickly flattened out and he looked down at the same time. I stayed flat for three counts. Then he looked away and I rose up. I stayed that way for five counts. Then I quickly flattened out and he looked down. I stayed flat for three counts. Then I rose up again and stayed that way until he yelled at me.

FORMULA JOKE

CREATING COMEDY FROM scratch can be difficult, especially for a beginner. Fortunately, it is not necessary to start entirely from scratch all the time. Comedy writers sometimes use a Formula Joke. That is a joke with a standard structure. Part of the joke is automatically written according to the structure, which also helps serve as inspiration.

The first formula joke everyone learns as a child is the Knock-Knock joke.

Here is one of my current favorites:

Knock-Knock
Who's there?
Cows Go
Cows Go Who
No silly, Owls go who. Cows go moo.

Here is another sample:

> Knock-Knock
> Who's there?
> Minnie.
> Minnie Who?
> Minnie Knock-Knock jokes are very dumb.

One year one of my grandsons loved repeating this joke.

> Knock-Knock
> Who's there?
> Interrupting Rooster
> Interrupting...
> Cock-a-doodle-doo

No matter how fast we tried to say the fourth line, he would start crowing before we finished.

Another well-known Formula joke is "My Hotel Room." It is so well known that audiences knew how to respond to it. The comic begins, "My hotel room was so small... (pause)"

The audience chants in unison, "How small was it?"

The comic concludes, "It was so small that the mice were hunchbacked." Another possible conclusion was "It was so small that I had to go outside to change my mind."

"It was so Cold" is a similar Formula Joke. The comic says, "It was so cold that..."

The audience knows to respond in unison, "How cold was it?"

"It was so cold we couldn't have conversations outside, because we had to wait for our breathe to thaw out in the spring to hear what anybody had said."

Another variation is "My hometown was so small."

"How small was it?"

"It was so small that when they put in a one-way street nobody could figure out how to get back into town."

The audience does not always participate in a Formula Joke. You will be working with some other formulas in later exercises.

How do you learn Formula Jokes? By observation of comedy. As you study comedy, you will begin to notice jokes that fit together into similar structures. Then you have discovered a formula. Analyze the structure to find out all of its elements. When you think you understand a formula, try writing original jokes to fit that formula. Assign a name to the formula. Make a list of all the formulas you discover so that you won 't forget them when you are creating comedy.

If you study a lot of material used by one performer, you will discover that they tend to use certain formulas. There are two reasons for this. First, performers find some specific formulas work better for them than others. Using a successful formula is one way of trying to insure a successful joke.

Second, some formulas become part of a performer's trademark. For example, Jo Ann Worley was known for her chicken jokes.

Once you've identified several formulas, and have practiced using them to create jokes, try those jokes out on an audience. Find out which ones work best for you, and then continue to use them.

EXERCISE

KNOCK KNOCK

WRITE AT LEAST ten Knock-Knock jokes. Write more if that minimum is easy.

> **HINT:** To write Knock-Knock jokes, start playing with phrases and song titles. Try to create puns with the first word or words of the phrase. When you find one, you have a potential Knock-Knock punch line. You can also play with names to inspire the pun.

COMMENTS

Part of the appeal of call and response Formula Jokes like Knock-Knock ones is that the audience knows their role so it is an easy way to get them involved in your show. Here are two examples of how they have been used by variety artists.

Wally Boag created the Traveling Salesman character for Disneyland's Golden Horseshoe Review. After telling several knock-knock jokes, he would tell the audience, "Okay, it's your turn. You go first."

The audience quickly chanted, "Knock-Knock."

Wally responded, "Who's there?"

The audience would erupt in laughter when they realized they didn't have a response and he had tricked them. The show was extremely popular. I saw it many times growing up. I know that many others in the audience had seen it before. However, I never saw anybody shout out the next line of a knock-knock joke even though they knew what was coming. I think repeat customers felt they were joining Wally in fooling the new audience members.

When I was a Cubmaster, I used Knock-Knock jokes frequently at Pack Meetings. It was a good way to recapture everyone's attention. It was also a good way to let the boys release some of their pent-up energy. I learned a routine from Leslie Akin that I used occasionally.

> After a series of Knock-Knock jokes, I would ask the boys, "Will you remember me tomorrow?"
> They would reply, "Yes."
> "Will you remember me next week?"
> "Yes."
> "Will you remember me next month?
> "Yes."
> "Will you remember me next year?"

"Yes"

"That's good. Okay, Knock-Knock"

"Who's there?"

"See you have forgotten me already."

SPOONERISM

A SPOONERISM IS THE transposition of letters or sounds in two words. The term comes from the name of the Rev. William Archibald Spooner (1844–1930) who was famous for unintentionally making that mistake. Here are some of his bloopers:

> He told a rector, "The vicar knows every crook and nanny in the parish."

> He invited members of Parliament to honor Queen Victoria with "three cheers for the queer old dean."

> In one of his sermons, Rev. Spooner warned his congregation that "there is no peace in a home where a dinner swells."

Another person prone to unintentionally make the same type of mistake was Mary Livingston who appeared on "The Jack

Benny Program." For example, once she was scripted to ask for a swiss cheese sandwich, but she ordered a "chiss sweese sandwich."

Don Wilson, the announcer on the Jack Benny radio and television program, was also prone to accidental spoonerisms. In one episode, Jack has purchased a new suit. When Jack asked Don how he knew about the suit, Don was supposed to say, "I read it in Drew Pearson's column." Instead, he said, "I read about it in Drear Pooson's column."

Frank Nelson appeared later in the episode as the doorman. When Jack asked if he was the doorman, Frank was scripted to say, "Who do you think I am in this uniform? Nelson Eddie." The writers got a note to him changing the script. To Jack's delighted surprise, Frank said, "Who do you think I am in this uniform? Drear Pooson."

While some people make these mistakes unintentionally, especially in time of stress, they can be purposely written into a script. For example, on the "Fibber McGee and Molly" radio program, Mayor LaTrivia, played by Gail Gordon, would slip into spoonerisms when he got upset because Fibber and Molly misunderstood him. The June 11, 1946 "Fibber McGee and Molly" broadcast introduced Fred Waring and his band as the program's summer replacement. Mayor La Trivia commented he thought Fred Waring's music was "old hat."

Fibber told the Mayor, "I don't think it is very nice to criticize Mr. Warring's hat because if he wants to wear an old one that is alright."

Mayor LaTrivia patiently tried to explain his comment, but Fibber misunderstood each explanation. LaTrivia finally said, "Now look here, Mr. McGee, I didn't say Mr. Hat was wearing an old Warring, I mean, if he wants to lead his hat in an old band, if wants to wear his bat to his handstand. (Pause) Now look, I was only trying to explain I made no reference whatsoever to Mr. Warring's hat. Have I made myself clear?"

Fibber said, "Yes, but Mr. Mayor, you might be more careful indulging in personalities, a man's hat is his own business."

LaTrivia shouted, "Oh, for heaven's sake! I didn't intend to Mr. harrings wat reference, heference to rarrings, refer, riffle, hafle... when I said that an old handleader has a bat, an old hat, has... you stated... nobody would... I was... we were... you... I..." After a long pause, LaTrivia concluded in a quiet voice, "McGee, good day!" Then he exited.

Archie Campbell (–1987), a country comedian and "Hee Haw" television show writer, was known for telling complete fairy tales in spoonerisms. One of his stories was Rindercella which concluded "and the storale of the mory is if you are invited to a bancy fall by a pransome hince don't forget to slop your dripper."

I have seen clowns do the same thing. Larry "Boozer" Luebben told the story of Rittle Led Hiding Rood. Most clowns that I have seen perform spoonerism stories read their script, but Larry performed his completely from memory. His verbal mistakes were motivated by his character's inebriation.

It can be hard to motivate a Spoonerism story. One of the best performances I have seen of the technique was Carol "CLaroL the CLown" Crooks at the 2009 Northwest Festival of Clowns. When CLaroL opened her giant story book, loose letters spilled onto the floor. She picked them up and jammed them back into the book, but supposedly got them into the wrong place resulting in her use of spoonerisms.

★ ★ ★

SPOONERISM

☞ Choose a favorite fable, fairy tale, story, or song.
Rewrite it so that it contains Spoonerisms.

☞ Create a list of announcements that might be given
at a meeting that you attend. Now turn them into
Spoonerisms.

☞ Give some further consideration to this technique.
How can you use a Spoonerism in your performances?
What would motivate your character's use of spoonerisms? How can you take advantage of a mistake made
by you or a partner during a performance?

Malaprop

Richard Brinsley Sheridan was a playwright at London's Covent Garden Theater. His play "The Rivels" opened on January 17, 1775. Sheridan incorporated his love of word play into the dialogue of all the characters. It was a flop, and closed after one performance. Sheridan listened to the audience feedback he received. One of the biggest complaints was that the constant word play was confusing. So, Sheridan limited its use to one character, Mrs. Malaprop. After eleven days of intense rewrites the play reopened on January 28, 1775 and was a tremendous success.

The technique Sheridan used with Mrs. Malaprop was using a similar sounding, but wrong, word. Here are some of Mrs. Malaprop's comments from "The Rivals":

Mrs. Malaprop said, "Ah! Few gentlemen, nowadays, know how to value the ineffectual qualities in a woman!" (She meant "intellectual qualities.")

She said, "He is the very pineapple of politeness."

Since the success of "The Rivels" this comedy technique has been known as a Malaprop.

Jane Ace starred in a radio program titled the "Easy Aces" from 1930 until 1948. Her use of Malaprops distinguished her from the other top screwball comedians appearing in the medium. She described a problem as "the fly in the oatmeal."

She said she had relatives "too humorous to mention" and hated to "monotonize the conversation."

Sometimes there was an element of truth in her mistakes. For example, "Familiarity breeds attempts."

Malaprops can be used to portray a character as trying to be more intelligent than they really are. They try to impress others by using big words without being sure of their exact definition. An example of this is Archie Bunker on the TV program "All in the Family." Archie would explain to a friend, "Oh, I could never do something like that! If I did, Edith would know right away. She's got woman's intermission."

They are also appropriate for child characters because kids actually do make this kind of mistake. Bil Keene utilized them in "The Family Circus" comic strip. For example, in one panel, the kids were playing in the backyard and their mother can be seen standing inside the screen door. The caption says, "Oh, oh! Mommy's at the scream door."

Elderly characters are sometimes portrayed as being prone to Malaprops. An example is the Crankshaft comic strip, written by Tom Batiuk. In the October 18, 2011 strip Ed, the grandfather, declared, "I can see twenty-twenty with my glasses and my perennial vision is great."

The Frank & Ernest comic strip, created and originally illustrated by Bob Thaves, and later by Tom Thaves, is based on word play. Sometimes on Sunday, the strip features Malaprop Man, a character dressed like a superhero. Each panel of that day's strip has a different malaprop.

The same idea can be presented in different ways. For example, a young child could joyfully sing, "A pretty girl is like a malady."

A musical clown playing a love sick young boy could create an entire parody of "A Pretty Girl is Like a Melody", the 1919 song written by Irving Berlin for the Ziegfeld Follies.

I wrote this monologue about thirty years ago when hillbilly characters were very popular at clown conventions. A woman would say, "My feller and I went to a weddin' last weekend. I have never seen anything so beautiful. When the bride came down the aisle in that gorgeous dress, I turned to my feller and said, 'doesn't she have a wonderful train.' He told me, 'she certainly does have a big caboose.' He wanted to know how a feller would know he was in love with a girl.' I told him that he would think about her all the time, his breath would be so shallow he would just sigh, his heart would race, his palms would get sweaty, his knees would be weak, he would lose his appetite, and he couldn't sleep because all he did was think of her.' He said, 'you mean she would make him sick?' I said, 'yes, haven't you ever heard that a pretty girl is like a malady?'"

Malaprops can be a very effective technique when entertaining family audiences if you use phrases that children are familiar with. They will get involved by correcting you.

★   ★   ★

MALAPROP

☞ Write at least ten sentences that each contain a Malaprop. Then describe what type of character would say each sentence. What would that character's use of a Malaprop communicate about them to an audience?

☞ How can you use malaprops in your own performances? What would motivate the mistake? What would it express about your character?

PUN

A PUN IS A play on words that sound the same or nearly the same. For example, on "Frazer", Roz, a character that came from Wisconsin, related how her relatives relished cheese puns. In one episode, she said, "My cousin would come up to me and ask, "Havarti?" I would reply, "I'm Gouda."

Puns are often used to entertain adults in a family audience. For example, on "Sesame Street" a singing character was named Placido Flamingo. It may have sounded funny to the kids, but it was more humorous to adults who realized it was a pun based on Placido Domingo, a famous opera singer.

Puns are frequently used in the patter for acts. Every joke book contains some examples of puns, and there are books devoted exclusively to them.

Because puns are based on sounds, they usually don't translate into other languages. I learned from Carolan Foerch that people who are deaf or hearing impaired are bilingual. They read English, but they speak and hear American Sign Language.

A clown skit titled "Banana Bandana" involves a clown being instructed to use a Bandana in a magic effect. They misunderstand and use a Banana instead. Carolan said people who are deaf or hearing impaired don't understand that skit because the signs for Banana and Bandana are not at all similar. She suggested that a skit involving apples and onions would work with this audience because those signs are very similar.

A joke is that the United States and England are separated by a common language. During a show in England, I performed my Scarves that Bekum Tide routine. It did not get much response. Afterwards, I asked a local clown about Tide. He said that Tide detergent is not sold in England so the audience did not know what it was.

★　★　★

EXERCISE

PHRASE VARIATION

☛ Appendix A is a list of popular phrases, cliches, and proverbs. Choose one of the phrases and see how many variations you can create. What type of character would use that new phrase?

Here are some examples based on the phrase "read any good books lately?"

- ★ One priest to another, "Read any Good Book lately?'
- ★ One bird to another, "Bred any good rooks lately?"
- ★ One woman hater to another, "Fled any good looks lately?"
- ★ One jail warden to another, "Fed any good crooks lately?"

Double Entendre

A Double Entendre is a line with two meanings, one of which is risqué. They are not appropriate for every audience. In almost any audience there will be some people who will be offended by a double entendre. There is really no place for them in family entertainment.

I was an instructor at a magic conference. The instructors performed a public show for a family audience. One of the other instructors normally performs in venues where a double entendre is accepted. He performed his act the way he usually does it. When he finished his act, he received notably less applause than any other entertainer in the show. When he came off stage, he told me that when he tried performing his act without including the double entendre jokes, it throws him off because he does not know what to say in their place. He said he would rather get a few laughs than no laughs so he does not edit his act. He told me that if somebody is offended by his act it is their problem, not his.

He is wrong. It is his problem. The conference organizers got so many complaints they were forced to promise to never book this instructor again.

Randy Pryor said that he doesn't use any joke that he feels might be inappropriate somewhere. That way he does not have to worry about editing his act for a particular audience.

Jack Benny was entertaining a group of men at a venue where double entendre jokes were not only considered appropriate, but were expected. He told a joke that fit that audience. However, he was embarrassed to later learn that a member of that audience retold that joke in a setting where it was inappropriate and had attributed the joke to Jack. Benny would not have told that joke in that setting. After that he made it his policy to never tell a joke that he would be embarrassed to have somebody repeat in any setting.

Steve Allen talks about conditioned response to comedy. He said that when a new audience member attends a comedy club, they hear others laugh at certain words. The new person laughs to fit in. They do this often enough that their automatic response is to laugh when they hear that word. This is why some comedians in comedy clubs get a laugh simply by using an obscene word when there is no humorous context. According to Allen, those comedians fail when they work for a different audience not conditioned in the same way. He said those performers have not learned the difference between making a reference to something and making a joke about it.

Charles Shows has said, "The cheap use of sex and violence is in lieu of the ability to write good humor. "

★　　★　　★

Incomplete Comic Strips

HERE ARE THE captions from some comic strips. In each case I've left them incomplete. Create at least two endings for each one.

My husband ran off with Shirley.
So did mine.
What does that worthless floozy have that we don't?
She has....

MAN: Can you explain women's intuition?
WOMAN: Certainly, it is the same as man's...

TEACHER: What function does February serve in our modern calendar?

STUDENT: February helps balance the calendar because....

MAN: So you think it's gonna be a boy! What are you naming him?

WOMAN: Well, he's already two weeks late, so we 're thinking of...

S: Oh, Great Guru, What is the secret to long life?

G: No booze and no cigarettes.

S: What about women?

G:.....

I'll have a B. L. T.

What's a B.L.T.?

Bacon, Lettuce and Tomato sandwich!

Oh! I'll have a B.L.T.P.B. , that's a....

WIFE: Why are you taking this bottle of whiskey with you?

MAN: That's my cure for travel sickness.

WIFE: Why are taking that photograph of mother?

MAN: That's my cure for....

There are several purposes to this exercise. First, it allows you to exercise your creativity without starting from scratch. There is a seed for inspiration.

Second, it demonstrates that there is no single ending to a gag. Sometimes when I use this as an exercise in a class, what students come up with is better than what the original creator wrote. Too often performers do the same routines in the same way because that is how they learned it.

☞ Take a fresh look at your routines. Where can they be changed, improved, made uniquely yours?

WORD DISTORTION

WORD DISTORTION IS an unusual pronunciation of a word. For example, a pretentious woman who calls everyone "dahling."

I heard a program discussing early comedy radio programs in Britain. Each host had his own unique way of pronouncing the word "hello." That became their trademark so their fans could instantly identify them when they appeared on radio. I had a friend who would answer the phone by saying "Jello" instead of "Hello."

Frank Nelson was a frequent guest star on the "Jack Benny Show" on the radio. He usually appeared as a waiter, doorman, floorwalker, or other person Jack might ask for assistance. Jack would start off by saying something like, "Pardon me." Frank's first word in response was a long-drawn-out Y-e-s-s-s-s. The studio audience always laughed when they heard that word because they recognized his character and anticipated the difficult time that he would give Jack.

Sometimes word distortion is used in cross cultural entertainment. For example, a British clown performing in Germany tries to say something in German, but purposely mispronounces it. The audience is flattered that the entertainer tried to speak their language. The audience also feels superior because the entertainer was not able to pronounce it correctly.

I used that in performing one of my original card effects at a venue where there were many people from Japan. In the original effect, I show that I have six cards, the Ace through Six of the same suit. I flip the cards over and show that the backs have the numbers one through six. I rotate the last card around so the numeral 6 becomes a numeral 9. I flip the card over, revealing that the face has turned into a Nine of that suit. When I performed it for one of the Japanese, I tried counting the cards out loud in Japanese while displaying the backs. I purposely made some mistakes. My audience would patiently correct me. Because they were concentrating on the language lesson, they weren't scrutinizing my actions. They were even more surprised than other audience members, when I revealed the transformation at the end. The routine got a much greater response than during other performances.

☞ How might you use word distortion? How would you change the pronunciation? What would motivate the change?

★ ★ ★

EXERCISE

WORD SWAPPING

SOMETIMES A JOKE can be created simply by swapping words in a phrase.

When I toured with the Carson & Barnes Circus in 1981, many of us were dispirited. One of the jokes we frequently repeated backstage was, "I want to run away from the circus to join a home."

One of my friends said that if he broke up with his girlfriend, he would send her a postcard saying, "The weather is here, wish you were beautiful."

☞ Write at least ten jokes in which you switch two words in the punchline. You can use your own phrases or select some from Appendix A.

ALLITERATION

ALLITERATION IS THE repetition of a sound.

Kids love it. They often delight in silly rhymes

Ali Bongo originated using "Hocus Pocus Chicken Bones Don't Choke Us" as a magic phrase to cause an effect to happen. That alliterative phrase was so successful it has been copied by family entertainers worldwide.

One formula joke consists of a definition or situation which is followed by a summary consisting of two rhymed words. For example, "Jim's Aunt Virginia was always very critical of anything he planned. He was tired of arguing with her and avoided her every chance that he got. He was definitely Anti-Auntie."

Here are some short examples:

* You could say that a fat cat is a flabby tabby.
* You could say that the alligator farm veterinarian is a croc doc.

★ You could say that the playground is a tot lot.
★ You could say that a woman hit with a pie is a mess Miss.

Alliteration is used heavily in circus announcements such as, "Astounding aerial achievements aloft. At the apex of the arena, the Amazing Armando."

Alliteration is often used in circus program act descriptions. The 1988 Ringling Bros. and Barnum & Bailey Circus Blue Unit program described a display of three animal acts as "An Assemblage of Astounding and Alluring Animal Acts Bringing A Bevy of Beautiful Beasts, Brutish Bears and Bemusing Baboons Together for a Three-Ring Tableau of Terrifically Talented Training." The same program described the comedy aerial cable car act as "Mountains of Magnificent Mid-Air Mirthmaking Alpine Adventures Abound Aboard a Teetering Tyrolean Tramway For This Fanciful Family of Funsters!"

Extended alliterative sentences can be difficult to pronounce so they are sometimes called tongue twisters. Vicky Miller and Joyce Quisenberry created an entire clown skit based on the two of them attempting to say tongue twisters. Their skit appeared in the September 1991 issue of *Clowning Around*, published by the World Clown Association. It was reprinted in the book, *The Best of Clowning Around*.

You can use a well-known tongue twister as a set up line and get a laugh by changing the ending. Here is one that I wrote. "Susie Sells Sea Shells in her She Shed."

Extended alliteration can be hilarious as in this excerpt from "Mouse in the House", the February 28, 1939 episode of the

"Fibber McGee & Molly" radio show. Fibber is talking to a big game hunter about a trip to Africa.

> **FIBBER:** I had a trading post in pygmy country. That 's how the expression this little pygmy went to market got started.

> **BIGAM:** You must have been a splendid companion on a long trek.

> **FIBBER:** That's what everyone used to say. I was really a card on a long trek. Card Trek McGee they called me.—Card Trek McGee, the cleverest khaki clad kid who ever kept a camp in the cruel climate of the carbon continent calmly collecting creeping cobras to classify and catalogue for keen eyed collectors, casually clicking cameras at carnivorous cats, continually convulsed at the cute conversational comebacks of cackling cockatoos, and concentrating on carving a career as the King Kong of the Congo from the Cape of Good Hope's cloudy dunes to carefree Cairo and the Cameroons

That entire speech, beginning with "Card Trek McGee, the cleverest..." was given with one breath in rapid fire. Its completion created cascades of cheering.

Technically alliteration means the beginning of stressed words in a line sounds the same. Assonance is a vowel sound being repeated in a line, e.g, How Now Brown Cow. Consonance is a consonant sound repeated in a line, e.g. Better Bitter Butter Batter. I think the majority of people refer to all three as alliteration. The main thing to know is that all three can generate laughter.

★ ★ ★

ALLITERATION

PLAY AROUND WITH Alliteration.

Can you write a joke inspired by each of these alliterative phrases? The alliterative phrase can be part of the set up or the punchline. You can change the phrases to another alliterative phrase. For example, instead of Tyrolian Troll Trolley you might write a joke about a California Cable Car.

* ★ Sandy Candy
* ★ Rubber Baby Buggy Bumper
* ★ Hoarse Horse
* ★ Better Bottom Button
* ★ Purple People Pager
* ★ Calm Clam
* ★ Crying Crab
* ★ Tyrolian Troll Trolley Toll

☛ Study the comic strips and panels that you collected. Can you summarize what happened in any of them by using two alliterative words?

☛ What is the longest alliterative sentence that you can write?

☛ Write an alliterative introduction to your act?

☛ What alliterative description of your act might appear in a circus program?

K Sound

COMEDIANS HAVE DISCOVERED that words containing the K sound tend to be funny.

Early in the 21st Century, Blackberry was a type of smart phone. I wrote a joke about them. I purposely created it to contain as many k-sounds as possible. Here is the final result. "What do you call someone who constructs high tech communication devices? A Blackberry Cobbler."

You can rewrite existing jokes so that they contain more K sounds. The March 6, 2003 "Bound and Gagged" comic by Dana Summers depicted two vultures circling over a clown crawling across the desert. The caption is "Fred and Biff Spot a Happy Meal." I turned that into this verbal joke, "What do cannibals call a kettle of clowns? A Happy Meal."

The K sound being funny is a tendency, not a rule. Using it does not guarantee laughter, but it increases the probability. The only way to know for sure is to test it in front of an audience.

★ ★ ★

K SOUND

☞ Rewrite each of these phrases so they contain as many K sounds as possible. As always, there is more than one possible correct response.

* ★ Sound of Train Wheels Passing
* ★ Alarm Clock Sounds
* ★ Youth Group Transportation
* ★ Smart Thief Arrested
* ★ Unpleasant Rural Relative
* ★ Playful Young Bear

☞ Look at your list of favorite comic strips and jokes. Can any of them be rewritten to include more K sounds?

Invented Words

THIS MEANS YOU create a new word to cover a situation. For example, "Property values have soared since they began redeveloping downtown. They are hoping to attract the rich and have just started building some new condomaximums."

The November 7, 2020 "Pickles" comic strip, by Brian Crane, showed Nelson listening to his grandparents talking. While they took turns saying something, they weren't actually listening to each other. When it was her turn, Opal talked about almond milk. When it was his turn, Earl was talking about the neighbor's dog. In the last panel, Nelson says, "I like listening to grandma's and grandpa's non-versation."

L. Rich Hall was famous for his Sniglets, which he defined as "any word that doesn't appear in the dictionary, but should." He performed them on the HBO series "Not Necessarily The News". Several books of them were published. Here is an example, "AIRDIRT (ayr' dirt) n. A hanging plant that's been ignored for three weeks or more."

Perhaps the most famous invented word is from Walt Disney's "Mary Poppins" film. That is supercalifragilisticexpialidocious. According to the song, that is a word you use when no other one seems to do.

Critics, like Alexander Woolcot, delighted in inventing wards as evidence of their intelligence.

However, they can also be evidence of a character's stupidity because they don't know there isn't such a word. For example, when Geech, Jerry Bittle's cartoon character, is asked by a salesman, "perhaps you 'd like this style of shirt in off-white?" he responds, "Does it come in off-blue?"

Invented words can fill other purposes.

It can be an exclamation. On "The Flintstones" TV series, Fred would exclaim, "Yabba Dabba Do."

When young kids laughed or made a comment, Andrew "Kooky" Stevens, would look at them and say, "You're a Rudy Prudy." Every time that I saw him perform, that comment increased their laughter.

Dante, the magician, created Sim Sala Bim as the magic command that he would use to cause magic to occur.

A special type of invented word is the Acronym, a word formed from the initials of the words in a phrase.

In 1990, a female member of the Orange County (CA) Magic Club performed a sleight of hand coin routine during a club meeting. She said, "Wham," each time she was going to reveal that a coin had vanished, appeared, transported, or transformed. At the end of the routine she said, "What I want you to remember from my routine is W-A-M, which means Women Are Magical."

In *Auntie Mayhem*, Mary Daheim described a convention of psychiatrists. The name of the group was the International Mental and Neurological University Therapists Society —IMNUTS.

In *Antiques Fate*, Barbara Allan uses acronyms for two groups of people. Men who have lunch together at a restaurant are the ROMEO's—Retired Old Men Eating Out. Three women who meet at a tea room every Sunday are the JULIET's—Just Us Ladies Into Eating Together.

Bureauspeech is another type of invented word. This is a complicated phrase used by a bureaucrat instead of a simple word. For example, an "infantry support and transport system" is a shoe.

★ ★ ★

INVENTED WORDS

☞ Play around with invented words.

★ Invent a word for each of these situations:
   ✴ A young person interacting with others only through technology instead of in person.
   ✴ A teacher announcing the test you didn't study for has been postponed.
   ✴ The moves you make while crossing hot asphalt in your bare feet.
   ✴ The soda that you can't get out of a pop top can.
   ✴ A child helping their grandparents with technology.
   ✴ Standing in line for an hour at an amusement park and then discovering the ride has just broken down.
   ✴ Losing your place in the book you are reading because you fell asleep.
   ✴ Reaching the grocery store without your shopping list.

* Watching the wheel, or dots, going around on your computer.
* Avoiding hearing the final score for a game you recorded to watch later.
* A dog or cat appearing in the background during a ZOOM meeting.

★ Invent a word for ten more situations.
★ Invent a word that your character would use as an exclamation.
★ Invent a word to use in order to make a magic event occur.
★ Create ten acronyms.
★ Create a bureauspeech word for a prop that you use in your act.

ᴀᴅ ʟɪʙ

ᴀɴ ᴀᴅ ʟɪʙ is a spontaneous response to something.

Some Ad Libs are truly original jokes created on the spur of the moment. I was touring with the Reynolds' Family Showcase Theater fall 1987 Tour. The show performed in gyms and on theater stages. One night we all went to dinner together. Bill Reynolds proudly announced that in a few days we would be performing on a stage in a historic vaudeville theater, and that Red Skelton had opened it. I immediately asked, "Oh, did he open it with his Skelton keys?"

At first, I couldn't figure out why everyone was laughing. I had to think back over the conversation to understand why my comment was funny.

The ability to create humor spontaneously is developed through exercise. If you work every day at creating humor, when an unexpected opportunity arises you will automatically create humor because it has become a habit. That is why the exercises in this book are so useful.

Another way to develop the ability to Ad Lib is to play improvisation games. That gives you exercise in reacting to new situations and thinking quickly. I take improvisation classes as often as possible when I attend variety arts conventions or educational programs. Sometimes I already know all the games that are taught, but I enjoy the opportunity to play the games with a new group of people. Occasionally, we have played improvisation games at social events.

What if you think of the perfect response after the show? It is never too late. Remember that response and use it the next time that situation comes up.

According to Milton Berle, "There are two kinds of ad-libs. The first is the truly impromptu remark... The second type of ad-lib is prepared. It is culled from ad-libs of the past or funny thoughts you've been able to come up with when not under pressure. The prepared ad-lib carries with it one caveat: Make it *sound* as if you've just thought of it!"

Jim Howle said, "Can I give you a moment on what makes a clown great? It takes a clown working every day of his life, experiencing, working in close proximity to an audience, and developing and working on routines, and over and over and over and over again, until they work absolutely perfect. And in the process of this he makes a few mistakes. And those mistakes are sometimes funnier than what he set out to do on purpose. He adds those things, he adds those ad-libs. He puts all those ingredients together. Now this takes time. You don't do this tomorrow afternoon. Then he goes out and he sees his friends working. And the more he works, the more people he works with, the more he travels, the more chance he has to see other performers working, doing their comedy in other forms. He sees a lot of theater, and he watches a lot of movies and television. He gets ideas from here and there. And he watches and he learns timing and he learns subtlety. If he keeps his eyes and ears open and he works at it for 30 years ... 35 years, he becomes a genius—at least in everybody's minds because if a situation arises, he knows how to respond to it. He's seen it over and over again, and he knows the funniest way possible to respond. It's not an innate gift. It's something that someone learns."

A prepared Ad Lib can be a planned response to a perceived potential problem or to a situation that you encountered repeatedly.

Marvin Hardy was on staff for the 1989 Laugh-Makers Variety Arts Conference. He was a balloon artist with a contract to represent Qualatex, a producer of balloons used in balloon sculpture. At the time, Ashland was the largest competitor of Qualatex. Marvin was the first person I saw create large sculptures by weaving together balloons similar to creating a wicker basket. Mike Decker was a conference participant. Marvin and Mike worked together to create a giant ventriloquist figure out of balloons. Mark Wade, a very talented ventriloquist, was also a staff member. He was cast as the emcee of the public show on the last night of the conference. Marvin and Mike asked Mark to use their balloon vent figure for one of his emcee bits between other acts. Mark got a lot of laughter when he brought the large balloon figure onto stage. He had just begun a dialogue with the figure, when suddenly the puppet's neck broke. The body fell to the stage floor while Mark continued to hold the head. Mark tipped the head down to stare at its body while the audience laughed. Then Mark had the head look out at the audience. The head said, "Hmmm, must have been Ashland balloons."

That remark brought a great deal of laughter from the conference participants who understood the reference. After the show, Mark told me that was a prepared Ad Lib. He said that when he tried out the balloon puppet, he thought that the neck looked weak and might not be able to withstand the movements he had to make. So, he figured out a line to use in case the neck broke. He was ready when it happened.

Mark predicted a specific possible situation. Other Prepared Ad Libs are created to take advantage of frequent situations. For example, jugglers will sometimes drop their props. Many drop lines have been created to cover that situation. Lee "Juggles" Mullally will say, "Must have been a sudden gust of gravity."

Randy Pryor advised his juggling students to choose a couple of drop lines and use them when they dropped while practicing. Then when they dropped during a performance, they didn't draw a blank trying to think of a response.

Your response does not have to be verbal. Audiences tend to not applaud while I am juggling. I think they may be trying not to create a distraction causing me to drop. Often, when I drop a prop, the audience will start applauding. They are not applauding the drop. They are applauding because the drop causes a pause allowing them to react to what I had done before the drop. I respond by tipping my hat acknowledging their applause. I pick up the dropped prop, resume juggling, and immediately drop the same prop again. Then I tip my hat as if I expected them to applaud that I had dropped. That always gets a lot of laughter.

Timing is the key to making it seem like you just thought of it. Don't repeat a Prepared Ad Lib immediately. Pause briefly as if you are taking time to think of your response.

Some variety artists claim that they don't like to practice routines because they want to maintain their spontaneity. That actually has the opposite effect. As long as you have to think about what comes next, you can't think about what is happening now. Practice is the foundation that supports your act. It allows you to think about what is happening at each specific moment.

☛ What is a situation you might encounter during your performances? How could you respond humorously to that happening? Rehearse responding that way during your practice sessions.

★ ★ ★

MEMORIZED MATERIAL

THIS IS AN exercise Ken Rugg assigned during a class he taught in children's theater at California State University – Long Beach. We chose a short monologue from a script and memorized it. We had to give Ken a copy of our monologue so he could identify it. Then we started a conversation with a group and tried to steer the conversation to the topic of the monologue. Then we recited the monologue as if it is something we just thought of by trying to keep the tone of our voice conversational. We were successful if the members of the group couldn't tell when we switched to the memorized material.

This is a good exercise if you are a member of a variety arts club. Each person takes turns trying to work something they have memorized for their act into a conversation without the others knowing when they start reciting.

QUOTATIONS

MARY PETTIBONE POOLE said, "The next best thing to being clever is being able to quote someone who is."

An appropriate quotation can add humor to your performance.

When I visit nursing homes as Santa Claus, I often notice residents reading a book. I quote a sign that I saw in a book store. I say, "Santa likes books. They are a present you can open again and again."

Another line that I use in that situation is "Groucho Marx said, 'Outside of a dog, a book is man's best friend. Inside of a dog, it is too dark to read.'"

Those quotes always get a laugh and are a great conversation starter.

If you quote a well-known and liked person, that reminds the audience of that person. The good will that they feel towards that person is then transferred to you. I was playing Pickleball when somebody said, "As Yogi Berra said, 'It ain't over 'til it's over.'"

Soon somebody else quipped, "As Yogi Bera said, 'The future ain't what it used to be.'" Then someone quoted him saying, "Cut my pie into four pieces. I don't think I can eat eight."

A juggler could quote Yogi Berra saying, "I'd give my right arm to be ambidextrous."

A magician could quote him saying, "It's tough to make predictions, especially about the future."

When I teach at an educational variety arts program, I like to end each of my classes with an appropriate joke or quotation. I always end my last class by quoting Oscar Wilde who said, "Some cause happiness wherever they go; others whenever they go." That always gets a laugh. Then I conclude, "Thank you for the happiness you have brought me during the time that we have spent together."

Books of quotations are available. They are usually organized by topic so they serve as a kind of gag file. You can search for quotations on line, but your computer will only find what you tell it to search for. That eliminates the possibility of serendipity providing valuable surprises.

Don't just collect quotations that might be potential jokes. Collect quotations for your personal inspiration and post them where you will see them. For example, a note on a bulletin board in my office says, "Finally, brothers, whatever is noble, whatever is right, whatever is pure, whatever is lovely, whatever is admirable—if anything is excellent or praiseworthy—think about such things. Philippians 4:8" (NIV Bible)

If you are involved in a Gospel Variety Arts Ministry, reading the Bible and making a list of relevant passages is important.

☞ Start collecting funny quotations that you might use in your performances.

★　★　★

INVENTED QUOTATIONS

BESIDES ACTUAL QUOTATIONS, you can invent your own. Here is a type of joke that was popular in radio that I have not seen anyone currently perform. Old ideas that everybody else has forgotten can seem fresh today.

Once, when Lou Costello agreed with someone on the Abbott and Costello radio show, he responded, "As Orville said to Wilber, 'You're Wright.'"

When Lou Costello wanted to put down another character, he said, "As Buster Crabbe said to Johnny Weissmuller, 'What dive did you come out of?'" (Crabbe and Weissmuller had each competed in diving at the Summer Olympics before becoming movie actors.)

On the April 27, 1945 broadcast of Duffy's Tavern, Archie, the manager, announces that he wrote a play. Heathcliff responds, "As the man said when he saw three oil gushers, 'Well, well, well!'"

Archie asks Heathcliff if he knows any jokes. Heathcliff replied, "Do I know any jokes? As the dog said leaving the flea circus, 'I've got a million of them.'"

After audience applause, the entertainer says, "As the cow said to the farmer, 'thanks for the warm hand.'"

☛ Write ten invented quotations. Use the names of current celebrities in some of them.

TOPPING

TOPPING IS THE technique of using the punch line of one joke as the set up for the next punch line. Instead of a routine having a pattern of set up, set up, punch, set up, set up, punch, the pattern is set up, set up, punch, punch. The laughter comes more often and builds.

This exchange between W.C. Fields and Charlie McCarthy is an example.

> **W.C.:** After the show I 'll take you piggy back riding on a buzz saw.
> **CHARLIE:** After the show you won't find me.
> **W.C.:** Yes, I will. You 'll be hanging in my window as a Venetian blind.
> **CHARLIE:** That makes me shutter.

The bit with Charlie McCarthy was first performed on an episode of the Chase and Sanborn radio show. It was repeated in the 1939 film "You Can't Cheat An Honest Man."

Here is a topped joke Joanne Worley told on an episode of "Laugh-In." "Why did the chicken cross the road?—"To see GREGORY PECK.—I know, that's a FOWL reason."

Jokes can often be topped in more than one way. For example, here are three possible toppers to "Why did the skunk cross the road?—For Scent-imental reasons".

* ★ "He's a little stinker."
* ★ "I know that joke smells."
* ★ "But that is another tail."

Topping is often thought of in terms of verbal jokes. However, it can also apply to visual routines. My wife topped a popular clown routine when she entertained adults at Steven's Hospital. She pulled two pieces of rope out of a lunch bag. After displaying them, she announced that they were going to become tied. She put them back into the bag, and then pulled out a laundromat size box of Tide detergent. That is how most clowns end that routine. She topped it by saying, "I am here to cheer you," as she pulled out a small box of Cheer detergent.

Topping was often a part of a script. However, topping another performer with an ad lib is considered a demonstration of intelligence and wit, Sometimes, when I am with other entertainers, we start trading jokes or brainstorming a routine idea. Everyone tries to top each other.

EXERCISE

TOPPING

WRITE AT LEAST one topper for each of these jokes.

Where do cows like to go on Saturday night? To the Moo-vies.

Did you hear about the fire in the shoe store? They lost 200 soles.

You're no bunny until some bunny loves you.

TEACHER: How do you spell rain?
STUDENT: R-A-N-E
TEACHER: That's the worst spell of rain that we have had in a long time.

What kind of hen spends all her time in the snow resort lodge? Chicken of the Skis.

Did you know that Superman can jump higher than the tallest skyscraper?
Big Deal! I can do that.
You can?
Yes, a skyscraper can't jump very high.

☞ Go over the list of favorite verbal jokes that you have been collecting. Can you top any of them?

☞ Look at your existing routines and jokes. How can you top them?

Put Down & Retort

THIS IS A special type of Topping. A put down is an insult, and a retort is a response to the put down.

This one is sometimes attributed to Winston Churchill. A woman said, "Sir, if you were my husband, I would put poison in your tea."

His retorted, "And Madam, if you were my wife, I would drink it."

Another example is a woman telling a man, "You are drunk!"

His retort was, "And you are ugly. Tomorrow, I'll be sober, but you'll still be ugly."

Trading put downs and retorts is sometimes done as a contest of wit between friends. At an organizing meeting for my trip to the World Boy Scout Jamboree, our Scoutmaster told Jim, my Patrol Leader, "You had better look out or I will bust you so low that you'll have to climb a step ladder to look an ant in the eye."

Jim's immediate retort was, "And you will be holding the ladder." That caused everyone to laugh, including our Scoutmaster.

Put downs and retorts were perhaps at the height of their popularity during the days of radio comedy. There were the famous feuds by Jack Benny and Fred Allen and by W.C. Fields and Charlie McCarthy. Bing Crosby and Bob Hope also put each other down, which carried over into their movies and television appearances.

Jack Benny was known as the first comedian to make himself the target of jokes, instead of the other way around. On "The Jack Benny Show", Jack was the target of put downs by all the other characters. Whenever Jack tried to put down somebody else, they always had a retort. Particularly Frank Nelson.

On the January 25, 1953 episode of the Jack Benny radio program, Jack and Mary were eating in a restaurant at a race track. Frank Nelson was their waiter. Benny asked Nelson, "Why did you have to be our waiter? You make me sick."

Nelson retorted, "Well, you're not penicillin to me."

Many standup comedians respond to a heckler by using a put down, known as a heckler stopper. In general, though it is dangerous to put down the audience. An entertainer's job is to make the audience feel good, and being put down is not a good feeling.

★ ★ ★

Fractured Proverb

A Fractured Proverb begins with a well-known phrase as expected, but has a different ending. For example:

- ★ A bird in the hand is...
- ★ ... going to be messy.
- ★ ... a fowl thing kept at arm's length.
- ★ ... cheating at badminton.

Fractured proverbs are a frequently assigned creativity exercise in schools. It is also an easy to write joke because the setup is already done for you. If the proverb is well known, the audience expects a specific ending. They are surprised when you provide something else.

☛ Write at least three endings for each of these proverbs.

★ Early to bed and early to rise makes you...
★ A penny saved is...
★ If you don't have something nice to say...
★ An ounce of prevention is...
★ A fool and his money...
★ Ask me no questions...
★ The early bird catches...
★ Laugh and the world laughs with you...

NON-SEQUITUR

A NON-SEQUITUR IS A comment that doesn't logically follow what has preceded it. The Marx Brothers used it frequently in their performances. An example is this line from "Duck Soup", a 1933 Marx Brothers film, "What is it that has four pairs of pants, lives in Philadelphia, and it never rains but it pours?"

Mike Course was a clown in ice shows that used non-sequitur to give his act a flow of consciousness feeling. In one routine, a bird song could be heard. Mike began prancing around flapping his arms like a child pretending to be a bird. Suddenly, the sound of a slide whistle was heard. Mike looked up and then wiped something out of his eye. Next the moo of a cow was heard. Mike looked up, screamed, and pulled the back of his collar up over his head. That made him look a little like a monk in a habit so he briefly acted like a priest. In another routine, he was crawling across the ice to get something. The theme from the film "Jaws" began playing. Mike looked behind him and then started acting like he was swimming. When the music ended, he yelled "Jaws!" Then he bit his partner on the ankle.

★ ★ ★

ALPHABET CONUNDRUMS

I DISCOVERED THIS JOKE formula in an Adam Forepaugh and Sells Bros Clown Songster circa 1902. These jokes were included on the first page under the title "100 Red-Hot Conundrums." I have decided to call them alphabet conundrums.

Here are some examples from that book that I have used to entertain current audiences:

- ★ Why is the letter K like a pig's tail? Because it's at the end of pork.
- ★ Why is the letter T like an island? Because it is in the middle of water.

★ Why is the letter A like twelve noon? Because it is in the middle of the day.

Here are a couple that I wrote:

★ Why is the letter R like our planet's core? Because it is in the middle of Earth.
★ Why are the letters I and N like a healthy person? Because they are In the Pink.

I thought that this was a forgotten formula joke. However, on January 14, 2022, the Kids Corner Mini Page in the *Seattle Times* included this riddle. "What is the center of gravity? The letter V."

Something written as a riddle does not have to be performed that way. For example, here is a possible bit of dialogue.

VARIETY ARTS INSTRUCTOR: In order to balance an object, you have to keep your base of support under the center of gravity.
STUDENT: What's the center of gravity?
VARIETY ARTS INSTRUCTOR: The letter V.

☛ Now write at least ten of your own alphabet conundrums.

REVERSAL

ONE DEFINITION OF reversal is to have a contrary or opposite direction, character, order, etc. In comedy three types of reversal are used: situation, character, and role.

Situation reversal means that the situation a character finds themselves in has been reversed. It can be very satisfying for an audience when a character they have identified with comes out on top. In "Grandma's Boy" (1922), the town bully pushes Harold Lloyd down a well at the beginning of the movie. At the end, after he has learned that the secret of courage is believing in yourself, Harold pushes the bully down that same well. The audience always greets this scene with cheers and applause.

Situational reversal can provide a sense of symmetry and balance. Buster Keaton used it extensively in his movies, usually signaled by a period of sleep about halfway through the film. For example, in "Seven Chances", Buster is informed by a lawyer that he must be married by the end of that day, or lose his inheritance. He rushes off to propose to his girlfriend, but she turns him down thinking he only wants to marry her for his money. Buster then proposes to every girl he sees, but is always turned down. His lawyer tells Buster to wait at the church, and he will find a bride for him. While waiting, Buster falls asleep in the empty church.

His lawyer plants a story about the inheritance in the newspaper. When Buster wakes up, the church is full of women waiting to marry him. Now every woman who sees Buster wants to propose to him.

The rest of the movie shows Buster fleeing mobs of women. His girlfriend regains her senses and marries Buster just in time to save his cents.

"The General", "The Navigator", "Steamboat Bill Jr.", and many of Buster Keaton's other films have this structure of situation, sleep, and reversal.

Situational reversal is often done through ingenuity, unorthodox actions, or by luck.

> ☛ How can you use situational reversal? What would be the original situation? What would cause the situation to reverse? What would be the final situation? Would the end mirror the beginning?

Character reversal means a character exhibits a trait contrary to what you would expect. The brilliant scientist who is absentminded is perhaps most frequently used. Disney's Ludwig Von Drake is a prime example. The little boy riding a skateboard who is a mathematical genius is also frequently used. Mel Tellis, the country singer who stuttered, was a real-life example, and he took comedic advantage of that. After he overcame his stutter, he had to do it on purpose in performances because it had become such a part of his stage character.

I conceived of Charlie as being a bumbling character who could not do anything right. Then in 1981, I was ordered by D.R. Miller, the owner of the Carson & Barnes Circus, to perform a juggling act in addition to my normal clown duties. Performing an entertaining bumbling juggling act requires more skill than a serious one because it takes more control to seemingly perform tricks that are out of control. I did not have that degree of skill, so I performed a straight juggling act. I was worried that was a contradiction to my character. By the time I moved to the Funs-A-Poppin' Circus, in 1982, my act had improved to the point that it was placed next to closing. My parents attended a performance of that circus. When I began my juggling act, they heard a woman exclaim, "Hurray! He can do something right!"

That was when I realized that my juggling was an important character reversal. I couldn't do anything else correctly, but I could do that. If the audience cares about a character, they want to see them succeed.

I changed my concept of my character to being an idiot savant. Charlie can juggle because he loves to do it so he spent time learning how to do it. That also changed the focus of my juggling act from attempting to impress the audience to sharing something that I loved with the audience.

☛ How can you use character reversal? What are the major attributes of your character? What unexpected trait would your character have that is the opposite of what might be expected? How can you make that contrary trait believable? If your character is an idiot savant, what would be their special ability?

Role reversal is somebody trying to play an unaccustomed role. It is usually used to illustrate the theme of not understanding the difficulty of somebody else's job until you try it. The most frequent role reversal was male/female with the husband taking care of the house while the wife gets a job. The "Job Switching" (S 2 Ep 1 Sept. 15, 1952) episode of "I Love Lucy" is built around this type of role reversal. Ricky stays home to take care of their apartment while Lucy tries to find employment.

Generally, the wife is shown inept at work, and the husband uses an unorthodox approach to cleaning and cooking which fails. The comic strip "Adam", by Brian Basset, updated the stock gags by including Adam's doubts about his role of stay-at-home househusband in the enlightened eighties. This type of role reversal is no longer used as often because women have demonstrated their competence in the workplace and boardroom.

Other roles can be reversed. In "Freaky Friday" (1976), mother and daughter magically exchange bodies. Now the mother must go to school where her daughter is captain of the field hockey team, and the daughter must stay home where she is expected to prepare a buffet dinner for corporate executives.

In "Fitzwilly", Dick Van Dyke plays a butler who runs the household of a woman who had been wealthy, but is now destitute. All the servants engage in illegal activities to earn money to support their mistress in the manner to which she is accustomed, including her philanthropy, without her discovering her true financial situation.

Perhaps the most famous role reversal story is *The Prince and the Pauper*, by Mark Twain. Tom Canty, youngest son of a poor family living in London, is born on the same day as Edward Tudor, the Prince of Wales. They meet as young boys and discover they look like each other. As they get to know each other, they are intrigued by the other's life. They decide to switch places. Edward has to learn to survive outside the palace and experiences the injustice to which the poor are subjected. Tom tries to adjust to the manners and expectations of life in the British Court. Those around him suspect that an illness has caused him to lose his memory. When Edward VI dies, Tom has to get ready to be coronated as the King. Just in time, the boys are reunited and their true identity is proven. Due to experiencing the cruelty of British society, Edward vows to rule with honesty.

The Prince and Pauper story has been produced many times on film and television. Some versions stressed the dramatic story while others were more comic. There have been several animated versions, including a 1990 Disney one featuring Mickey Mouse in the dual role.

☞ How can you use role reversal? What role would your character normally occupy? What new role would they assume? Why would they take that new role? What complications would they encounter? What new approaches would they attempt?

★ ★ ★

COZY TITLES

A COZY IS A mystery novel genre. The protagonist is usually a woman, and she often is single, at least in the beginning of the series. There is a romantic interest, often with a police officer. There is very little graphic violence. There is often a great deal of humor. This is signaled to readers by book titles that are puns. A series will often have a title theme.

The Cozy novels by Carolyn Haines all include the word "bone" as part of the title. Her titles include *Rocka Bye Bones, Bone Appetit, Bone to Be Wild* and *Bonefire of the Vanities.*

The Cozy novels by Donna Andrews include the name of a bird as part of the title. Her titles include *Toucan Keep a Secret, Some Like It Hawk, Stork Raving Mad, Swan for the Money, Cockatiels at Seven, Owls Well That Ends Well, We'll Always Have Parrots,* and *Terns of Endearment.* Her holiday stories in the series include *How the Finch Stole Christmas, The Night-*

ingale Before Christmas, Duck the Halls, Six Geese A Slaying, and *The Twelve Jays of Christmas.*

Sometimes the puns are in chapter titles. *Antiques Ravin',* by Barbara Allan, is set in a small town during a festival honoring Edgar Allen Poe. The chapter titles all incorporate Poe's name. Here are some samples, "Poe Blow", "Poe Bono", "Poe With the Flow", "Poe, Poe, Poe Your Boat", and "Poe Me a Merlot".

☞ In addition to attempting to write humor, you should be studying existing humor. That helps you understand humor and can serve as inspiration. Visit a bookstore or public library. Go to the mystery section and look for examples of Cozy novels with puns in their titles. Which ones do you like best? Why do those titles appeal to you?

☞ Choose some of the series that you discover. Now write at least some additional titles that would fit into each series.

☞ Choose a theme for your own series of Cozy novels. Now write at least ten titles with puns for your series.

☞ An alternative is to choose a setting for a novel and create at least ten chapter titles with appropriate puns.

DEFLATION OF AUTHORITY/ POMPOSITY

THIS IS THE flip side of reversal. If people enjoy seeing the underdog triumph in the end, they also enjoy seeing an authority figure or pompous character knocked off their pedestal.

The Keystone Cops is an example of authority figures deflated by their portrayal as incompetents. Mack Sennett not only had the Keystone Cops, but also the Keystone Fire Department. They did the same kind of gags, were portrayed by some of the same actors, but the firemen weren't as popular as the cops. One of the theories explaining this is that at that time firemen weren't as much an authority figure as policemen; therefore, the firemen being bumbling and silly looking does not involve the same degree of authority deflation. This made them less satisfying than the cops to the audience.

Part of the appeal of a character flaunting authority is the audience vicariously enjoying the character getting away with something they wish they could, but didn't dare do. In 1918, Mack Sennett said, "Nearly every one of us lives in the secret hope that someday, before he dies, he will be able to swat a policeman's hat down around his ears. Lacking the courage and the opportunity, we like to see it done in the movies."

The humor of something depends upon the character it happens to. Charlie Chaplin said that if he dropped an ice cream cone from a theater balcony and it landed on a rich socialite it would be funny, but if it landed on a cleaning woman it would be tragic. A comedian's target is usually rich, or better yet, pompous and conceited. Audiences love to see a character proven not as good as they think they are.

Deflation of authority is part of the role of the traditional Auguste character. Either the Whiteface clown or the circus Ringmaster represented authority. In a traditional nineteenth century one-ring circus gag, after an exchange with the Ringmaster, the Auguste started to leave the ring. The Ringmaster would stop him and declare that he would never follow a fool. As the Ringmaster led the way out of the ring, the Auguste announced, "I always gladly follow one."

According to legend, this gag started when a courtesan refused to let Mathurine, a French female court jester, leave the court first. The courtesan announced that she would never follow a fool. Mathurine told the King that she was glad to follow a fool. Then she turned and followed the other woman out the door.

You Can't Do That Here is another traditional circus deflation of authority routine. Many famous clowns have performed some variation on it. The clown enters the ring to perform some action. It might be playing a music box, blowing bubbles, or some other activity. The Ringmaster tells them that they aren't allowed to do that here. So, they exit. They return to perform it in another part of the ring. Again, they are chased away. In the end, the clown overcomes the Ringmaster's authority, often in an unexpected way. For example, in the music box variation, the Ringmaster may vent their anger at the clown's obstinance by smashing the music box and dumping it into a trash can. The Ringmaster covers the can with a lid. Sadly, the clown opens the trash can to look at the wreckage, and the music begins playing again. Despite his best efforts, the Ringmaster failed to stop the music. Leaving the trash can uncovered, the clown triumphantly dances out of the ring.

Wally Boag performed a nice variation in Disneyland's Golden Horseshoe Revue. When Wally made his first entrance, he was wearing a full head gorilla mask. Fulton Burley, the tenor, ordered him to take off the mask. Wally removed the mask, and performed his Travelling Salesman act. When Wally entered a second time, he was wearing the mask again. Fulton ordered him to take off the mask. Wally removed the mask, and performed his Pecos Bill routine. Wally was wearing the mask a third time when he entered for the finale and curtain bows. Fulton demanded that Wally remove the mask and give it to him.

Wally followed his orders. What Fulton did not notice was that Wally was wearing a full head old man mask under the gorilla mask. So, Wally was triumphant in the end. (I got two masks and recreated Wally's routine in his honor during circus performances on Halloween when I was touring with the Family Showcase Theater.)

★ ★ ★

CHARACTER MIRROR

THIS IS A group exercise. In the comments I will explain some solo implications.

These instructions are for the person leading the exercise.

Pair up the participants. If there is an odd number, you will be the partner of one of the participants.

Each pair decides who will be number one and who will be number two.

Explain that they will be the mirror image of each other. For example, they will do everything with their right hand that their partner does with their left hand. The person who is leading should start slowly so their partner can easily follow. The goal is to work together, not to fool each other. Announce that number one is the person who will start off leading. After a little time, announce that number two will now be the leader. Let them lead for a short period. Then announce that number one will be the leader again. Switch back and forth until you observe that most participants can handle both being the leader and follower. Then tell them to switch who is leading when they think it is appropriate.

Tell the group to relax while you give them new directions. Explain that they are going to continue being their partners mirror image, but that you will identify the person using the mirror and the reason for doing that.

Here are examples of the directions that I give.

* Number one, you are a man shaving.
* Number two, you are a teenage girl getting ready for a date.
* Number one, you are a young bride-to-be trying on a wedding dress.
* Number two, you are a teenage boy tying his tie for the prom.
* Number one, you are a clown applying makeup.
* Number two, you are Madonna in your dressing room, and the assistant director has just announced that they are ready for you on the set of your music video.
* Number one, you are the Queen from Snow White. You look into your magic mirror as you drink the magic potion that will turn you into the ugly old hag.

Then I have the participants discuss what they have just experienced.

COMMENTS:

Participants usually notice that the room is completely silent when they are performing abstract movements in front of the mirror, but that when they are imitating a task done by a specific character there is a lot of laughter. I point out that people are interested in other people. The more your routine is based on being human the more the audience will relate to it. I also point out that humor is based on the actions of a human character, and that a specific character generates more laughter. When somebody portrays Madonna, they often do something specific related to one of her well-known costumes. That is what draws the most laughter in that segment.

I started using this exercise in 1987 and repeat it frequently in my classes. I have varied the characters and tasks. However, I make sure that each person leads portraying at least one male and at least one female character. I try to make sure that there are tasks that they may have done themselves, tasks they have observed others doing, and tasks that they might not know anything about. Participants say most familiar tasks are the easiest to do.

Something else that participants usually notice is that the exercise becomes a lot easier when I give them a task to do. That is because in the beginning they don't have any source of inspiration for the abstract movements. When they have a task to perform, they immediately know how to begin.

When people perform a mirror exercise, or utilize it as part of a routine, they usually don't make a sound. However, it does not have to be done silently. Sometimes when people are playing a music star in their dressing room, they will call out a comment to the person at the door. Frequently, they will start to cackle when transforming into the witch. You can mirror speech if you slow the pace slightly and exaggerate your facial expressions while carefully enunciating your words. If you are mirroring actions in a rehearsed routine, it is easy to speak in unison.

Comments for solo entertainers:

For a solo entertainer, in order to connect with your audience, try to think of a normal activity that somebody would be involved in. For example, a well-known magic effect is to wrap a piece of rope around your neck. Suddenly, you pull on the rope which penetrates your neck. Why would somebody do that?

I don't remember the entertainer's name, but the most effective presentation that I have seen of this effect was using a man's tie. The entertainer was having trouble tying the tie. He got tangled up in the strip of fabric. Finally, in frustration he yanked on the tie and it penetrated his neck so that it came off completely. He reached into his pocket and pulled out a clip-on tie which he donned.

☛ Pick a task that people frequently perform. How can you turn that into a comedy routine? What problems might you encounter? How would you solve that? How might you incorporate your variety arts skills? If you are a juggler, how might you manipulate the objects that would be involved? If you are a puppeteer or ventriloquist, how might you turn any of the objects into a puppet? If you are a magician, what effects could you perform with those objects? What would motivate you to perform those effects?

CHARACTER

ℰARLY ANIMATED FILMS followed an anything-for-a-laugh philosophy with little attention paid to character. Walt Disney's success resulted from his realization that character was vital. People might laugh at gags, but gags alone would not hold their attention. People were more interested in watching characters that they liked.

Charlie Chaplin, speaking about his start in movies, said, "Little as I knew about movies, I knew that nothing transcended personality."

Neil Simon has said, "It's not just the situation, it has to be the character in the situation. "

According to Goodman Ace, "It is more important to develop a situation and to build up a character than to go for big belly laughs. I 'll throw away a sure-fire joke anytime rather than sacrifice character. Once you develop a good, recognizable character, you get yuks even with soft lines. "

Tom K. Ryan, the creator of the Tumbleweeds comic strip said, "Well, I think any good strip is based on the characterization involved. The people have to be able to relate to the characters, and they have to be human enough for the people to like."

But what is character? It is a role that you play. We all play many roles in our lives. Everyone is a child, and no matter how old they are they will always be the child of their parents. You may also be a spouse, a parent, an employee or employer, a coach, or other roles. Different actions are appropriate for each role. Each role draws upon different aspects of your personality. The same is true of your entertainment character. It draws upon the appropriate aspects of your personality.

Animation Director, Chuck Jones said, "As you become acquainted with a character you are creating, you add parts of yourself that are pertinent to that character... I have come to know Bugs (Bunny) so well that I no longer have to think about what he is doing in any situation. I let the part of me that is Bugs come to the surface, knowing, with regret, that I can never match his marvelous confidence."

Magician Duane Laflin defines your stage character as a slight exaggeration of the more entertaining parts of your personality.

Richard Snowberg said, "Use what makes you unique to make your character unique."

I had a friend who struggled to find her character. She was the manager of a fabric store. She became a success when I helped her become a seamstress clown. She performed magic effects with a sewing theme during a show at birthday parties. Then following the show, she led the young guests in completing an age-appropriate sewing craft.

When I began clowning, I worked as a church janitor. So, Charlie started off as a janitor clown.

Some people refer to clown makeup as a mask that allows you to become somebody you are not. They refer to a clown as a fantasy or cartoon character. It is true that while in clown character a person who normally is quiet may become boisterous. However, what is happening is that the clown façade allows them to express the boisterous part of their personality that they usually suppress.

An effective clown makeup design is not a disguise. It enhances the natural expressiveness of your face. It makes it easier for the audience to see and understand your expressions.

Animation Director, Chuck Jones said, "Character always comes first, before the physical representation. Just as it is with all living things, including human beings. We are not what we look like. We are not even what we sound like. We are how we move; in other words, our personalities. And our personalities are shaped by what we think, by where we come from, by what we have experienced. And that personality is unique to each of us."

Brenda Marshall originally performed as a Whiteface clown character she named Flower. She specialized in performing at Vacation Bible Schools and would work for the same clients many years in a row. One year, she changed her appearance to an Auguste style clown, and changed her name. When she introduced herself by her new name at VBS programs, the kids contradicted her. They said, "No, you're Flower." They knew that she looked different, but her personality was still the same.

Jeff McMullin said, "Don't talk about a clown costume. That implies that you are pretending. Talk about your clown's clothes."

Just as you wear different clothing in your daily life while remaining the same person, you can wear different clothing as an entertainer while remaining the same character. That is why I have included illustrations in this book of Charlie wearing different clothes. Whether I am dressed like a pirate, a cowboy, jester, or Tramp clown, I am still Charlie.

Charlie

Your clothing is not your character, but it is an expression of your character. In the theater, the term "justification" means explaining the choices you make based on the character's personality. What you wear as an entertainer helps your audience understand your character's personality.

Character development is not something that you do once and forget about. Allow your character to evolve over time. Early in my career, I created a fantasy story about the origins of my character. Part of that story was that when he was young, Charlie kept hearing people say, "Now, you listen to me." He noticed that nobody listened. So, he learned to listen instead of talking. Initially, I never spoke when performing.

Later I discovered that there were times when I needed to speak. When I first started adding verbal routines to my repertoire, I worried that they broke my character. I asked a friend, who is a magician, about that after he watched one of my performances. He responded, "Charlie can speak when he needs to, but most of the time he doesn't need to."

Based on that feedback, I sometimes incorporate verbal routines into my performances. The reason they don't contradict my character is that they are original routines based on my actual personality and experiences.

Kenny Ahern said, "Let your experiences in your private life change your character. Let your experiences as a clown change your private life."

George Burns and Gracie Allen originally performed a boy meets girl act. Gracie's onstage character was single and would chase every man she thought was attractive. In their vaudeville act, and in the early seasons of their radio program, George was just one of the men around Gracie.

At first, Burns and Allen were very popular, but their popularity began to decline. George realized that the public had become aware that they were married and had two young children. They thought Gracie's actions were inappropriate for a young mother. So, George reworked their act making them a married couple. They became even more popular than before. At first their characters were childless. When Ronnie and Sandra, their children, got old enough to be interested in acting, they were cast playing bit parts in the television show. Sandra did not particularly like acting, but Ronnie loved it. The format of the show changed again, and suddenly they had a son, played by their actual son, who was studying acting in college.

★　★　★

Favorite Comedy Characters Part One

☛ Make a list of your favorite comedy characters. They can be from comic strips, television shows, and movies. They can be live action or animated.

☛ Try for at least ten characters. However, the second part of this exercise will be more effective the longer your list is.

Action/Reaction

At the first workshop that I attended on clowning, Bill "Pinky" Greene said, "A clown must be in action and reaction."

Pinky said that if all you do is wear a costume, you are just a model. To be a clown, you have to do something. He said that starts an action/reaction chain. The audience then reacts to your action. Their reaction is actually an action, which you then react to. Your reaction is an action, that the audience reacts to.

Humor is not what happens to you. It is how you react to it. That reaction can be exaggerated or understated, but is usually not realistic. Your reaction reveals your personality.

The 1927 Laurel and Hardy short film "Battle of the Century" ends with a massive pie fight. A pie lands face up on the sidewalk. A rich society debutant in a dress, played by Anita Garvin, slips on the pie. As she falls, her dress billows out so that she sits on the pie. She pretends that nothing happened because it is beneath her dignity to be involved in such foolishness. She starts to walk away. She stops, lifts one leg slightly, and twitches her hips a little trying to dislodge the pie stuck to her derriere. That is all she can bring herself to attempt to minimize her discomfort. I think that short bit is hilarious.

According to Academy Award winning actor, Morgan Freeman, "I read somewhere, and I think it might have been the book *An Actor Prepares*, that one of the keys to acting is reacting, and in order to react, you have to listen."

Listening to your partner is important in a variety act. In the standard clown version of Banana Bandanna, a clown is told to get a bandanna in order to perform a magic trick. They misunderstand and get a banana instead. I saw it performed one time where the clown giving the instructions held up a bandanna, and said, "Get one of these."

Their partner looked at the bandanna and then got a banana. I could tell that most of the audience could not figure out what was going on because the word bandanna had never been used. The clown reacted in the way they had rehearsed. They did not react to what was actually said.

Jack Benny listened to the cast of his radio show, and was quick to react when one of them made a mistake. In one episode, his Maxwell car was being worked on by a mechanic. Mary Livingston was supposed to say that the car was on a grease rack. Instead, she said, "grass reek."

Benny immediately challenged her to use that phrase in a normal sentence. She was not able to do so at the time. However, a week later the show's writers had her read a letter from her mother. The letter said, "A skunk ran across our lawn last night, and boy did the grass reek."

If the audience can hear or see something, you had better react to it. Mark Wade was doing his ventriloquist act in front of the grandstands at a county fair. In the middle of his act, a train passed on a nearby track. Mark knew that the train would drown out anything that he said. He didn't get mad. He stood there quietly as his puppet kept looking from one side to the other. When the sound of the train faded away, the puppet looked at Mark and said, "That sounded cool! Do it again."

During a clown workshop, I was performing on a stage in a hotel banquet room. The stage backed up to a divider wall. There was another group meeting on the other side of the wall. Suddenly there was loud applause behind me. I stopped what I was doing, turned around so I was facing the wall, and took a bow. That caused my audience to laugh. I turned to face them, and took a second bow. They reacted with applause. During the rest of my show, when the other group applauded, I would point to my audience. They then tried to applaud louder than the other group. I don't know what the other group thought, but after my show concluded several people in my audience commented on how impressed they were by my response to being interrupted.

You can have selective hearing. If an audience member makes a comment that you think is inappropriate, you can choose not to respond by pretending that you didn't hear it.

You can also have superior hearing. In many of my routines, I respond to a comment by audience members. In the vast majority of my shows, somebody makes the comment that I want. On the few occasions that they don't do that, I pretend that somebody in the front row has made the comment. I react as if I have heard it. The rest of the audience assumes that somebody made the comment so softly that they didn't hear it. That also cues the audience. Somebody always makes the next comment that I expect to receive during that routine.

Action also aids in improvisation. Sometimes I am called upon to fill an unexpected break in a show. That means I have to improvise. I have learned that if I stop and try to think of an idea, the pressure creates a mental block. Instead, I look around for something that I can start cleaning. Right Mode Thought is where your memories are stored and where ideas are recombined. Right Mode Thought is also part of dance and other physical activity. I find that if I begin an action, it opens up Right Mode Thought and an idea will come.

★　　★　　★

Favorite Comedy Characters Part Two

AFTER EACH CHARACTER in your list, write down what it is that you like about them.

Next, look for things that those characters have in common. That tends to be something that resonates with your own personality. That may be something that you can use in your own performing character.

My wife struggled for many years trying to find and understand her clown character. Then she realized that Gracie Allen was one of her favorite characters. She began thinking of her clown as being a version of Gracie. That gave her a hook that she used for a while. She didn't do an identifiable imitation, but when she was developing new material, she thought about how Gracie would do it. Eventually, her character evolved into something different, but her Gracie period gave her the confidence that she needed to continue.

Sometimes you can imitate or incorporate something from your favorite characters. For example, when I was growing up two of my favorite characters were Charlie Brown, from the Peanuts comic strip, and Charlie the Tuna, from the Starkist Tuna television commercials. I liked that they both kept trying no matter how many times they failed. They never gave up. I wanted my clown character to have that same quality. So, I choose Charlie as the name for my character. I think it worked. There was a time in the late 1980's when kids would tell me "Sorry Charlie!" exactly as it was used in the TV commercials.

Here are two more examples. I loved the Tumbleweeds comic strip by Tom K. Ryan. When I was asked to create a cowboy clown costume for the 1981 Carson & Barnes Circus spec, I used the oversized hat worn by the strip's title character as inspiration. I measured the head of Tumbleweeds and figured out the proportions of his hat. Then I measured my head and figured out the size of a hat that fit those proportions.

Two years later, the owner of Raging Waters asked me to create a clown swim suit to use during my appearances at Raging Waters. On many days, I went swimming with the guests. I love Disney's Goofy. So, I made a costume inspired by the swim suit that Goofy is depicted wearing in "Hawaiian Holiday", a 1937 cartoon.

Nobody ever told me that they recognized the inspiration for those two costumes. However, I enjoyed wearing them because of the associations involved. A principle of showmanship is that the audience enjoys seeing you perform something that you enjoy. Anything that you can do to increase your enjoyment will improve your audience response.

Patty Wooten loved Robin William's performance of Mrs. Doubtfire. So, when Patty created her Nurse Kindheart character, she used a British accent similar to the one Williams used as Mrs. Doubtfire. I did not realize that until Patty told me that was the origin. Then I recognized the similarities between the two characters.

Kenny Ahern said, "You must always be aware of the fine line between being inspired and copying someone's character or material."

Sometimes clowns do imitate one another too closely in the early stages of their character development. Somebody saw a photo of a clown in a magazine and asked me when my wife had changed her clown name. She hadn't. It was a picture of somebody else. The clown in the photo admired my wife and copied her appearance, including a distinctive head band that my wife used. As this clown got more experience, she began making changes in her appearance. Eventually she developed her own style and no longer looked like my wife. Imitation is a step in the learning process. Those who succeed are the ones who go beyond that step.

It is said that having unlimited possibilities makes it difficult to make a decision. This exercise narrows the possibilities so you can choose something. It may work for you. If it doesn't work, it can point towards something else that will work.

> ☞ Look at your responses to this exercise. How can you incorporate trends into your performances? Is there something that you can imitate or copy from one of the characters that will help you portray that? Is there something that will help you express your character's personality to your audience?

TWISTED LOGIC

ARTHUR PEDLAR SAID, "Clowning is different than all of the other circus arts because it is the only one that is based on thought."

I have heard it said many times that comic characters don't do funny things. They do things for funny reasons. They have their own way of thinking that is different from others.

In one episode of the "The Burns & Allen Show" on television, George saw Gracie putting salt into the pepper shaker, and pepper into the salt shaker. When he asked Gracie why she was doing that, she said, "Well, people are always picking up the wrong one, and this way when they 're wrong, they 're right. "

In another episode, George saw Gracie putting a pea into each compartment in an ice cube tray. Then she put it into the freezer. When he asked her what she was doing, she replied, "I'm growing frozen peas."

She had her own way to time her baking. She opened the stove to put in a cake pan. Another cake pan was already in the oven. When George asked her why, she said, "I always burn the cake when I cook it. This way when I smell the first cake burning, I know the second one is done." (In another episode, she put one roast in five minutes before starting a second roast for the same reason.)

In a number in the Ice Capades, the female skaters were carrying flower garlands on poles that arched from hand to hand over their heads. Mike Course entered carrying one of the garlands. The right side slipped out of his hand. The pole supporting the garland was flexible so it partially straightened out. Mike couldn't reach the other end with his right hand. So, he climbed up onto a chair trying to reach higher. Of course, since he was holding the other end in his left hand climbing onto the chair also raised the garland. Not being able to reach the garland, Mike decided that he needed to be higher yet. So, he climbed onto a pedestal table, which tipped spilling him onto the ice. When he got up, he held the garland so the right end was the proper height but too far in front of him. He skated forward trying to grab it, but it retreated from him. He started skating faster trying to catch up with the end of the garland. Finally, he ran into his partner. When the end of the garland hit his partner's chest, the pole began to bend further. Now it was bent far enough that Mike could grab the right end. Finally, he skated off triumphantly holding both ends of the garland.

In the Golf routine that I performed in the circus, I kept missing when I tried to swing and hit the ball. So, finally, I got down on my hands and knees to sight along the club handle lining up the shot. Then I used the club as a pool cue and shot the ball into the can I was using as my target.

Justification is a theater term meaning the choices that you make are based on your character. There are two ways to approach it. One is to make a choice, and then figure out why your character would do that. The other is to start with your character, and then make an appropriate choice.

My clown shoes are mismatched. One is solid black and the other is a brown and white saddle shoe. I originally decided on wearing mismatched shoes because as a tramp I would find them separately. Shoes don't wear out evenly. When one shoe is too worn to continue wearing, both shoes are thrown away even though one could still be worn. Also, if you leave your shoes on top of your car when you drive away, one may fall off before the other. So, I originally made my choice of shoes based on my character. Sometimes kids ask me why my shoes don't match. My original justification is too complicated to explain to them. So, I had to come up with a new justification. I tell kids that my shoes are different so I can tell which one goes on which foot. That makes sense to them and they will frequently nod their head in understanding. Parents find their children's reaction to be particularly funny.

EXERCISE

PHOTO CAPTIONS

Reader's Digest and Boy's Life are two magazines that print an unusual photo in each issue. For example, the October 2021 issue of Reader's Digest had a photo of a man wearing pajamas and a robe seated at an upright piano. The man had fallen asleep and was leaning forward with his face pressed against the sheet music.

The magazines challenge readers to submit humorous captions for the photos. The editors select some of the captions to be published in an upcoming edition.

There are other sources for unusual photos. On October 1, 2021, The Seattle Times newspaper published a short article about a man who went to a city park to feed ducks at the same time every day. In the accompanying photo, he is seated on a bench. A flock of ducks is clustered around his feet. There is one duck seated upon his head. The photo did not have a humorous caption, but one could certainly be written.

Find ten unusual photos and write ten captions for each one. Try to go beyond the obvious response. Surprise the audience, and yourself, with what the caption says.

There is no time limit for this exercise. You might choose to use the Reader's Digest photo each month and submit your best captions. That would inspire you to continue writing comedy each month. You might also have the satisfaction of seeing your writing in print.

If you are a member of a local variety arts club that meets once a month, you can bring an unusual photo to a meeting and challenge everyone to try to create humorous captions. The advantage to this format is that you have an available audience for immediate feedback on the success of your writing attempts.

GETTING IT ALL WRONG

THIS INVOLVES A character giving a wrong explanation for something, either through misunderstanding or pretense.

A common comedy character, going back to Doctore in the Commedia del Arte, is a person who pretends to know everything but is really ignorant. No matter what you ask them, they have an answer.

For example, on the "Fibber McGee and Molly" radio program, Teeny asked Fibber McGee what makes grass green. He answers, "Grass is a very ambitious vegetable, and wants to be tall. Whenever it sees a tree, it just turns green with envy. "

The little girl knows that is false, and explains to Fibber that the color green is due to the presence of chlorophyl.

The premise for the December 24, 1944 episode of "The Edgar Bergen/Charlie McCarthy Show," is that Edgar has promised Charlie a special gift if the boy memorizes "Twas The Night Before Christmas."

Charlie is too lazy to learn the poem, but he still wants the gift. He tries to bluff his way through reciting the poem. Edgar prompts him, but he gets it wrong. Here are some examples:

EDGAR: It was the night before Christmas and all through the house not a creature was stirring, not even a...
CHARLIE: Louse.

EDGAR: In hopes that Saint, Saint who...
CHARLIE: Saint Vitus, Saint Bernard, Saint Paul, Minneapolis

EDGAR: The stockings were hung by the chimney with care...
CHARLIE: In hopes that the laundry man soon would be there.

EDGAR: Surely, you know the part about Santa Claus and how he flies through the air...
CHARLIE: He flew through the air with the greatest of ease the jolly fat man in the red DVDs.

The know-it-all never admits an error. When proven wrong they just change their story. An example is this portion of the May 16, 1944 episode of the Fibber McGee and Molly radio show.

FIBBER: Sleep mask. Is that what that thing is? It looks like one of those false faces that you wear to a macaroon.

MOLLY: You don't mean macaroon, dear, you mean masquerade.

FIBBER: I don't mean any such thing. Masquerade is that black lipstick that women put on their eyelashes. The stuff that makes her look like she spent the day shoveling coal.

ALICE: No, Mr McGee, that's mascara.

FIBBER: What are you gals doing? Giving me the old razzmatazz? Mascara is the capital of Russia.

MOLLY: Ah, McGee, that's Moscow.

FIBBER: Dad drat it, then what's a macaroon?

ALICE: It's a small cake or a cookie.

FIBBER: Of course, it is, and they are always serving them at masquerades. So, lay off of me.

You can apply this to variety arts by identifying what you are doing, and then misidentifying something. For example, while juggling three clubs you pass one club under your right leg as you say, "Under the leg." You pass one club under your left leg as you say "Under the other leg." You pass one club around your back from the left to the right as you say, "Around the back." You pass one club around your back from the right to the left as you say, "Around the other back."

Gijon Polidor was a featured clown with the Ringling Bros. and Barnum & Bailey Circus. He worked in a freelance manner strolling around the tent while other acts were performing. He would sometimes interact with an act, with their advance permission. He would also tell audience members, "Watch carefully. This act is going to...." His predictions never came true.

EXERCISE

ANSWER MAN

THE ANSWER MAN is a commonly performed improvisation game.

During variety arts classes, I like to divide the participants into groups of four to play this game. One person is designated as the Answer Man. The others each take a turn asking them a question which they answer. Their answer can be serious or comedic.

For example, "What is a black hole?" A serious answer is "a star that has collapsed so far that its density means its escape velocity is greater than the speed of light." A comedic answer might be "a black hole is what is left when you finish eating a chocolate doughnut."

After the Answer Man has responded to a question from each person in the group, the role of being the Answer Man then goes to the person on their right. Continue until everyone has been the Answer Man.

TIPS

It is best to ask questions that begin with "why," "how," or "what is." For example, "why is the sky blue?" That provides the Answer Man with a little more inspiration. Try to avoid questions with a yes or no answer.

APPLICATIONS

During class discussions, participants usually comment that it is easier to come up with the answers than it is to think of questions. That is because when you are asking the questions there are unlimited choices and no obvious source of inspiration. When you are asked a question, it limits the possibilities and can provide direct inspiration.

The best entertainment is an interaction with your audience. Questions and answers can be a tool in creating that.

I try to develop planned ad libs for the questions that kids most commonly ask me.

I also like to ask audience members questions. When distressed jeans with holes in the legs became popular, I would ask girls, "How do you know when those jeans are worn out?"

When the "Hannah Montana" television show was popular, girls dressed like the title character. When I recognized that somebody was wearing that style, I would ask, "Oh, do you like Hannah Indiana?" That always got a laugh, and sometimes led to an interesting conversation.

When I moved to the Pacific Northwest, the Bon Marche was an upscale department store in downtown Seattle. When I was performing as Santa Claus, and a child didn't know what they wanted for Christmas, I would ask, "Are you waiting for the Bon Marche catalog to come out?" That usually got a laugh from the adults who were listening. Sometimes it started an interesting conversation with the child about the type of catalog they liked to look at.

Cathy Gibbons was excellent at using questions to create audience interactions. When she appeared as Sweetheart at a mall, she might approach somebody, and say, "I decided to go shopping today for a princess dress. What color should I buy?" If somebody answered that she should get a pink one, she would remember that. When somebody suggested that she purchase a blue dress, she would ask them to come with her. When she found the first person, she would say, "This person told me that I should buy a blue dress, and you told me to get a pink dress. How come?" Then she would coax them into defending their suggestion. Soon she would have a group of people discussing what color dress was most suitable for her.

When Randy Pryor was doing atmosphere entertainment, he would ask kids to tell him a joke. He warned them that if they didn't tell him one, they would have to listen to one of his.

A question frequently asked of children is "how old are you?" Some entertainers have a prepared response. For example, if a child says they are eight, the entertainer says, "That is amazing. I was eight when I was your age." That gets a laugh, but it tends to end the conversation.

I prefer to ask follow up questions. After a child tells me their age, I ask, "And how old were you when you were born?"

Art Linkletter was a master at interviewing children on his TV shows. The interviews became known as "Kids Say the Darndest

Things." Books of his questions and the kid's responses were published. If you can find them, they are a valuable resource.

Here is how I used questions related to my Visual Puns as conversation starters.

When I worked at Raging Waters, I didn't speak while performing, so I would sometimes use notes and signs. One of my props was a large badminton shuttle cock in a bird cage. I would show people a note that said, "This is my Birdie. What should I name him? Or is he a she?"

That got some great responses. One little girl told me, "Call him Rudolph because his nose is red."

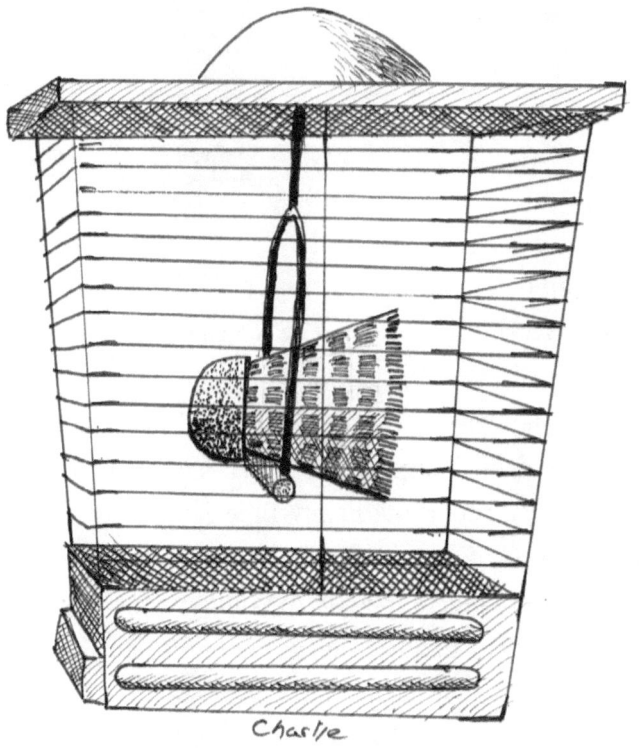

Charlie

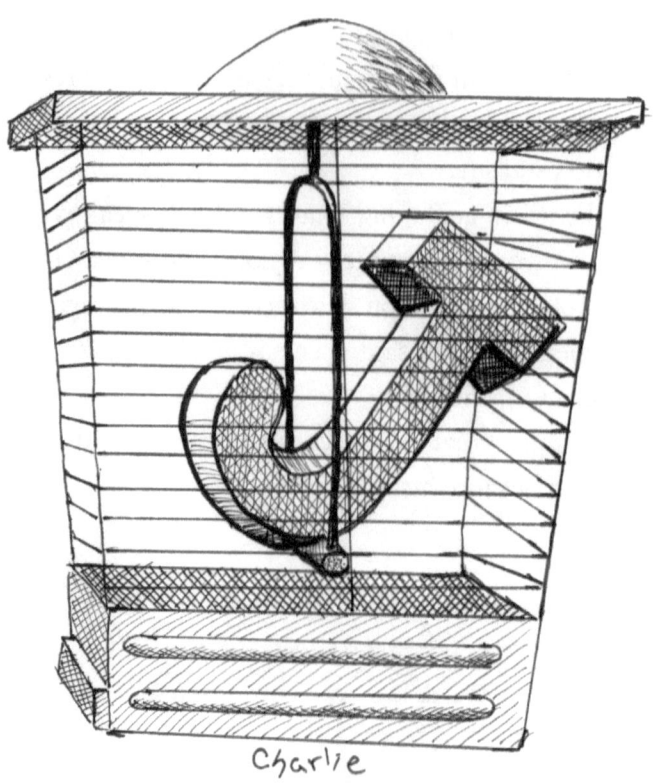

Charlie

A woman told me in very serious tones, "Of course it is a he because it is a shuttle cock. If it was a she it would be a shuttle hen."

My Blue Jay was a large 3D letter "J" painted sky blue. I carried it in a bird cage. One day at Raging Waters, a man commented that he thought my Blue Jay was a little pale. I wrote a note asking him what he thought was wrong with it. Soon there were several people surrounding me discussing my bird's health. They finally reached a consensus that he was love sick, and needed a girlfriend. They suggested that I find him an O-riole. That inspired a new gag. I put a package of Oreo cookies in my bird cage the next week. That got a good reaction. The best reaction came from the people who had been discussing my Blue Jay the previous week. They were delighted that I had followed their suggestion.

In a class on Caring Clowning, Richard Snowberg advised looking around when you enter a resident's room in a nursing home. Then ask a question about something that you see. For example, ask about a photo on the wall or a book on the table. That starts a conversation. Sometimes the conversation provides the opportunity to ad lib some humor. At other times it is a serious conversation that allows me to form a connection with them. Then they are more interested in seeing some of my comedy routines.

☛ How can you incorporate questions and answers into your performances? What prop do you have that you can ask audience members about?

LITERAL MEANING

TAKING THE MEANING of a phrase literally, especially an old saying, is useful in comedy. It can be used to point up the humor of what we all say and don't pay attention to.

For example, one summer when I was performing at Raging Waters, frequently kids would greet me by saying, "What's up?" I responded by pointing at the sky which they thought was funny. Sometimes kids would patiently try to explain to me that they really weren't asking which direction was up, but that they were just saying hello. Their parents would grin when they heard that.

One time I was part of a car pool of entertainers going to an event. When the van reached my house, everyone got out to talk about our plans for the evening. When the driver said, "Well, it's time to hit the road," I bent down and rapped my knuckles on the asphalt. It took a moment for them to realize what I had done, and then everyone started laughing.

Literal meaning can also be used to demonstrate a character's stupidity.

On Edgar Bergen's radio show, he advised Mortimer Snerd to keep his shoulder to the wheel. Mortimer replied, "Which shoulder?—uh, what wheel?

This type of humor was used extensively by George Burns and Gracie Allen. George said the key to Gracie's success was that we all think like her at times, but we congratulate ourselves on realizing how silly it is before we say it out loud.

In an episode of the Burns and Allen television show, Gracie was leafing through a book. When George asked her what she was doing, she said, "I'm looking for my spot so I can keep reading."

George responded, "Didn't I tell you to leave a book mark where you are when you stop reading?"

Gracie, "Yes, and the book mark is right there on the seat of that chair."

George: "Because that is where you were when you stopped reading."

In one of his monologues George Burns said, "And what about this piece of advice. 'Let a smile be your umbrella.' I tried that once. I had pneumonia for six weeks and shrunk a $450 suit."

Here is a way circus clowns use this technique. The Whiteface clown says, "Take the hammer. I'll hold the nail. When I nod my head, you hit it." The Auguste clown holds the hammer expectantly. When the Whiteface nods his head, the Auguste hits him on the head instead of hitting the nail.

One way is to point out the humor is to explain that you don't mean something literally. In *Antiques Ravin'*, by Barbara Allan, Sherriff Vivian Borne is describing supervising two crime scene technicians at work. She says, "for the next hour, I went between them wearing protective blue booties, watching as they worked. (I was watching, not the booties.)"

★   ★   ★

METAPHOR

METAPHOR IS AN unrelated word or phrase that is used to point out the characteristics of another. It is similar to a simile except that the words "as" and "like" aren't used.

When I was an Alley Leader at Clown Camp, my group performed a skit where each person repeated a complaint that they had. Every person repeated the same line, except for one. He performed variations of his boss telling him how stupid he was. The first time he said, "My boss told me that I am a slice of bread short of being a full loaf." The next time he said, "My boss told me that I'm six ants short of a picnic." The next time he said, "My boss told me that I'm a bulb short of a pack."

Here are some other stupidity metaphors.

★ "He is a half bubble off level."
★ "His train of thought left the station without him."

★ "His body is in the batting box, but his brain is still in the on-deck circle."

☛ Create ten metaphors for how stupid somebody is.

☛ Now reverse it and create ten metaphors for how smart somebody is.

☛ Create ten more metaphors for any subjects that you choose.

DISCIPLINES/RULES

A COMIC CHARACTER IS distinguished from others by their own set of rules or disciplines. According to animation director Chuck Jones, "The rules and disciplines are properly difficult to identify. But there are—there must be—rules. Without them comedy slops over the edges. Identity is lost... All comedians obey rules consistent with their own view of comedy."

In my Sorcerer's Apprentice act, the magician's props are set on stage but he does not appear when he is introduced. The emcee exits to find the magician, leaving Charlie, the janitor, in charge of the props. Here are my rules for the act.

1. Charlie tries to clean the stage, but out of curiosity he plays with the props.
2. Charlie does not know how to be a magician so he does not cause the magic to occur. The magic resides in the props and the atmosphere.
3. Charlie is as surprised by what happens as the audience.

4. When Charlie invites audience members to play with him, they are successful.
5. Charlie does not speak.
6. Charlie listens to suggestions from audience members and tries to follow them.
7. While I perform technically difficult magic, I keep that a secret. I make everything look easy as if I am expending no effort in causing it to happen.

Because I established the rule that Charlie does not speak during a performance, I can decide to make exceptions to that rule or change it entirely when I feel that is appropriate.

When you enter a competition, you must follow the rules of that competition. Rules are the basis of judging criteria. The nature of a competition is that participants are eliminated until just the winners are left. Breaking a rule may mean you are eliminated. Remember those rules are only valid for that one specific competition. Be sure to investigate the rules because each organization has their own competition rules, and they can vary from year to year. I rarely enter clown competitions. One time I placed second because the rules specified "effective use of voice" as one of the judging criteria and I did not speak. The points that I lost on that one rule lowered my overall score enough that I did not place in first.

Outside of variety arts competitions, you are free to establish your own rules for your character and acts.

☛ What rules apply to your character? What specific rules do you follow in one of your acts? What exceptions do you make to those rules?

EXERCISE

LIMERICK

HERE IS AN exercise with rules.

A limerick is a comic five-line poem. The first, second, and fifth lines rhyme. The third and fourth lines rhyme.

Most people just follow the rule associated with the rhyme. Technically, there are also rules about the rhythm of sounds and length of the lines. In poetry a foot is two short or unaccented syllables followed by one long or accented syllable. In a formal limerick the first, second, and fifth lines are three feet long. The third and fourth line are two feet long. The first line has nine syllables.

Here is an example:

As a beauty, I'm not a great star.
Others are handsomer by far,

But my face—I don't mind it
Because I'm behind it.
It's the folks out front that I jar!

☛ Write at least ten limericks.

RECIPROCAL DESTRUCTION

RECIPROCAL DESTRUCTION IS a stylized, escalation of violence, a perpetual cycle of revenge. I do something to you or destroy something of yours. You do something to me or one of my possessions to pay me back. I do something worse to pay you back, and so on.

Reciprocal Destruction follows a definite set of rules.

1. The participants take turns seeking revenge.
2. When it is not their turn, they do nothing to try to stop the damage.
3. The amount of damage gradually builds.
4. Bystanders may get drawn in or they can simply be innocent observers.

This is a technique closely associated with Laurel & Hardy. It is used prominently in their films "Big Business", "Two Tars", "Your Darn Tootin'", and "Battle of the Century".

The reaction of the victim is an important part of this technique. The victim is a good sportsman. Curious about what will happen next, the victim doesn't try to avoid or prevent it. The victim politely waits for their turn to retaliate.

Reciprocal destruction can escalate into a mob scene of chaos. If a character misses the intended target, hitting an innocent bystander, the bystander is given a chance to retaliate and join the cycle. The bystander may miss their target, and hit another innocent bystander. This is how the pie fight in "The Battle of the Century" builds.

However, in "Big Business" the bystanders are not involved. They are spectators, and nobody, including a cop, does anything to interrupt the retaliation cycle. The cops only reaction is taking notes for the report he will eventually write.

There is often a kind of logic to the retaliation that is taken. In "Big Business", Stan and Ollie are trying to sell a Christmas Tree to James Finlayson. Their car is parked in front of his home when the fight begins. James Finlayson tears a headlight off the boys' car, and throws it through their windshield. They tear off his porch light and throw it through his living room window. He pulls the driver's door off their car. They demolish the front door of his house.

The popular Laurel & Hardy Reciprocal Destruction films were silent, projected with musical accompaniment. The modern performances of reciprocal destruction routines are usually done silently with musical accompaniment to recall that style. Dialogue does not seem to fit that style.

Laurel & Hardy's reciprocal destruction films are almost always on lists of favorite silent movies. The appeal of the technique has been proven, but it is seldom seen today.

☛ How might you use Reciprocal Destruction? What would cause the initial act of revenge? How would the cycle of retaliation build? What would be the final act of vengeance?

SIMILE

A SIMILE IS A comparison using either "as" or "like." They can be used as a joke. Here are some examples.

Organizing clowns for a group photo is as difficult as nailing Jell-O to the wall.

Josh Billings said, "I enjoy a good laugh—one that rushes out of one's soul like the breaking up of a Sunday School."

Bob Ross said, "A leader without a sense of humor is apt to be like the grass mower at the cemetery—he has lots of people under him, but nobody is paying him any attention."

Mary Daheim, in *Dead Man Docking*, wrote, "A platinum-haired beauty in a silver satin evening gown that clung to her curvaceous body like melted cheese on hot toast."

Start a page of similes that you like. Collect them as sources of inspiration, not something that you will copy in your own shows. Studies have shown that jokes can serve as a mental warm up for creative activity because they often create one mental image and then force you to suddenly switch to another mental image. A simile causes the same mental flexibility. Collecting serious similes can have that effect.

Here is a serious simile. Carolyn Hart, in *Walking on My Grave*, wrote, "A seashell is like a memory. The life is gone. The beauty remains."

A cliché is to say, "he is as nervous as a cat in a rocking chair factory."

Laura Childs, in *Eggs on Ice*, wrote, "as nervous as a ceiling fan salesman with a bad comb-over." (Childs used many similes in her mystery novels.)

☛ Write 10 similes describing being nervous.

☛ Write 25 other similes on topics that you choose.

Slosh Act

IN THE CIRCUS, any clown act using water or soap suds is known as a slosh act. These acts sometimes, but not always, follow the Reciprocal Destruction rules.

Soap suds are used for wall paper paste, paint, batter, and cream pies. Professional clowns don't use whipping cream for pie fights because it can turn rancid which is unhealthy. Also, whipping cream can stain clothing. Instead, a bar of shaving soap is grated into a bucket. Water is added. Then the soap is whipped up using a paint stirring attachment on an electric drill. Shaving cream from an aerosol can is sometimes used for small amounts.

Charlie Cairoli was the resident clown at the Blackpool Tower Circus for many years. Each year he created two featured acts, a musical act and a slosh act. He said that the challenge was properly motivating water or soap being spilled for the first time.

Often it starts off as an accident. For example, in a paper hanging act, the wall paper keeps rolling back up before paste can be spread on it. So, the boss decides to hold down the other end of the paper while his assistant applies the paste. The assistant gets distracted and when he reaches the end of the paper, he continues applying paste to his boss's sleeve without realizing what he is doing.

Here is a slosh act that I produced for Circus Kirk in 1977. Prop boys placed Scotty's garden in the center of the circus ring. It was a piece of plywood painted green with a row of plastic flowers and a row of imitation vegetables. Scotty entered first carrying a watering can. He stopped to admire his garden. I followed him. I removed my hat to beg for some food. Scotty pushed me away. He continued across the ring to where two buckets were sitting just outside the ring curb. He poured water from one of the buckets into his watering can. While he was busy, I knelt down and began picking his flowers. He returned and began flirting with a woman in the audience. He began to water his garden without paying attention to what he was doing. He actually poured all of the water onto me. He turned away to put down his watering can. I stood up. When he turned back, I offered him the bouquet of flowers. At first, he was delighted by my gift. Then he recognized the flowers as being the ones that he had grown. He threw the flowers down in anger. I turned towards the bandstand and began wringing the water out of my tie. Scotty turned in the opposite direction and decided how to get his revenge. He picked up one of the buckets of water. We simultaneously turned towards each other. I took one step forward just as he threw the contents of the bucket at me. The water hit me in the chest and splashed upwards. During the evening show, the drops glistened in the lights. I ran across the ring and grabbed the other bucket. I chased Scotty into the bleachers. When I threw the contents of my bucker, Scotty ducked. Popcorn flew from my bucket and landed on some of the audience members.

Clowns working in outdoor shows often use popcorn instead of confetti. Popcorn is inexpensive and easily available. On Circus Kirk, we got one bag of stale popcorn from the concession trailer every morning. Also, popcorn does not have to cleaned up outside while bits of paper would. When I appeared at the Raging Waters amusement park I would sometimes pretend to throw or spill a bucket of water. In that setting, I would use mylar streamers tied in a bundle and attached to the bucket by a length of fishing line.

I think there are several reasons for the popularity of slosh acts. First, kids are taught not to make a mess. Seeing adults making such a big mess is a type of forbidden subject humor. Adults are prevented by proprietary from being able to make a mess like that. So, they vicariously enjoy the clowns doing something they wish they could do.

Audience members don't want to be the victims of a clown's practical joke which is why the cliched squirt boutonniere and squirt camera aren't very effective. However, water can be effective if properly motivated. Before Charles "Doc" Boas founded Circus Kirk, he had toured as a circus clown known as Professor Onions. He had a successful walkaround where he would begin slicing onions. Suddenly water would begin streaming from the rims of his glasses because the onions made him cry.

When I appeared at Raging Waters, I would hold up a large book titled Moby Dick. Opening it revealed a painting of a white whale. Suddenly water began streaming out of the whale's blow hole. I used an adult enema syringe (a large blue squeeze bulb), aquarium airline tubing, and a plastic eyedropper to propel the water. If I did not include Moby Dick in one of my shows, season pass holders would ask why I had left it out. Because it was so popular, I had a back-up plumbing set so if my regular one broke I could continue performing the routine.

When I began traveling by air to many of my performances, I had a weight limit for my props. To make my Moby Dick gag lighter, I changed it from a book to a framed picture. That was not nearly as effective as the book version. I concluded that the routine really did need the double set up. However, this time it was a verbal set up followed by a visual set up. Also, using the book gave me greater control of the timing. When I was holding up the framed painting some people glanced at it briefly and had looked away before the water began squirting. By using the book, I delayed the audience seeing the picture. Everyone saw it at the same time, and the water began squirting before they lost interest.

When performing a squirting gag, keep the stream of water moving from side to side. That way no person gets hit with very much water. Sweeping the stream from side to side ensures that at some point it will be at an angle to show up in the lights for each audience member. If you are working inside, be sure that you don't allow the water to cause a hazard by pooling in any one location making the floor slippery.

☞ How might you use soap suds or water in a routine? What would motivate it? How might it escalate? What would be the finale of the routine?

★　★　★

Tom Swiftly

A TOM SWIFTLY IS a formula joke where you quote someone and use a verb or adverb that relates to the quotation. Here are some examples:

* ★ "I made my wife stay home with the kids," he said ruthlessly.
* ★ "I was hoping they would have the pencil sharpener fixed," he said disappointedly.
* ★ "I think they are installing a new gas main," he hazarded a guess.
* ★ "I was sure the Ouija board would have worked tonight," he said dispiritedly.
* ★ "It's oil! We struck it rich! We struck it rich!" she gushed.

Write twenty-five Tom Swiftly jokes. Here are some prompts to help you get started.

* ★ .... Said Tom dryly.
* ★ ... Said Tom intently.
* ★ ... Said Tom gravely.
* ★ ... Said Tom hoarsely.
* ★ ... Said Tom figuratively.
* ★ ... Said Tom weakly.
* ★ ... Said Tom...

The person speaking is often identified as Tom when this formula is used. You can use another name. You can change the gender of the person speaking.

The name from this formula is supposed to be due this type of verb and adverb use in a series of children's books about a character named Tom Swiftly. However, the one Tom Swiftly book that I have seen did not use that structure.

IMPERSONATION

IMPERSONATION IS A character pretending to be somebody else, or having a skill that they don't possess. The performer starts out doing as accurate an impersonation as possible, and then little flaws creep in which reveal the duplicity.

For example, the clown concert pianist who can't play, but has a recording or another pianist hidden backstage. In the beginning, the clown hits the proper keys in time with the music. After playing the first song things begin to go wrong. He finishes a song, stands to take his bow, and the piano starts playing the chorus over again. When he hits the keys to start another song, no sound is heard, and he has to wake up his backstage accomplice.

The 'Mirror Routine is a classic impersonation gag where a clown breaks a mirror and tries to impersonate the owner's reflection. Harpo Marx excelled at this routine. He can be seen doing it in the film "Duck Soup", and in the "Harpo Marx" episode #124 of "I Love Lucy" television show.

Objects can be impersonated. In the "New Neighbors",
episode #21 of "I Love Lucy", a couple is moving into the building where the Ricardo's live. Lucy is snooping in their down-
stairs apartment. They come home unexpectedly, and Lucy hides
in the closet. Lucy hears Tom O'Brien and his wife rehearsing
a play. She doesn't know that they are actors so she mistakenly identifies them as spies and saboteurs. She listens as they
describe killing the couple in the apartment upstairs, assuming
their identity, and blowing up the capitol. When Mrs. O'Brien
starts to open the closet to hang up her coat, Lucy, dons a slip
cover in order to impersonate a chair. There is a yoke in the top
of the slip cover so it approximates the appearance of a chair.

Lucy puts her arms in the arms of the slip cover to complete the chair shape. She kneels down to be the proper height. When the door is left open, Lucy tries to escape using her chair disguise. She gets about three quarters of the way across the room before she has to stop.

Mrs. O'Brien gives her husband a stack of books that are tied together with twine. He sets the books down on the seat of the chair. Since there is nothing under the seat of the slip cover, the books fall to the floor. Tom picks them up and returns them to the seat. They fall again. He picks them up again, and without looking tosses them onto the seat of the chair. Lucy grabs them with her arms creating a pinched looking chair. She carefully lowers the books to the floor. When Tom finds them on the floor once again, he puts them on the mantel.

Tom sits in the chair. (I think Lucy has raised one leg so he is sitting on her knee.) While talking to his wife, he pounds his hand on the arm of the chair for emphasis. Lucy shakes her hand trying to get rid of the pain. Neither of the O'Brien's notice that the arm of the chair is moving. When Tom stands up, Lucy dashes out of the open apartment door. He sits down again landing on the floor. He slowly looks around trying to find the chair that he had just been sitting on.

Impersonating a chair has been used in many clown acts on stage and in the circus. They are usually motivated by one clown trying to convince another that they are in a haunted house.

A ghost is another frequent impersonation. A script to "Pete in the Well," a nineteenth century medicine show routine, is included as an appendix in *Step Right Up*, by Brooks McNamara. It is a variation of an older routine called Dead and Alive. The

Doctor convinces Jake that he has killed Pete. He orders Jake to dispose of Pete's body by throwing it down the well. Pete is more alive, then dead. He thwarts Pete's efforts to move his body. Eventually, Pete dashes off the stage. Jake is horrified that the body has disappeared. The Doctor returns to the stage, and congratulates Jake on disposing of the body so quickly. Pete puts on a sheet, and returns to the stage as a ghost. After some comedy bits, the Doctor and Pete are frightened off the stage. Pete jumps onto Jake's back to ride off.

☛ How can you use impersonation in your performances? Who would you pretend to be?

☛ What skill would you pretend to possess? What would you do to make the audience think you really are skillful? What errors would begin to become evident? How would you try to cover them up?

★　　★　　★

CRAZY WORDS

FOR A CHANGE of pace, here is an exercise allowing you to play around with words and images. This puzzle form is referred to by many names, but I like to call it Crazy Words. Some people call it word puzzles. In its purest form, only words are used, but here you can include rebuses. The position and alignment of words and pictures depict common phrases. Can you decipher these examples?

```
┌──────────────────────────┐
│  PINEAPPLE ƎʞⱯƆ           │
│                       1   │
└──────────────────────────┘
```

```
┌──────────────────────────┐
│  CROALONEWD              │
│                       2   │
└──────────────────────────┘
```

HEART

3

LO HEAD HEELHEEL VE

4

GNIKNIHT
PAST

5

Aa B Cc Dd Ee Ff Gg Hh
Ii Jj Kk Ll Mm Nn O Pp
Qq Rr Ss Tt Uu Vv Ww Xx
Y Zz

6

7

ANSWERS

1. Pineapple Upside—down Cake 2. Alone In A Crowd 3. A Broken Heart 4. Head Over Heels In Love 5. Thinking Back Over The Past 6. A Little Boy Is Lost 7. Writing A Friend

CELEBRITY IMPERSONATION

THIS IS DEMONSTRATING your skill in imitating a person your audience will recognize.

Rose Marie did an excellent impersonation of Jimmy Durante. On the March 31, 1948 episode of "The Jimmy Durante Show" on radio, there is a knock on the door. Someone enters who sounds just like Durante. The two begin a conversation. At one point, Durante says, "This is confusing. I'm not sure which one is me."

The routine ends with Durante announcing, "That's enough of this. Let me introduce a fine entertainer who does a better impersonation of me than I do, Rose Marie."

Then Jimmy tells Rose Marie, "I have heard your recording of my song 'Chicory'. You do a fine job with it. How about singing it with me now? We could make it a duel."

Rose Marie responds, "Don't you mean a duet? A duel is when you try to harm each other."

"You have never sung with me," Durante replies. Then the two sing the song together.

Impersonations of celebrities and politicians has been a standard part of the "Saturday Night Live" format on TV.

Here is how Peter Pitofsky used impersonations during the 2017 performance of Circus Venardos near Seattle, WA. He puffed out his cheeks to impersonate "for children a blow fish snoring, or for Jazz fans Dizzy Gillespie snoring." Then he impersonated a bull dog. Next, he compressed his lips together in his impression of Cher. During his impression of Robert De Nero eating a lemon, he contorted his face in distaste as he prepared to try it. However, when he licked the sour fruit, his face broke out into a big smile. He took off his clown shirt revealing a black tank top and donned a black hat to impersonate Sylvester Stallone as Rocky. He ended that impersonation by shouting "Adrian." He explained that in his last pantomime he will slowly lower his IQ. He began impersonating an upper-class Englishman, then an expression of doubt crept across his features, then he adopted a silly expression, and finally transitioned into a very good gorilla imitation. The routine concluded with the gorilla grabbing the black hat and yelling "Adrian." During his act people are so busy laughing that I don't think they appreciate that he is a very skilled pantomimist.

★ ★ ★

WRITING CRAZY WORDS

HERE ARE SOME phrases associated with being a variety artist. How would each one look if you turned it into a Crazy Word like those in the previous exercise?

* Alone in the Center of the Spotlight
* A Rabbit Out of a Hat
* In the Center Ring
* A Pie in the Face
* Three Ring Circus
* Cutting A Woman in Half
* Flying Trapeze
* Multiplying Balls
* Makeup

COMMENTS:

Here are some ideas for ways to use Crazy Words.

* During the 1990's, I created a promotional piece that was Fun Riddles, Jokes, and Puzzles for Kids. It was a three-fold-brochure that fit into a Number 10 envelope. It included jokes, pencil mazes, dot-to-dot pictures, and crazy words. One year I sent then out to every family that I had done a birthday party for during the previous twelve months. When I had a booth at a showcase for entertainers, I had a stack of them on my table. My goal was to demonstrate that I was a fun person. I did get some bookings from them.

* I did several corporate banquets as Santa one year. As an extra service for my clients, I provided them with a page of Carol and Christmas Songs Crazy Words. They were distributed to everyone when they arrived so they could work on them while waiting for their food to be served. The people at one banquet did not know everyone, so working together on the Crazy Words served as an ice breaker.

* Most organizations have newsletters, and their editors are desperate for material, including fillers. You might offer to provide a Crazy Word Puzzle

each month. It is good publicity, and would give you experience in meeting a writing deadline. You can target your humor by forming Crazy Words of phrases used specifically by that group. Create more material than you need, and submit what you think is the best.

★ During the 2020 Pandemic, people were looking for humorous content on the internet. Parents were looking for activities for their children while staying at home to prevent the spread of the virus. I know that several sets of Crazy Word puzzles were circulated through Facebook. I shared them to my page, and they were extremely popular.

☛ How will you use Crazy Words? Who will your audience be?

☛ Now create ten additional Crazy Words specifically targeted for that audience. What words or phrases would that audience be familiar with?

☛ If possible, deliver your Crazy Words to that audience. What kind of response do they receive?

ⒶNIMAL ⒾMPERSONATION

Ⓙ OSEPH GRIMALDI IS considered the Father of Modern
Clowning. He grew up performing in shows with his father,
who was a British clown. According to Grimaldi's memoirs, in
1782, at the age of four, Joseph appeared in a theater impersonating a monkey. His father led him around by a chain leash which
he used to swing the boy around in the air at a rapid speed.
During one performance the chain broke and young Joseph
flew far into the audience where he landed unharmed in the lap
of a gentleman.

Grimaldi expert Richard Findlater, in his book *Grimaldi
King of Clowns*, says, "Monkey tricks were a traditional line
of business for theater children until the twentieth century... In
young Grimaldi's time, and for another century to come, animal
impersonations were a child actor's apprenticeship to the stage.
Skinwork provided a more or less pleasant initiation into the

charlie

mysteries of the family profession... disguised
as a monkey or a dog, a boy acquired the
rudiments of a theatrical education."

In "The Play House" (1921), Buster Keaton plays a stage hand
in a vaudeville theater. When he accidentally allows a young
orangutan to escape, he decides to take the animal's place. He
applies makeup, including large false ears, to look like a monkey.

He dons the monkey's suit. He enters with the trainer, sits in a chair at a dining table, rings for the maid, eats a salad, and smokes a cigar. Next, he jumps into a bed and covers himself with a sheet. The trainer uncovers him revealing that he is eating fleas off the mattress. He discovers a flea on his trainer. He escapes the stage by climbing into a box seat. The man seated in the box flees, but the woman, looking through opera glasses, doesn't realize how close he is. He sits on the railing staring back at her. When she puts down her glasses, she is shocked to see him. He jumps onto the proscenium arch and climbs it to the top. He rides down on top of a piece of scenery that topples to the floor. His final trick as the monkey is to ride a bicycle weaving around two wine bottles. When he crashes, he picks up a bottle, and is disappointed to find it empty. He escapes the stage again by diving through a hidden slit in a backdrop painted like the sea.

I participated in a mime class taught by Tony Montanaro at the first Motionfest in 2000. Montanaro said that when he wanted to imitate a giraffe, he originally tried to make his neck as long as possible. However, nobody understood what he was doing. When he changed his emphasis to portraying the grace and dignity of the animal, it suddenly clicked with the audience.

He taught us how to do a monkey impersonation. He said that instead of trying to move like a monkey, we should try to think like a monkey. Then the movements would come naturally.

I performed a monkey impersonation once when Randy Christensen and I were the instructors for the 2009 Next Step Clown Ministry workshop. During a midweek children's worship service, Randy asked me to assist him in a skit that he had written. Randy was performing the straightman role as the pastor. Randy started to talk about transformation. I misunderstood thinking that meant imitation and began acting like a monkey. Randy corrected me and explained that transformation was not an outward change but was a "renewing of your mind." (Romans 12:2)

A specific type of monkey impersonation act is called a Gorilla Parody. In this routine a gorilla is performing an act in the circus ring when it suddenly escapes. Sometimes it grabs a popcorn box from a vendor and tosses the corn into the air. Then the gorilla steals a purse from an audience member. The woman who loses her purse is actually another performer planted in the audience. The gorilla retreats to the center of the ring and begins going through the purse pulling out its contents. Often the gorilla finds a container of baby powder and begins shaking it in the air. Another standard bit is for the gorilla to find a brassier in the purse which they put on their head like a hat. During the act ,the animal's trainer prevents the woman from entering the ring explaining that the animal is just too dangerous. Finally, she dashes into the ring and grabs her purse. Sometimes the gorilla rips away her skirt leaving her standing there in a slip. She begins hitting the gorilla over the head with her purse and chases the animal from the ring and out the performer's entrance.

Another special type of animal impersonation is two men in a costume portraying a four-legged animal. In England, and other countries that are part of the British Empire, this is known as a Pantomime animal because it was associated with a particular style of holiday show. In America, it is known as a Jargo.

I have performed in a Jargo routine once in my career. When the Funs-A-Poppin' Circus did some winter spot dates, Phil Sherer was temporarily added to the cast. He performed a Jargo act where he was the trainer. His girlfriend was the front end of a giraffe. He asked me to play the back end. It was fun performing a little different style of comedy.

A technique sometimes used to add comedy to a Jargo is called Squash and Stretch. I first heard this concept discussed in terms of animation. A bouncing ball is a classic example. When a ball hits the floor, the force on the bottom of the ball immediately stops the bottom from moving. However, the top of the ball is still moving downward so the ball squishes until the force of compression halts its momentum. When the outward force of compression is great enough the top of the ball begins moving upward. The ball stretches out as the top moves upwards until finally the bottom of the ball is pulled off the floor. Animation students often animate a bouncing ball to practice their use of squash and stretch.

Here are some ways Squash and Stretch can be applied to a Jargo performance. Starting from a standing position, the front person begins moving forward first. The back person stays in place as long as possible, and then they hurry to catch up. It is kind like a cat stretching as they get up from a nap. When the Jargo turns a corner, the back person follows a wider curved path stretching the costume out sideways. When the front person stops, the back person continues walking forward and may straighten up as far as the costume allows as they "bump" into the front person.

An opposite technique, simultaneous movement, is also often used in Jargo performances. Audiences often laugh at movements performed in unison. This could be as simple as the Jargo marching with the front person and back person in perfect step. It looks humorous because animals don't really move this way.

A gag that was frequently performed in Pantomimes was for a Jargo animal like an elephant to split in half. The back half would then wander around trying to find their front end.

It seems that a giraffe is the most popular form of Jargo in American circuses, but different animals are performed in other venues. One of the members of the original 1940 Ice Capades cast was Al Surette, a tramp clown who also specialized in Jargo acts. He often performed as a dog or horse. Frequently a Jargo animal in an ice show would begin crying so that water sprayed out over the audience.

Sometimes a Jargo character has a puppet head. A famous Jargo character is Mr. Snuffleupagus on Sesame Street. The Muppet character's body is supported by aluminum backpack frames worn by both performers. The performer in front manipulates the character's head and expressions.

Basket Animal/ Carry

A COSTUME/PROP THAT MAKES it look like the entertainer is riding an animal is called a Basket Animal. The animal's body is hollow. The clown's legs extend down through the animal's body and the clown is actually walking on the ground. A set of dummy legs straddles the animal's body making it appear that the clown is sitting astride the animal. The name comes the British Pantomime productions where the body of the animal was woven out of wicker similar to how a basket is constructed.

In the early 1990's, the Carson & Barnes Circus clown alley rode basket horses for a race around the hippodrome track. At the conclusion, the neck of one of the horse's was extended so that its rider won by a nose.

Mark Anthony pioneered the art of carving foam rubber props and made a series of Basket Animals. Diamond Jim Parker performed with a Mark Anthony constructed Basket Camel which was rigged so water would squirt out of the animal's hump.

Often the performer's actual legs are hidden using a blanket worn by the animal or some other type of drape, but other options are possible. During the opening montage of circus acts in the 1952 film "Cecil B. DeMille's Greatest Show on Earth", two Indian clowns, wearing Paper Mache masks, ride a Basket Horse pulling a travois. The horse has four visible legs because each rider wears a pair of pants that matches the fabric covering the animal's body.

The performer's legs can be visible in an animal with two legs. Basket birds are common. I have also seen Basket Dragons, Dinosaurs, and a rearing horse walking on their hind legs. Here is Mark Anthony riding an ostrich.

Sometimes humor is derived by what is used to encourage the animal to move. A clown riding a horse may use a fishing pole to dangle a carrot in front of the horse's nose. Mark Anthony carved a giant peanut for another clown to carry in front of the person wearing his Basket Elephant.

A similar concept is for a person to be in a vehicle pulled by actual animals. Often the vehicle is a barrel on wheels similar to what street sweepers use. The performer stands in the bottomless barrel so they can move it by walking. Dummy legs sticking out the top of the barrel make it appear that they are sitting on top of it. The animals are harnessed to the front of the conveyance and the performer follows them. Joseph Grimaldi was known two hundred years ago for his cat carriage. Many contemporary rodeo clowns perform chicken carriages. Paul Wenzel performed a goose carriage gag. His carriage was a box on wheels with a goose harnessed in front.

From the beginning of the circus, equestrians would do a two-high trick with somebody balanced on the shoulders of the rider on the horse. Baptiste Dubois, a French clown appearing in British theaters and circuses, performed a parody of this trick in the mid-eighteenth century. In *The Book of Clowns*, George Speaight describes Dubois' most popular act which was called "Frolics of my Granny." In this routine a horse enters the ring ridden by an elderly woman wearing a "bonnet and black bombazine skirt." A young man seated on her shoulders waves his arms attempting to maintain his balance and nearly falls off several times. Finally, it is revealed to the audience that there is only one rider standing on the horse. According to Speaight, "The lower part of his body is hidden in a wicker frame covered in an old woman's skirt; the old woman's head and body, and the young man's legs, are dummies."

"Frolics of my Granny" is an example of a Carry. That is a prop that makes it appear that one person is carrying another.

Richard Snowberg performed a Carry, constructed by David Heim, which looked like a janitor carrying him out in a trashcan. Having a container makes the construction easier because it hides the junction between the two characters. In this carry, the trashcan was bottomless. The janitor's body from the waist up was attached to the front of the trashcan. Richard's legs extended down through the trashcan into the legs of the janitor's coveralls. Richard's torso stuck up through the top of the trashcan.

Trading Places is a company that specialized in manufacturing Carry props. Their products included a magician in a hat carried by a rabbit, a hunter in a square cage carried by a gorilla, and a bird watcher in a bird cage carried by a parrot.

I have seen photos of clowns with the Ringling Bros and Barnum & Bailey Circus portraying a character carrying a container on their head. For example, a pygmy balancing a pot containing a hunter. In another variation, a woman was carrying a basket of laundry on her head with her husband seated in the basket.

Oleg Popov introduced a routine he called "The Pasha" in 1952. Playing an oriental character, he was seated cross-legged on a sumptuous palanquin. His concubines danced around him while the palanquin was carried in.. He turned and bowed majestically to his audience. In his autobiography titled *Russian Clown*, Popov wrote, "The solemn, serious atmosphere is transformed into a comic one when, wanting to change the position of my legs, I discover that they are not my legs, but papier mâché ones that won't obey me, and, besides this, I am not sitting in the palanquin, but standing upright on my own legs which have been disguised. This sketch was performed with gaiety and simplicity." Popov concluded the sketch by opening the side of the palanquin and walking away leaving his dummy legs behind.

Many clowns have performed variations of this. For example, playing a wrestling fan seated on a box or barrel. They get carried away by the spectacle and end up tying their own legs in knots. Another version is for a contortionist seated on a platform getting tangled up in their own legs.

Steve "Steve the Pretty Good" Hamilton is a magician who uses a flying carpet while doing strolling or atmosphere shows at fairs and festivals. A blue circular drape hanging below the carpet hides his legs. Wearing a bush pilot's outfit, he "sits" cross-legged on the carpet. A flag on the back of the carpet announces a magic show. Not only does the appearance of the flying carpet attract attention, but it also serves as a portable table top that he can utilize in presenting some of his magic effects.

★　　★　　★

EXERCISE

PROFESSION

IN ABOUT 1990, a friend asked me to critique and act called
the Magic Plumbers. They wore white overalls and all of their
props were plumbing related. They performed a linking ring
routine with three toilet seats. They levitated a toilet tank valve
float. It was an unusual and very funny act.

The Hanlon Lees were a famous theatrical clown troupe active
from 1860 through 1890. In one scene of their show "A Trip to
Switzerland", they play hotel waiters trying to disrupt a dinner
party. They juggle and spin the plates. They juggle loaves of
bread and other food. One of the members juggles three eggs,
a knife, and a plate.

Comedy waiters have been a popular act. Kenny Ahern and
Steve Russell currently perform as the Zany Waiters at banquets.

My clown character was originally a janitor. I carried a mop
and bucket in many of my performances. The bucket was gim-

micked with parachute cord forming a square a little below the rim. (I drilled eight holes, a pair every quarter of the circumference that the cord was threaded through.) When I stepped into the bucket, the cord would bend out of the way so my foot would enter. When I tried to withdraw my foot, my heel would hook on the cord so my foot became stuck.

I also created a gimmick that was a piece of elastic, two lengths of fishing line, and two s-hooks. The gimmick was threaded through the front belt loops of my pants. I placed my bucket on the ground open side up, and sat on it. I began waving to people in the audience. I would secretly hook the gimmick to the points where the handle attached to the bucket. Then when I stood up, the bucket was stuck to my pants. I would unsuccessfully look for it, I sat down again in frustration. When I realized that the bucket was under me, I excitedly jumped up. I turned around to pick it up, but it was gone again. When kids told me where it was, I tried to get it off, but it remained stuck to the seat of my pants. Finally, I had somebody take hold of the bucket. I secretly released the gimmick. Now they could easily remove the bucket for me. I would take it from them, tip my hat in gratitude, and then move to a different part of the audience where I would repeat the routine.

During my career, I have also been a cowboy clown and a pirate clown. My character didn't change. I was still Charlie. I was just Charlie as if he had been employed by a ranch and a pirate captain. I have also played other professions briefly.

Circus clowns frequently perform acts based on a profession. I have seen clown acts portraying chefs, hotel porters, doctors, dentists, auto mechanics, painters, carpenters, symphony conductors, and other jobs.

☞ Choose a profession as the basis for an act. What do people in that profession wear?

☞ What objects are associated with that profession? How can you incorporate those objects into your act?

☞ What kinds of actions do people in that profession perform?

☞ What is that profession's shop talk? How can you use that as the basis for verbal humor? What cliches are associated with that profession? How can you take advantage of them?

☞ Write a sample script or running order for that act?

FEMALE/MALE IMPERSONATION

IN CLOWNING, THERE is a difference between female impersonation and appearing in drag.

A female impersonation is a male performer playing a female character. Barry Lubben's Grandma is a good example of that. It used to be common for male clowns to play "realistic" mother characters in the circus. Lou Jacobs was known for his female impersonation roles.

John Travolta played a female impersonation role as Tracy's mother in the musical film "Hairspray".

Beulah was the maid on the Fibber McGee and Molly radio program in 1944–1945. When you listen to the recordings of the program, there was always a great response, including laughter, from the audience when she was summoned. Her first line was always "Somebody ball for Beulah." That line was not what caused the reaction. It was not widely known that Beulah was performed by Marlin Hurt. It was a brilliant piece of vocal female impersonation. During the broadcast, the studio audience was shocked when they heard Beulah's voice coming from a man. Eventually Beulah was spun off into its own radio program. Hurt initially continued playing the character. However, after Hurt died of a heart attack, a succession of women performed in that role.

RONE and Gigi, two women from Japan, are the founders/directors of Open Sesame, Japan's Theatrical Clown Troupe. They perform male impersonation. Their two little men are so realistically portrayed that I thought they were actually men the first couple of times that I worked with them.

A British Pantomime tradition was the role of the Best Boy, a woman playing a male character. One explanation for its popularity was that many of the female characters wore long dresses while male characters wore doublets and tights. That meant that playing a male character allowed a female performer to display her shapely legs.

I have seen video of European clown acts that includes male impersonation. Usually, they are either music or acrobatic routines. At the end of the act one of the entertainers reveal that they are a woman by pulling off their wig allowing their actual long hair to cascade down.

Appearing in drag means a performer plays a male character pretending to be a woman. Robin Williams played a drag role in the film "Mrs. Doubtfire".

A stock clown drag gag is to have balloon bosoms that are burst during the act. Hans Leiter was known for his drag act performed in ice shows. When one of his balloon breasts broke, he would center the remaining balloon on his chest. Then, because it was filled with helium, it would rise up out of his V-neck dress. Then he would sadly wave goodbye to his breast as it floated away.

Sometimes the person in drag really is a female performer playing a male character pretending to be a woman. During the 1980 Carson & Barnes Circus season, Maddie Lou "Flip" Flippen Bayliss performed a washer woman routine assisted by her sister, Edie. Although she was a female clown, she performed the act in drag. She used balloons to form large breasts. Both women sat on low stools while washing clothes in buckets. Edie hit Flip on the back with a wet towel. She fell forward onto her chest. One of the balloons burst. (She carried a pin to make sure it popped when she wanted it to.) When she stood up, she leaned to the side because of her lopsided bosom. She took her remaining balloon and shifted it to the center of her chest. Then she could stand up straight. Next Edie hit her in the chest with the wet towel breaking that balloon.

I performed in drag one season. The 1976 Circus Kirk clown alley had five members, three men and two women. One of the acts we did was a beauty pageant. Woody entered first carrying a box camera. When the Ringmaster stopped him and demanded to know what he was doing, Woody responded, "I'm here to photograph the winner of the beauty pageant. Send in the contestants!"

Then Doug and I would prance into the center ring. Doug had an actual dress that he wore for the act. The wig that he used could have been worn by a man or a woman. He had large balloon breasts. I was a Tramp character with a painted-on beard, so I knew nobody would believe that I was a woman. My dress was a sheet wrapped around my body and held in place with a flower broach. I plopped a string mop head on top of my hair to serve as my wig. I used two nerf balls for my tiny breasts in order to be a contrast to Doug. The two of us would start to flirt with some of the men in the audience.

Then the two female clowns would enter impersonating men. They wore white union suits covered by leopard skin caveman costumes. They had balloon biceps. They would demand that men be allowed to enter the competition.

After some comedy about getting us posed for the photograph, Woody took our picture. A starter pistol hidden inside the camera caused the sound of an explosion. Our outer costumes broke away leaving all four of us in comedy underwear. After we ran out in embarrassment, the Ringmaster and Woody did a commercial for the clown photo studio on the midway where people could pose for a Polaroid photo with a clown.

EXERCISE

Oh, You Can't...

HERE IS ANOTHER formula joke from my Boy Scout camp-fire days. Mr. Stevenson was our Scoutmaster so this was deflation of authority humor.

> **LEADER:** Repeat after me. Oh, you can't get to heaven
> **GROUP:** Oh, you can't get to heaven.
> **LEADER:** In Mr. Stevenson's car.
> **GROUP:** In Mr. Stevenson's car.
> **LEADER:** Because Mr. Stevenson's car.
> **GROUP:** Because Mr. Stevenson's car.
> **LEADER:** Won't go that far.
> **GROUP:** Won't go that far.

Then a different boy became the leader. He might say:

Repeat after me. Oh, you can't get to heaven
On Mr. Stevenson's skates.
Because Mr. Stevenson's skates.
Roll right past the gates.

☞ How might you adapt this formula to your own use? What task would you be attempting? Would you use a character's name? Would you use it as a call and response routine? Could you turn it into a dialogue between two characters?

☞ Write at least ten "Oh, you can't..." formula jokes.

COMEDY IMPERSONATION

THE PERFORMER ANNOUNCES that they are going to do an impersonation, but it is not a realistic impersonation. It often involves a visual punchline.

For example, Jim Howle would announce that he was going to perform his impersonation of Elvis Presley. Then he would lie down on the floor and cross his hands on his chest.

Jim would announce that he was going to impersonate a stick of chewing gum. He would pantomime removing his wrapper as if he was a stripper. Then he would make chewing sounds as he contorted his body. Finally, he would pick up a nearby chair and put it on his head.

Ted "Suds" Sudbrack was another entertainer known for doing this type of impersonation. He self-published a pamphlet describing many of his impersonations.

★ ★ ★

_____

Answer Machine

THE ANSWER MACHINE is an improvisation game related to the Answer Man. It is frequently used in classes and I have seen it many times in improvisation shows. It will help you learn how to work with other performers.

Even solo entertainers should learn how to work with others. Sometimes a show will require that two entertainers work together during a transition to fill a break while props are set. Often shows will conclude with all of the entertainers performing a finale routine. I have worked in many shows where a magician needed another assistant so I joined the act temporarily.

Even when it is not a necessity, two solo entertainers might perform a routine together as part of a variety show. It creates the image that they are equal colleagues not competitors. I often greatly enjoy those opportunities.

Also, the most effective solo entertainers don't actually work alone. They interact with audience members. In effect, the audience becomes their partner in that particular performance. Any exercise that helps you discover how to work with other entertainers will also help you discover how to interact with audience members.

Instead of a single person answering questions, a small group of people comprise a machine that will answer. Each person provides one word of the answer. The person next to them provides one more word. Punctuation is provided by a person saying the name of the punctuation mark. For example, "comma." Participants continue adding words until one of them decides that the answer is complete. Then that person says "period" or "exclamation point."

Usually there is a game referee who then picks an audience member to ask the next question.

TIPS

It helps to restate the question. For example, the machine is asked, "why is the sky blue? The first person says, "The." The second person says, "Sky." The third person says, "Is." The fourth person says, "Blue." The fifth person says, "Because." Then the next person has to supply the first word in the creative answer. This establishes a rhythm to the responses. It also gives people a moment to think of an answer.

Don't decide on your answer too soon, and don't try to control the machine's answer. This game requires you to be flexible. The others will surprise you by the words they decide to add to the sentence. Listen to your performing partners and react to the last word that is added.

If you can't think of something right away, add a word to keep the momentum going. If you think too long, you may get a mental block. Conjunctions like "and," "when," or "but" moves it along and gives the next person something to respond to. You can also add a punctuation mark like "dash."

APPLICATIONS

This game expands your ability to listen and to work with others. Because you don't control the outcome, you cannot try to impress anyone else with the word that you add. However, you can add a word that makes it easier for the next person to respond. Instead of trying to look good yourself, you work to make the entire group look good.

☛ Is there some way you could use the Answer Machine principles in your performance?

|MITATION

THE DIFFERENCE BETWEEN Impersonation and Imitation is not real distinct. Some people use the terms interchangeably. I think it helps to separate the two for purposes of discussion. To me the difference is intent. In Impersonation you are trying to fool someone, either the audience or another character. In Imitation you are openly copying somebody else.

In the classic Whiteface and Auguste clown act, the Whiteface demonstrates how something is to be done. Then the Auguste tries to imitate them.

An excellent example, is a scene in the 1960 Disney film "Toby Tyler or Ten Weeks with a Circus." Gene Sheldon plays Sam Treat, an Auguste clown. Sam tries to imitate a Whiteface who is performing a magic trick. The Whiteface gestures dramatically to show that his hands are empty. Sam copies his actions but isn't as graceful. With a flourish the Whiteface opens his black coat and pulls a blue scarf out of the breast pocket of his grey and black striped vest. Sam nonchalantly reaches into his plaid jacket and removes a red scarf. The Whiteface waves his scarf in the air so it flutters gracefully. Sam awkwardly copies him. The Whiteface begins to stuff his scarf into his left fist. Sam copies him. The Whiteface clown's poker face indicates how seriously he is taking his task. Sam is having so much fun that he grins at his audience. After tucking the scarf entirely into his fist, the Whiteface turns to his left and raises his left hand high. He dramatically opens his fist by slowly moving one finger at a time to reveal that the scarf has vanished. Sam is surprised by what the Whiteface has accomplished. Sam opens his fist rapidly and is amazed that his scarf has also vanished. Quickly Sam checks both hands, looks into his sleeve cuffs, and pats his pockets looking for the red scarf. He can't find it. The whiteface reaches into his inside jacket pocket and removes a duplicate blue scarf. The Ringmaster whistles the clowns off. The Whiteface marches off triumphantly holding his scarf aloft. Sam follows him carrying their prop table.

Record acts were popular in vaudeville and night clubs. The entertainer would imitate a singer while lip syncing to songs played on a phonograph. They would not perform a realistic impersonation. Instead, they would greatly exaggerate their facial expressions and movements.

An example of this occurs in the "White Christmas", a 1954 film. Rosemarie Clooney and Vera Ellen play the Haynes sisters, a singing act. Bing Crosby plays Bob Wallace. Danny Kaye plays Phil Davis. Wallace and Davis are a song and dance team. The men meet the Haynes sisters in a night club where the women are appearing. The women sing "Sisters". Just before their next show, a Sherriff arrives to arrest the women. In order to give the women time to escape, Bob and Phil imitate them while lip syncing to a recording of the women singing "Sisters". The Sherriff can hear them on stage so he thinks he can wait until the sisters finish their act in order to arrest them. (From the Sherriff's point of view, Bob and Phil are doing an impersonation.) Bob and Phil don't try to fool the night club audience into thinking they are the sisters. For example, they roll up their pants to bare their legs instead of wearing dresses. (From the audience's point of view, they are doing an imitation.) It is a very funny routine. When they exit the stage, the Sherriff is furious that he had been fooled.

Frank "Slivers" Oakley was famous for his baseball pantomime. It was a classical pantomime act meaning that he portrayed all of the characters. He played the pitcher, catcher, outfielders, base runner, and umpire. The act ended with the base runner being called out at home and getting into an argument with the umpire. Slivers took turns playing both participants in the argument. Finally, the umpire ejected the runner from the game. Discouraged, Slivers made his exit. As he played each position, he copied mannerisms of a famous player who currently played that position.

Sometimes the imitation is performed as a tribute. I knew and worked with Don Burda for about 30 years. We had both been core staff members of Clown Camp, and we had also been instructors at various clown conventions and conferences. After Don Burda passed away, I received several requests to perform tributes to him. There were two of his routines that I could imitate. He taught me how to inflate a heart shaped balloon so it seemed to happen by magic. He gave me permission to perform and teach it.

The second routine that I performed in tribute to Don Burda was his vanishing elephant act. Don would announce that he was going to make an elephant disappear. Then Dee, his wife and performing partner, would enter carrying a box of Barnum Animal Cookies. Don would use his right hand to take an elephant shaped cookie. He would do a clumsy false transfer of the cookie to his left hand. Everyone knew that the cookie was still in his right hand. He would visibly squeeze his right hand several times. Then he would announce that he had to sprinkle a little Woofle Dust on the elephant. He held his right hand above his left hand while letting the cookie crumbs pour out of his right hand. Then he dramatically opened his left hand as he proclaimed, "The elephant is gone!"

Sometimes I will briefly imitate an audience member as a way of connecting with them. For example, if I notice that somebody in the audience has their chin on their right hand, I will pause, look at them, and briefly put my chin on my left hand. I wait until I see them recognize that I am mirroring them. This proves that I see them as an individual, not just as a part of the crowd. Then I move on to doing something else.

Be careful not to overdo it. For several years, a mime at Sea World, in San Diego, CA, worked the Come In for their shows. He would get behind somebody entering the seating area without them knowing he was there. Then he would imitate their walk. That entertained the audience. However, he carried it too far. Sometimes he continued after the person became aware of his presence. Other audience members could see that his victims were annoyed by his actions. I also noticed that later in the day, people would look for him before they walked into the seating area because they did not want him to make fun of them.

Kenny Ahern reverses this approach. He asks audience members to imitate him. No matter how well they are able to copy his actions, he leads the audience in applauding them. He performs a very charming routine with a young audience member. While music is playing quietly, Kenny gives the child a duplicate of the hat and glasses that Kenny wears. Then the two of them sit side by side on Kenny's small prop case. Kenny has the child copy him in doing things like taking off their hat and pretending it is the steering wheel of a car. He does some hat manipulation moves that they try to copy. He flips his hat up so that it lands on his head. When they flip their hat up, he catches it, and places it on their head. It is a very charming interaction.

EXERCISE

CROSSING

A FORMULA IS "WHY did the _____ cross the ____?
The most common version is "why did the chicken cross the road? To get to the other side."

It can be changed to other animals, for example, "Why did the turtle cross the road? To get to the Shell Station."

Instead of animals, you can have a famous person or character cross the road.

Why did Johnny Cash cross the road half way? He wanted to walk the line.

Why did Frankenstein's monster cross the road? He wanted another shoulder.

Other objects can be crossed. Why did the whale cross the ocean? It wanted to get to the other tide.

This is one of my personal favorites. When he forgot his script, why did Jack Nicholson cross the "As Good As It Gets" movie set? To go to Helen Hunt for it."

☛ Write twenty crossing jokes.

ANTHROPOMORPHISM

ANTHROPOMORPHISM IS ATTRIBUTING human qualities to non-human objects.

Henri Bergson wrote, "the comic does not exist outside of what is strictly human.... You may laugh at an animal, but only because you have detected in it some human attitude or expression."

This was part of the secret to the success of Walt Disney's True-Life Adventures. The films were shot by naturalists. The actions of animals were natural. However, during the editing process, human motivations were sometimes given to the animals. For example, in "Walt Disney's Living Desert", (1953), two scorpions were shown fighting. Square dance music was added to make it seem that the insects were dancing.

"Son of Paleface" is a 1952 film starring Bob Hope, Jane Russell, and Roy Rogers. In one scene, Bob has to share a bed with Trigger, Roy's horse. Trigger keeps reaching over and pulling the covers off Bob because the horse is feeling cold.

Walt Disney said, "Portrayal of human sensations by inanimate objects such as steam shovels and rocking chairs never fails to provoke laughter."

An example of this approach is the "Johnnie Fedora and Alice Bluebonnet" section of the 1946 "Make Mine Music" Disney film. The two hats meet in a department store display window. They immediately fall in love. Johnnie is devastated when Alice is sold. When he is sold, he rides around on his owner's head searching for Alice. When he spots her in the distance, he is blown off his owner's head. He encounters many difficulties. Finally, he is plucked from a flooded gutter by an iceman. The iceman punches two holes in Johnnie and puts him on the head of one of the horses pulling his wagon. To his delight, Johnnie discovers that Alice is perched on the other horse's head. The two are reunited for the happy ending.

That cartoon inspired this routine that I helped Dottie "Fiddlesticks" Goldfarb develop. She was a classically trained violinist who became a clown. She turned a sombrero into a marionette that hung from the end of her violin. Then the puppet bounced around as if dancing while she played "The Mexican Hat Dance" on her instrument.

Anthropomorphism was used in the "Love Bug" series of movies. Herbie, a Volkswagen Beetle, is intelligent and capable of acting on its own. It forms an emotional bond with its owners. This formed the basis of an act in the "Disney on Parade" arena show where Goofy confronts Herbie. The act ends with Herbie opening his front hood, swallowing Goofy, and carrying him off.

This was actually a topical version of a traditional clown routine. In this routine, a clown drives an old car into the ring.

The car breaks down. The driver gets out to try to repair the car. The car comes alive, moves on its own, and chases the clown out of the ring. It was accomplished by having a driver hidden in the back of the car. George Cook created and patented the original "Funny Ford" in 1926. He built it out of a 1913 Model T. His son, Merle Cook, took over the act in the 1940's. By 1967, Jack Cook (real name Jack Cugnin), Merle's son, started doing the act. He eventually replaced the car that he used in performances. Jack restored his grandfather's original car and donated it to the Circus World Museum in Baraboo, WI.

Norm Nelson performs a famous version of a floating routine known as Zombie. In his version, a violin plays while it floats around in front of Norm. Norm leaves the stage at the end of his act. When he returns to take his bow, a robot version of the violin rolls along following him. When they get to the center of the stage, they both turn to face the audience. Then when Norm bows by bending at the waist, the neck of the violin tilts forward in its own bow. That got a lot of laughter when I saw Norm perform one year in the Academy of Magical Arts and Sciences award banquet.

I used that as inspiration in my Floating Cane routine. I have given the cane a personality, and interact with it during the routine as if it is another character. At the finish of the routine, I let the bottom of the cane rest on the stage floor, and then as I take my bow, the cane tips forward in its own bow.

At the 1991 World Clown Convention in Bognor Regis, England, a clown from Germany taught me one of his short routines and gave me permission to perform it myself and to teach it to others. You explain that you have asked a friend to help you lead the group in calisthenics. His name is Corky. Then you hold up a cork screw which has levers on either side. Directing your audience to copy Corky's actions, you pull down on the center screw which causes the levers to rise upward. Members of the audience lift their arms above their head. You release the center so the levers lower and audience members lower their arms. Repeat several times. Then pull down on the screw just enough so the levers rise to horizontal position and stay there. Holding onto the screw, you turn the outer part of the cork screw creating the illusion that Corky is turning at the waist. Audience members follow Corky's actions as they twist from side to side. Lower the levers completely. Now hold the outer part of the cork screw steady as you turn the screw so the top handle turns from side to side. Instruct your audience to turn their head to the left, forward, to the right, forward, to the left, and forward. Then tell them to turn their head all the way around as you rapidly spin the screw.

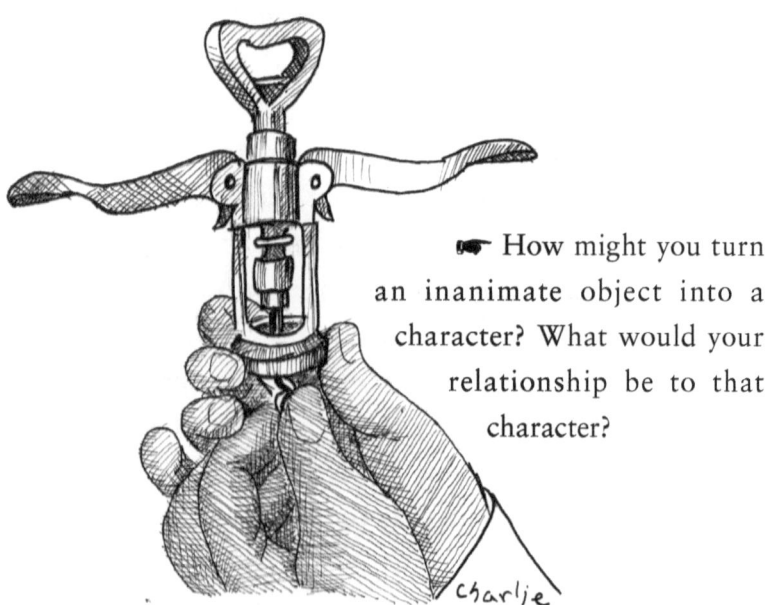

☞ How might you turn an inanimate object into a character? What would your relationship be to that character?

Charlie

EXERCISE

#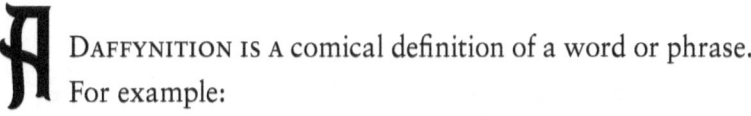

A DAFFYNITION IS A comical definition of a word or phrase. For example:

* National Anthem—Country Music
* Mousetrap—A device mice use to attract cheese
* Bigamist—A man who leads two wives
* Adolescence—The age at which children stop asking questions because they know all the answers
* Cash—The poor man's credit card
* Economics Expert—A man who knows tomorrow why the things he said yesterday didn't happen today

Usually in performance you let the word come up in conversation, ask the audience or another character if they know what that is, and then give the definition. For example, Bob Hope, talking to a USO audience, said, "Last week I was riding in a taxi, you know what a taxi is, it's a civilian jeep."

Johnny Hart, in his "B.C." comic strip, simplified it to a character looking up a word in Wiley's Dictionary or the Book of Phrases. The illustration was a book lying open on a rock. A character would be standing there staring at the book. The joke was in the caption. For example, on September 4, 1985, the caption was, "Cash Flow—In one teller and out the other."

WRITE YOUR OWN DAFFYNITION OF THESE WORDS:

* ★ diet
* ★ lecture
* ★ baby
* ★ antique
* ★ bachelor
* ★ committee
* ★ father
* ★ middle-age
* ★ pedestrian
* ★ marriage

☛ Now choose at least ten more words and write their daffynition.

MISTAKEN IDENTITY

THIS IS CHARACTERS mistakenly identifying other characters or objects. The audience knows the true identity.

It is a favorite technique of comic opera, and classic comic theater. Shakespeare's "Twelfth Night" is based upon mistaken identity.

A character, realizing they have been mistakenly identified, may feel compelled to impersonate the person the others think they are. This happens in "The Court Jester", the 1955 film starring Danny Kaye. Danny plays Hawkins, an innocent forced to impersonate a court jester. The villains mistakenly think that he is Jachomo, an assassin that they have hired. The mistaken identity is complicated by the fact that he has been hypnotized by a witch to think that he is Jochomo. He switches back and forth from Hawkins to Jochomo when he hears somebody snap their fingers.

The "New Neighbors" episode of "I Love Lucy" (episode 21, March 3, 1952) is another example of mistaken identity. Convinced that the people moving into an apartment are spies, Lucy reports them to Sergeant Morton. The policeman doesn't believe her. Lucy, her husband, Ricky Ricardo, and their friends, the Mertzes, barricade themselves in the Ricardo apartment. Ricky shoots a shotgun when somebody knocks on the apartment door. The hole blasted in the door reveals that Ricky nearly blew off the Sergeant's head. The four of them end up in jail.

The humor of mistaken identity derives from the inappropriate responses characters make to the character they have misidentified, and from the complications that result.

The audience's superiority at knowing the truth adds to the appeal of this technique.

Objects can be misidentified. In the July 1, 1985 Adam comic strip, by Brian Basset, Adam is attempting to clean the bath tub. He is shaking the contents of a cylinder into the tub. He is puzzled about why the tub isn't coming clean. Then he looks more closely at the label of the container. He discovers that he had been using Parmesan Cheese instead of cleanser.

I use mistaken identity in my juggling act. While juggling clubs, I turn towards my prop case. I drop one of the clubs so that it lands in the case. I turn, look at the audience, and shrug. Without looking into the case, I retrieve the club. I begin juggling again without realizing that I have grabbed a rubber chicken instead of a club. The audience is always quick to point out my mistake.

When I was in college, we went to an evening of Comic Opera performed by a troupe from Italy. In one of the numbers, two noblemen challenge each other to a duel. The coward substitutes a banana for one of the pistols. His opponent grabs the fruit thinking it is a gun, and arrogantly brandishes it while he tries to intimidate the other man.

Mistaken identity is the premise of a clown skit called Banana Bandana. (The basic idea was created by magician Tom Ogdon.) The performer is listening to directions for performing a magic act with a bandana. They misunderstand, and use a banana instead. Most of the humor comes from folding up the banana.

★ ★ ★

EXERCISE

WHAT IS IT?

T HIS IS A popular improvisation game that I call "What Is It?"
It is related to fifty uses exercise that you completed earlier.
I frequently use it as a classroom exercise. I like to divide the
participants up into groups of six to ten people. Each group
stands in a circle. I give them an object. Their task is to use
that object briefly as if it is something else. For example, use an
inflated balloon as a crystal ball to tell someone's fortune. Then
it is given to somebody else. They may polish the balloon like
an apple and pretend to take a bite out of it. Then they give it
to another person who uses it as a different object.

HINTS:

Pass the object around the circle at random. If you go in order
around the circle, somebody on the opposite side may disen-

gage because they think they don't have to come up with an idea yet.

Pay attention to eye contact and body language. If somebody makes eye contact, especially if they are leaning towards you or have their hands raised, they hope that you will send the object their way because they have an idea that they want to use. Give them the object. If somebody avoids making eye contact, they are hoping that you will choose somebody else because they don't have an idea. Don't give them the object right away.

If you draw a blank, begin moving the object around. Often a mental block is caused by judging ideas which is associated with Left Mode Thought. Movement is associated with Right Mode Thought, which is also the source of new ideas. So, moving the object may help you switch from Left Mode Thought to Right Mode Thought and start a flow of ideas. Also, when you begin moving the object, that may remind you of something else that moves in a similar manner.

Try to think of more than one idea. It is common for more than one person in a group to think of the same idea. If you have fixated on just one idea, you are at a disadvantage when it is used before you have a chance.

If you are directing the exercise, change the object before the group has too much difficulty coming up with additional ideas.

I know entertainers who play this when they get together for a party just because they think it is fun and usually generates some laughter.

This game is frequently included in shows performed by improvisation groups. The group lines up across the stage with a stool or small table in front of them. The director puts an object on the table. When somebody has an idea, they step forward and demonstrate how they would use it as something else. Then they step back into place and another player steps forward. When the director thinks the ideas are tapering off, they substitute a new object and the game continues.

The 2016 Northwest Comedifest included an improvisation show performed by all of the instructors. Mary Pat McCoy was our director. She and I started a running gag while playing What Is It? I used the first object as a hat. When she switched objects the first time, I used it as a hat again. When she chose the third object, she made eye contact with me and let me see it before she put it on the stool. I immediately stepped forward and used it as a hat. For the rest of the game, no matter what object she put on the stool, I was the first person to step forward. Each time I used it as a hat. Then later in that round, I would use that object as something else. Mary Pat began having fun by selecting objects that might be difficult to use as a hat. Each time I was able to find a way to turn it into a hat to the delight of the audience. Not only did our running gag entertain the audience, but it gave my partners on stage a few moments to think of an idea which made all of us look good.

Randy Pryor said, "Our job is to create an atmosphere of play, and invite the audience to play along."

This exercise helps create a sense of play. Sometimes I announce that I need an assistant from the audience. Then I hold one of my juggling clubs as if it was a telescope while I look for a volunteer. When I select somebody, I use the club as a microphone while I briefly interviewed them. I hold the club in front of my mouth while I ask a question, and then extend the club towards them. Usually, they will play along and speak into the end of the club.

RONE and Gigi, directors of Open Sesame, Japan's Theatrical Clown Troupe, made it a planned part of one of their shows. They invite an audience member to join them on stage. Then they demonstrate the game to their volunteer using a baseball cap. RONE and Gigi alternate using it as if it was a different object. After they have each done that twice, they hand the cap to their partner from the audience. No matter what that person does, they react with amazement and led the audience in applauding them.

I often play this game solo while working on new material. For example, I played it using a magic wand. A breakaway wand is a magic prop that tends to be overused. However, by playing this game with a wand I came up with a list of other possible objects that could be substituted. I have built breakaway pencils, paint brushes, and spoons by adding to the ends of a

breakaway wand and repainting it. I have also built a breakaway juggling club by cutting an actual club apart and then altering it so it worked like a breakaway wand. The breakaway juggling club has remained a popular part of my permanent repertoire. I also made a breakaway tennis racket that I used for many years in a juggling routine with a racket and two tennis balls.

This game can lead to ideas for mistaken identity material. Instead of pretending that a juggling club is a microphone while playing with a member of the audience, you can accidentally pick up a club without looking at it and try using it as a hand-held microphone. The easiest way to set that up would be to have your props on a table or in a case. You would use the microphone, and put it down next to your clubs while you do a different routine. When you finish the routine, without looking, you accidentally pick up one of the clubs instead of the microphone.

> ☛ Take one of the props that you use in your per-
> formances. Use that prop to play the "What Is It?"
> game by yourself. What new ideas can you discover
> for using that prop? What new ideas can you discover
> for building a similar prop?

Comic
Inventiveness

Comic inventiveness has two aspects, using a common object in an uncommon way, and creating an unusual invention.

In the "Job Switching" episode of "I Love Lucy", Ricky demonstrates his new invention to Fred. Ricky has attached a music stand to the top of a vacuum cleaner's motor. Ricky has a newspaper spread out on the music stand so he can read while cleaning the rug.

Unusual uses for common objects have long been used in comedy, particularly clowning. In the early Nineteenth Century, Joseph Grimaldi would knock out Pantaloon in order to steal his cheese. He piled the cheese on Pantaloon's back. Then Grimaldi would use a broomstick as the axle for a wheel of cheese. He placed the broomstick in Pantaloon's hands to turn him into a wheelbarrow for carting off the rest of the cheese.

Joseph Grimaldi would use objects to create a parody of something else. For example, he used coal buckets as boots when imitating a soldier.

I used this early in my career when I appeared in parades as a janitor clown. Before the parade started, I would go around entertaining the other units as we all waited. To entertain marching bands, I would imitate the Drum Major by putting my bucket on my head as a hat and using my mop as the staff.

Paul Jung produced baseball circus acts with the catcher wearing a bird cage as his protective mask.

The What Is It improvisational game that you just completed is a great way to generate ideas for this type of comic inventiveness.

In some cases, comic inventiveness would be motivated by need. In my file of comics, I have an undated panel drawn by Bernhardt. A couple are changing a light bulb in a ceiling fixture. The husband is standing on a piano stool holding a light bulb over his head. His wife is spinning the seat around.

Many standard clown gags involve a demonstration of an invention made by the clowns. One of these, the hair cutting machine that works too well, is included in the 1968 film "Chitty Chitty Bang Bang". Caractacus Potts, an eccentric inventor, needs money. So, he takes his pedal powered hair cutting machine to a county fair. He places a bonnet over his customer's head. He gets carried away as he pedals the machine. By the time he stops, his customer has a bald ring separating a fringe of hair and a top knot.

"It's A Gift", is a 1934 short film starring Snub Pollard. He is an inventor, and the film is full of comic inventiveness. One of his inventions is a motorless car. It is powered by pointing a large magnet at other moving cars. The short is included in the 1960 compilation film "When Comedy Was King".

charlie

Often the comic inventions are unusual-appearing versions of common machines, for example a vacuum cleaner. Frequently the comic machines are designed to look like they have a face or are actually given eyes, especially if the machine is intended to act like it has a mind of its own.

RUBE GOLDBERG

A CERTAIN TYPE OF comic inventiveness is called a Rube Goldberg. Its name comes from Reuben Goldberg, an artist famous for his Professor Lucifer G. Butts series of cartoons featuring amusing and complicated mechanical set-ups for accomplishing simple tasks. For example, his Simple Alarm Clock consisted of "The early bird (A) arrives and catches worm (B), pulling string (C) and shooting off pistol (D). Bullet (E) busts balloon (F), dropping brick (G) on bulb (H) of atomizer (I) and shooting perfume (J) on sponge (K)—As sponge gains in weight, it lowers itself and pulls string (L), raising end of board (M)— Cannon ball (N) drops on nose of sleeping gentleman—String tied to cannon ball releases cork (O) of vacuum bottle (P) and ice water falls on sleeper's face to assist the cannon ball in its good work. "

Jennifer George, Rube Goldberg's granddaughter, defined a Rube Goldberg as "an overly complicated machine that does a very simple task hopefully in a comical way."

Rube Goldberg devices are featured in several Warner Bros. cartoons, usually as a trap. In "Homeless Hare", a cartoon set in a building under construction, Bugs drops a hot rivet down a pipe. The rivet goes through a series of pipes and comes out a faucet, landing in a rain gutter. It rolls down the gutter landing on a load of bricks carried by a workman. When the load of bricks is dumped, the rivet bounces over the edge of the floor, falls onto a board, rolls to a flight of stairs, and bounces down them. Then it enters another pipe, drops onto a ladder, bounces down the steps, and finally lands on a rope passing over a pulley. The rope burns through, and drops the steel tank it is supporting onto Bug's enemy, the foreman.

Another version of a Rube Goldberg device occurs earlier in the same cartoon. The foreman hits Bugs with a beam knocking him silly. Bugs wanders along a beam and just as he gets to the corner a hook from a crane hits his leg turning him onto the next beam. He walks off the end of that beam, and lands on another beam being hoisted into place. He walks off the end of that beam, and lands on another beam being hoisted to the next floor. He reaches the end of the beam just as it is put into position. He walks across that floor, and up a board leaning against an upright. The board teeter totters and be falls to a rope. He walks, but doesn't get anywhere because the rope is playing out through a pulley. Just as the rope ends, a large pipe is hoisted past, and Bugs walks through it, being deposited on another floor. Bugs walks towards an open elevator shaft and the freight elevator arrives at the same time he does. He continues across the floor and off the edge, falling into a rain barrel which revives him.

Often a Rube Goldberg human gag involves a person knocked out of their senses or sleep walking, but it doesn't have to be. Ken Berry played bumbling Captain Parmenter on "F Troop." His own clumsiness could motivate a Rube Goldberg. In one episode, he fell over a hitching post, landing in a chair, which toppled over backward, somersaulting him towards the next object to fall over.

Milton Berle did a TV sketch where he read a newspaper while walking instead of watching where he was going. He wandered into a construction site, onto a freight elevator which took him up in a tower, and then the tower toppled precipitating him into the next fall. That could be turned into a topical routine by somebody not noticing where they are going because their attention is focused on their smart phone.

The popularity of the Rube Goldberg device is attested to by the longevity of the Mousetrap and Crazy Clock games which are Rube Goldberg toys.

The Los Angeles Museum of Science and Industry had a Rube Goldberg device to demonstrate potential and kinetic energy. The exhibit was always surrounded by enthralled spectators. In recent years I have seen Rube Goldberg devices on display in museums in Bloomington, IL, Coupeville, WA, and West Springfield, MA.

Jennifer George oversees an annual Rube Goldberg competition. Each year a task is assigned for the Rube Goldberg Machine Challenge. The goal for the 2014 competition was to zip a zipper.

The original task for the 2020 in person competition was going to be turning off a light. When the pandemic made in person events impractical, the goal was to submit a video where ten to twenty steps were used to drop a bar of soap into some-one's hand. There were 450 videos submitted from 12 countries for the competition.

I saw several other Rube Goldberg ideas posted on the inter-net during 2020. One of them featured a variety artist. Unfor-tunately, I don't remember his name. He started off riding a unicycle. When he ran into a table, he stepped off the unicycle onto a board on top of the table. The board was propped up on a cylinder. He moved forward so that the board was balanced on the cylinder. He did some short Rola Bola stunts. When he stepped off the other side of the board, he landed on a Rolling Globe. He walked on top of the globe as it rolled across the floor. It ended up under a tight wire. He walked the wire to the next apparatus that he performed upon.

According to Jennifer George, Rube Goldbergs were so popular during the pandemic because so much of life was outside our control. She said, "This was controllable, the coronavirus may be raging outside, but inside you could control building your machine."

A type of living Rube Goldberg contraption occurs near the end of the 2017 film "The Greatest Showman". During a circus performance, P.T. Barnum is going to give his top hat to Philip Carlyle, his protégé and new partner, to signal that Carlyle would now be in charge of the circus. Instead of giving it directly to his partner, he hands it to an elephant. The elephant takes the hat in its trunk and raises it up in the air. An aerialist circling above the ring on a web grabs the hat. After she has gone around twice, she flips it down to a giant. He hands it to Jo Jo—the Dog Faced Boy who does a flip across the ring and places the hat on a dancer's upraised leg. The fat man removes the hat from her foot and tosses it across the ring to the Siamese Twins. They let it roll down one arm, across both of their shoulders, and down the other arm. It is caught by the bearded woman who hands it back to Barnum. He leaves the ring and presents it to Carlyle. Carlyle dons the hat and runs into the ring where he takes Barnum's place as Ringmaster.

Joe Cook appeared in Vaudeville and Broadway musicals. His live performances on stage included Rube Goldberg devices like an elaborate method to call the hired man to dinner.

A Rube Goldberg is usually thought of as a sight gag. However, Joe Cook, performed convoluted verbal routines that led to a simple conclusion. They could be thought of as a type of Rube Goldberg. His most famous routine was the "Four Hawaiians." He would say, "I will now give an imitation of three Hawaiians. This is one (whistles), this is another (strums a ukulele) and this is the third (taps his foot). I could imitate four Hawaiians just as easily, but I will tell you the reason why I don't do it. You see, I bought a horse for $50 and it turned out to be a running horse. I was offered $15,000 for him and I took it. I built a house with the $15,000 and when it was finished a neighbor offered me $100,000 for it. He said my house stood right where he wanted to dig a well. So, I took the $100,000 to accommodate him. I invested the $100,000 in peanuts and that year there was a peanut famine so I sold the peanuts for $250,000. Now why should a man with $350,000 bother to imitate four Hawaiians?"

☞ How can you use the Rube Goldberg principle? Would it be an actual machine? What task would it perform?

☞ If you were caught in a Rube Goldberg series of actions, what would be the motivation for your character? What would your character experience in moving from one place to another?

☞ How could you use the Rube Goldberg concept in verbal comedy?

★   ★   ★

COVERING THE SITUATION

THIS FORMULA IS called "Covering the Situation. Two different stores are told. The punchline is a single phrase that summarizes both stores. For example, At Betty Hack's eighth wedding, Old Man Duggan predicted, "The marriage will only last three months. He was subsequently proven right.

Mr. Kitzle has been driving a New York Taxicab for 40 years. This past year was his worst ever. He was mugged six times and rear ended five times. His wife can't convince him to retire because he loves his work.

What phrase covers both situations?

"Once a hack, always a hack."

☛ Create ten of your own Covering the Situation jokes. Use your own punchlines or chose phrases from Appendix A.

COMMENTS

Covering the Situation jokes can be performed for their own merit. In 1986, a disc jockey for a Los Angeles radio station included one in his show each day. They were very popular. Puzzle fans tried to guess the punch line before he revealed it.

I included it in this exercise for an additional reason. There is more than one way to set up a punch line, some better than others. If you have what you think is a funny punch line, but it doesn't get the response you expect, the problem may not be the punchline. It might be how you set it up. Change the set up, and try it again.

Imagined Predicament

This is another form of misperception in which a character reacts to a danger which is imaginary.

In the movie "Never Say Die", (1939) Bob Hope plays Kidley, a hypochondriac whose test results gets switched with those of Kipper, a dog. Kidley's doctor diagnoses that he has Acidosis Cannes, a disease where his stomach acidity equals a dog's enabling him to digest bones. The prognosis is he will gradually digest himself from the inside eventually shrinking to nothing. The doctor tells Kidley that he has a month to live. The movie shows how Mr. Kidley reacts to this mistaken predicament. Although previously a coward, he now becomes brave because he believes that he would not live long anyway.

This mistaken medical diagnosis has been used in several other comedy movies. Other imagined predicaments are possible.

In the 1941 film "Look Who's Laughing", Fibber McGee is in trouble because he has been promoting an airplane factory being located in Wistful Vista. A political rival is arranging for it to be built in a neighboring town. Edgar Bergen gets lost piloting his private plane and lands in Wistful Vista. Edgar tries to help Fibber keep the factory in Wistful Vista. He shares Fibber's despair at losing the factory and Fibber's corresponding loss of prestige in his home town. At the end of the film, Edgar's accountant comes to town. He tells Edgar, "If you want the factory located here just give the order. You own the company."

The most famous example of imagined predicament is Chicken Little believing the sky was falling.

Imagined predicament can be motivated by a mistaken identity. For example, a gun fighter backing into a tree limb which they think is a gun barrel shoved into their back. They begin acting as if a villain is menacing them.

★　★　★

REPEAT

☞ Look back over the previous exercises. Choose one to repeat.

☞ Which one was the most difficult for you? Perhaps the experience and knowledge that you have gained since then will make it easier now.

☞ Which one was your favorite? How could you challenge yourself to go beyond what you did when you completed it the first time?

JUXTAPOSITION

THIS IS ANOTHER type of misinterpretation.

Juxtaposition means two characters think they are discussing the same topic, when they are really talking about two different things.

Here is an example from a "Burns & Allen Show" TV program. A running gag in several episodes is that George Burns suddenly starts singing an obscure song titled "Tying the Leaves on so They Won't Fall Down." In this episode, George talks about performing that song during a recent performance in Las Vegas. Gracie Allen wants a famous physicist to be her guest at a dinner party. He explains that he is limited on time so he is only meeting people who were in Las Vegas during the recent atomic bomb test. Gracie exclaims that George was there. The physicist thinks George is a scientist too. The scientist meets George at their home.

SCIENTIST: Your wife told me about your wonderful work.

GEORGE: Thank you, and it's a great honor to talk to a great scientist.

SCIENTIST: Ah, yes, it is.

GEORGE: That's a modest little opening line.

SCIENTIST: Your wife told me you were in Las Vegas.

GEORGE: Las Vegas?

SCIENTIST: Yes, during the atomic bomb test.

GEORGE: Oh, yes, I was there.

SCIENTIST: That's why I'm anxious to talk to you. Tell me, exactly what were you doing when the bomb fell?

GEORGE: "Tying The Leaves So They Won't Fall Down"

SCIENTIST: I want to drink a toast to you, my friend, the greatest scientist who risked his...

GEORGE: Hold it, Hold it, who's a scientist?

SCIENTIST: You are, are you not?

GEORGE: No, I 'm an entertainer.

SCIENTIST: This is terrible.

GEORGE: How do you know? You haven't heard me yet?

★ ★ ★

JUXTAPOSITION

☞ Try writing a short juxtaposition scene. Which two characters are having the conversation? What is the first character talking about? What is the second character's topic? What initial lines could fit both topics? When would the misunderstanding become apparent? How would the conversation end?

INCONGRUITY

INCONGRUITY IS COMBINING things that do not normally go together.

Incongruity was frequently used on "The Muppet Show". In one episode, vacationing penguins turned up in the middle of a musical number set in a jungle.

Combining two different acts can be very effective.

Incongruity is also included "I Love Lucy" episode titled "The Ballet" (S1/Ep 19, February 18, 1952).

Lucy learns that Ricky has openings for two performers in his night club show, a ballet dancer and a burlesque clown.

Lucy is determined to fill one of the openings. First, she goes to a ballet class with disastrous results. Then that afternoon she hires a burlesque clown to teach her a routine. He teaches her a traditional clown act called. Slowly I Turned. He talks about planning to go to Niagara Falls with Martha, but she jilted him. Now every time that he hears the name Martha, he goes crazy.

Lucy mentions Martha, and he hits her with a bladder. She asks why he hit her. He explains that it was because she said "Martha."

Lucy asks why he hit her when she said Martha, and he hits her again. She starts to say, "Why don't you like M—Oh, Oh, I almost said it."

"Said what?"

"Martha." He hits her again.

She takes the bladder away from him. The next time she says "Martha," he pulls a seltzer bottle out of a coat pocket and squirts her. She grabs the bottle, and he gets a cream pie out of his suitcase. She yells, "Put that down!"

He asks, "Do you want me to drop it here?"

She replies, "No! Give it to me!" He hits her in the face with the pie ending the routine.

That evening one of the ballet dancers can't go on. Ricky asks Ethel to call Lucy as a replacement. When Ethel tells Lucy that they need her for the show because she knows the routine, Lucy asks, "You mean, slowly I turn?"

Ethel responds, "Yah, all that turning stuff."

Lucy arrives at the night club in costume for the burlesque skit, rushes onto stage, and discovers she is in the middle of the ballet being danced to a song titled "Martha" sung by Ricky. She joins a female dancer and two male dancers on stage. Every time Ricky sings the name Martha, Lucy starts hitting the other dancers with the bladder, and then returns to attempting the choreography. Eventually when Ricky sings "Martha", Lucy starts spraying everybody with the seltzer bottle. At the end she grabs a pie off a customer's table, but before she throws it at her partner, he picks her up to carry her off stage. Just as they exit, they pass Ricky who gets the pie in the face.

In the "Lucy Meets Orson Welles" episode of "I Love Lucy" (#155, Oct. 15, 1956), Lucy is invited to assist Orson Welles in his act at Ricky's club. Lucy assumes the act consists of scenes from Shakespeare, and proudly invites Miss Hanna, her high school drama teacher. Lucy had played Juliet in a high school production of "Romeo and Juliet". However, Welles is performing a magic act. Welles performs a magic effect called a broom suspension. Lucy does not want to disappoint Miss Hanna. So, while she is hanging in midair, Lucy begins performing the balcony scene from "Romeo and Juliet".

Here is one way that I have used incongruity. I announce that since time is running out, I need two volunteers because I will be performing two magic effects at the same time. I give the first volunteer a piece of paper and ask them to tear it up. Then I ask the second volunteer to select a card from an animal rummy deck. I have the first

Charlie

volunteer drop their pieces of paper into a bag. I turn to the second volunteer and ask them to name the card that they selected. They announce that they choose a dog. I ask the first volunteer to reach into the bag and remove the contents. They pull out the paper that has not only been restored, but folded into an origami dog that matches the appearance of the dog on the animal rummy card.

Music can he used incongruously. In "A View to a Kill" (1985), James Bond is riding a snowmobile while being chased by alpine soldiers on skis. They shoot his machine and it is destroyed. James jumps onto the front skid and rides it like a snowboard down the mountain. When he begins sliding on the skid, the sound track changes to the Beach Boys singing "Wish They Could All Be California Girls". I thought the stereotypical Southern California surf song being played in a snow-covered mountain scene was hilarious.

★ ★ ★

GENE PERRET CHART

THIS IS AN exercise based on one created by Gene Perret. It can lead to a routine incorporating incongruity.

Choose an event or activity as a topic for a possible skit or variety routine. Now list everything you would expect related to that topic. List people, things, actions, phrases, and music. Then after each item on your list, write down its opposite. Now attempt to write a routine that includes some of those opposites.

As part of a course that I taught on clowning, a pair of students chose a picnic as their topic for this exercise. They ended up creating a routine with a Whiteface clown appearing as a society woman using her best china and crystal while going on a picnic. Her partner played a hobo clown stopping for a meal and sitting near her. Everything that he did was in contrast to what she did. For example, when she unfolded a linen napkin, he smoothed out a scrap of newspaper. Their reactions to each other were what made the routine so funny. Their punchline was the hobo turning to her and asking, "Pardon me, but do you have any Grey Poupon?"

☞ If you are a clown, what role would you play? If you perform with a partner, what would be their role? What would be the punchline for the skit?

☞ Study the list of things related to your topic. If you are a juggler, could you manipulate any of them? If you are a magician, could you perform an effect with any of the objects? What if you turned some of them into puppets?

✦ ✦ ✦

ANCIENT/MODERN

T HIS IS AN ancient idea in a modern setting or a modern idea in an ancient setting. For example, Wilma Flintstone using a baby Mastodon as a vacuum cleaner. The "Flintstones" relied heavily upon this technique.

The Hanna Barbara studio reversed it when they created "The Jetsons" set in the future. For example, instead of taking Astro, their dog, outside for a walk, they put him on a treadmill.

In "Hercules", the 1997 Disney film, two children are trapped under a boulder and one of them yells, "Call IXII." (Those are the Roman Numerals for 911.)

I have sometimes seen clowns portraying caveman characters. This technique would work with them. In my idea notebook I have sketches for a basket animal prop where I would ride a Triceratops as if it was an elephant in a circus production. My design included a Snaggletooth Tiger blanket. While riding the dinosaur I would juggle clubs, except that they would be wooden caveman clubs instead of modern style juggling props. I never built the props. It remains one of my favorite unrealized ideas.

I have seen magicians specializing in Renaissance Fair performances utilize this idea. They sometimes say that their magical powers allow them to see into the future when something will be done a certain way. Sometimes they refer to a modern prop as having been conjured up from the future.

EXERCISE

WHATSITS

DURING THE 1980'S, *Laugh-Makers* magazine ran Jim Kleefeld's Whatsits column, which were abstract pictures with a caption identifying what is pictured. For example, here is one of mine.

What is it?

* ...a checkerboard for hermits.
* ...a child's eye view of a man wearing a checked suit.
* ... a race car drivers final sight before his crash at the finish line.

This is a common creativity exercise that was assigned to me in many different classes in school. They are also a humor formula. Roger Price created a series of Droodles books with humorous captions for abstract drawings.

☛ Here are some abstract pictures for you to caption. Write at least one caption for each picture, but try for two or more for each one.

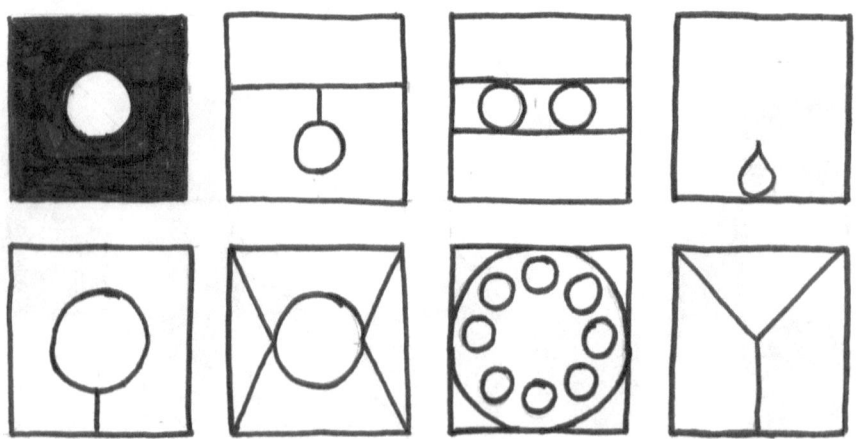

Sight Gag

A SIGHT GAG IS based on appearance instead of words.

I directed the International Gala Show at the 2013 World Clown Association Convention in Borneo. Arthur Pedlar, a clown from England, was in his eighties. He had performed a unicycle act for over fifty years. He could no longer perform his entire act, but he still wanted to do something on a unicycle. His character was a dotty old man, and he knew many people in the audience were aware of his actual age. So, he entered the stage using a walker, known as a Zimmer in England. He pushed the walker forward, and then turned the peddle on his unicycle a half turn. He pushed the walker forward a little further, and then turned the unicycle peddle another half turn. The visual of an old man needing a walker to maintain his balance while riding a unicycle was hilarious.

Bluch Landolph was famous for a sight gag. He would walk along with a board balanced on his head. Suddenly he would stop, spin around, and continue in the opposite direction. The board didn't turn when he did. It is a startling thing to see. The gag depends upon the inertia of the board. Some clowns place flowers in pots on the ends of the board. This additional weight at the ends increases the inertia making it easier to perform.

Paul Jung was known for sight gags incorporating Little People. Jim Howle told me that during his first tour with the Ringling Bros. and Barnum & Bailey Circus, he was cast in a recreation of Jung's Sawing a Woman in Two using Jung's original props. Jim said that he played a woman. He climbed into a box on a draped table. Once in the box, he exited through a trap door in the bottom of the box. He was hidden by the table cloth. The box was sawn in half. Then Jim pushed two Little People up into the box. When the box was opened, the woman's torso ran off in one direction, and her dress ran off in another.

A similar sight gag is a female clown wearing a vintage dress with a large bustle. When the woman turns a corner, her bustle detaches and continues going straight ahead.

There are many families performing as clowns. Sometimes the children appear as miniature versions of their parents. The Paul Jung sight gags could be easily adapted for performance by these families.

Not all of Paul Jung's sight gags required Little People. In his Steam Roller act, the machine rolled over a tall clown leaving behind a flat oil cloth version of the character. Other clowns carried out a stretcher, tenderly picked up the flattened clown, and transported him away. (The steam roller was a lightweight shell with a dummy driver. A person inside the shell walked along pushing it. The clown who was run over, simply started walking hidden inside the shell.)

When multiple ring circuses were introduced in 1870, circus clowns began relying more upon sight gags. They were the dominant form of gag in American circuses in the Twentieth Century. Books on the Golden Age of the Circus have photos that will provide many ideas for sight gags.

★ ★ ★

ORIGINAL COMIC PANELS

NOW WE WILL build upon the previous exercises by creating seven original comic panels. They can be a single panel or an entire strip. Play around with the techniques that you use in your original comics.

The idea is important, not the artwork. You can use simple shapes and figures for your characters. Let them inspire your captions or dialogue.

IT HAS BEEN
A WHILE
SINCE I HAVE
SEEN YOU
A ROUND!

Will You Please
Hurry Up And
Get To The Point

However, if you like to draw, you can create a parody of one of your favorite comic strips. Copy the structure and drawing style. However, change the characters enough that you aren't violating the trademark that protects them. Change the title of your parody strip or panel. The short introduction comic at the beginning of this book was my parody of the Mother Goose and Grim strip by Mike Peters.

☞ Here are some of my other original comic strip parodies: Can you identify the comedy technique that I used in each one?

This is a parody of the Family Circus by Bil Keane.

THE FAMILIAR CIRCUS

"A pretty girl is
like a malady..."

This is a parody of Marvin by Tom Armstrong.

This is a parody of Willy 'N Ethel by Joe Martin.

VISUAL PUNS

A VISUAL PUN IS a particular type of Sight Gag.

Puns are generally thought of as a literary or verbal form, but they can be presented visually. For example, placing an oversized sausage and bun in an invisible dog leash gives you a pet Hot Dog.

A sign is frequently used to set up the joke by identifying the object. Sometimes, the object is kept hidden to make sure everyone in the audience has read and understands the sign first.

When my wife entertained adult patients at Stevens Hospital, she kept her props out of sight inside a cart. She would announce that they were serving chicken and dressing for lunch. Then she pulled a rubber chicken wearing a doll's dress out of her cart. She continued by saying, "and of course we will have gravy and green peas." Then she revealed the letter V cut out of grey fun foam and two letter P's cut out of green fun foam.

Bob "Captain Kangaroo" Keeshan said, "Kids are not less intelligent than adults. They just have less experience."

I performed my version of a traditional clown visual pun when I appeared at Raging Waters. I created a small wooden treasure chest with the word "Diamonds" carved into the lid. Opening the lid revealed that it was full of poker cards of the Diamonds suit. Adults thought it was funny. Young kids never laughed. I realized that they didn't have enough experience with poker decks to know the names of the suits. So, I put a comedy prop called an Electric Deck in the chest behind the Diamond cards. I used the visual pun to get the adults to laugh, and then immediately performed a gag with the Electric Deck which drew laughter from the children. Because they were laughing, they forgot that there was something that they didn't understand.

After that experience, I have tried to be sure that any visual pun that I perform for family audiences uses objects that children are familiar with.

Sometimes visual puns are presented using a sign board. I painted a picture of a castle on one side of a board. I would display the castle, and ask audience members if they would like to see the royalty. Then I turned the board around revealing a large capital letter T with a crown painted on top of it.

In another sign board gag, the front looked like a chalkboard at a diner. It said, "Today's special Chicken Dinner $1.25." Turning the board around revealed an ear of seed corn that was attached to it.

Visual puns can also be represented as a book. A gag that I used with great success at Raging Waters was a box shaped like a book. The title was *The History of Aviation Volume One*. The author's name was Emma Byrd. Opening the book revealed a giant plastic fly. (The fly was sold in joke shops under the name Texas Fly.)

After seeing my book prop, Dena Piraino created one of her own. The title was *Fishing for Beginners*. Opening the book revealed a can of tuna and a can opener.

Sometimes a visual pun will inspire additional related ideas. Randy Christensen created a routine in which he entered with a Domino's Pizza box. When he opened the lid, the audience saw several tiles from a Domino game spread out on imitation pizza dough. Dena Piraino expanded that into a series of pizza jokes. Take-out pizza boxes often have a plastic support to keep the lid from being smashed into the top of the pizza. Those supports are round and have little legs holding them up. Dena put tiny checkered table cloths on several of the supports and glued them onto imitation pizza dough. Then she put her prop into a Round Table Pizza box. Her Numeral Uno Pizza was the imitation dough formed into a large number 1. She created several other pizza gags that she would use as a running gag. When she performed at a company picnic, she would walk around trying to deliver one type of pizza. Then she would return to her car and get the next type of pizza.

Raging Waters had many guests with season passes. That meant I might see some people once or twice a week. I wanted to have something new for them on repeat visits. So, I created a series of bird visual puns. I carried around a bird cage which would have a different bird each week. I started with a Blue Jay, which is a large letter J painted blue. That is a traditional clown gag. Then I found an oversized badminton shuttle cock which was my Birdie. I built a small foot stool that I attached to a hanging perch which was my Stool Pigeon. I told my friend Mary Beth Martin about my visual puns. She went to a Catholic book store and purchased a little statue of a Cardinal which she put in her cage.

Visual Puns are often associated with clown performances, but they can be used by other variety artists. Randy Pryor used them in one of his juggling performances. He did a few juggling tricks with clubs. Then he announced that he had a club collection. He put the top of a Mickey Mouse sippy cup, sold at Disneyland, on the end of one of his juggling clubs, and identified it as his Mickey Mouse Club. He did a few more juggling tricks. Then he stuck a roof on one of the clubs, and identified it was his Club House. He did a few more tricks, and then he stuck an elastic band with a feather sticking up on one of his clubs. He identified that as his Indian Club. Part of the entertainment value was people tried to guess what the prop represented before he announced it.

I was part of a three-person juggling show one season at Raging Waters. We worked with an emcee. After we did some ball routines, he would ask, "Can you juggle clubs?" That inspired me to build a juggling club visual pun. I cut three rectangles out of plywood and painted then so they looked like playing cards that were the Ace of Clubs, Two of Clubs, and Three of Clubs. When the emcee asked his question, I nodded yes, and pulled out the giant poker card clubs and juggled them. That inspired our emcee to create some verbal puns. He would respond, "Charlie, you are a real card. Now do it right or I will deck you." Then the three of us got out actual juggling clubs and performed a series of routines with them.

Details are important. When my wife performed the chicken dinner gag during her hospital appearances, she used a take-out box from Kentucky Fried Chicken which strengthened the set up. She announced that she had a three-piece chicken dinner. Then let her audience look into the box where three kernels of seed corn were glued to a napkin.

When I performed my hot dog routine at Raging Waters, I added a name tag to the collar identifying him as Frank. Adults thought that was hilarious.

I carried my props in a large treasure chest for my performances at Raging Waters. I posted humorous signs inside the lid of the trunk to provide additional humor. One of them was a picture of a fish with holes going through it. The caption on the picture was "Holey Mackerel." I took the time to research the appearance of mackerels and used that in creating the picture. I took great pride in knowing that I had been accurate. Most people just knew that it was a picture of a fish. Once I heard a man exclaim, "That really is a mackerel." That response made the effort worthwhile.

EXERCISE

VISUAL PUNS

Now explore some visual puns. Sketch what you think each of these objects would look like.

- ★ Jail Bird
- ★ Diamond Ring
- ★ Baseball Bat
- ★ Horse Fly
- ★ Honey Bee.
- ★ Catfish
- ★ Watch Dog
- ★ Saw Horse
- ★ Hero Sandwich
- ★ Horse Shoe
- ★ Rubber Band
- ★ Submarine Sandwich

☞ Now create ten more visual pun ideas.

☞ How would you present each of your visual pun ideas? Would you use it as if it was the real object? What kind of a container might you carry it in? Would you present it using a sign board? What details would you add to it to increase the entertainment value?

☞ Look at the props that you use in your performances. Can any of them be turned into a visual pun?

TRANSFORMATION

TRANSFORMATION IS A special type of sight gag where one object or person suddenly turns into another.

In the early Nineteenth Century, Joseph Grimaldi specialized in transformation scenes. The set location might suddenly change to someplace else due to flaps on the set walls and flat pieces of scenery that would slide up and down through slits in the stage floor.

I saw this technique used in a melodrama performed in the Birdcage Theater at Knott's Berry Farm. When the curtain opened, the set depicted a hunting lodge in the winter. The actors began their first scene, but the references were to a tropical local. An actress stopped the scene to say, "I think we are in the wrong place." Instantly flaps on the walls fell, and the furniture was spun around changing the setting to a grass hut.

Cathy is a member of Open Sesame, Japan's Theatrical Clown Troupe. At a World Clown Association Convention, she performed a Cinderella routine. She entered wearing a ragged dress.

She played a song on a melodica. At the conclusion of the song, she spun around and did an instantaneous costume change to a ball gown. Instant costume change acts are popular in magic shows and circuses. Clowns can do them as well. The difference is that the clown has a reason for performing the change.

There is not always a mystery to how a clown performs a transformation.

A Bend Over is one type of transformation frequently used in the circus. Two or three clowns are on the hippodrome track. One of them is wearing a cape. Their partners momentarily hide them by holding up a drape. When the drape is lowered, the clown has been replaced by an animal. Jackie LeClaire told me that his father performed one where he changed into Sparkplug the Horse, a popular character from the Barney Google comic strip by Billy DeBeck. Jackie said that it was a natural choice because Sparkplug was always shown wearing a blanket that extended down to the ground.

You can see a Sparkplug transformation being performed in "The Circus Clown", a 1933 film starring Joe E. Brown. It occurs near the beginning of the film when Happy goes to see the circus.

To perform this, the clown has a dummy head attached to the seat of their costume. Their cape covers it up in the beginning. When they are hidden, they turn sideways, bend over, and pull their cape up over their head. The cape is reversible. The other side of the cape forms a blanket that hides the clown and appears to be the body of the animal. The dummy head is then visible to the audience.

In addition to the horse, I have frequently seen Bend Over elephants. One of the most unusual that I have seen was in a fairytale routine. The princess kissed a handsome prince who transformed into a frog sitting on a rock.

Another type of transformation is known as a Lift or Kick Up. At Clown Camp, I saw Jackie LeClaire perform a routine that was built and originally performed by his father early in the Twentieth Century. Jackie entered dressed as a Settler woman in a long dress. Suddenly he hooked his right foot under the hem of the dress and kicked up sideways so he could reach the him with his right hand and hold it. He repeated that on the left side. Then he lifted up on the hem turning the dress inside out and raising it until the fabric covered his head. The reversed skirt formed a turban. A dummy head was attached to his chest. Dummy shoulders and arms were attached to about the bottom of his rib cage. He had on a short pair of pants with the waist worn low. The image it created was that of a little Turkish man. He did a funny little dance as he spun around. Then he dropped the dress covering up the little man and made his exit.

This was actually a version of a routine performed on stage in 1785 by John Durang, the first American born circus clown.

Durang performed the routine in reverse. He entered the stage as the Little Turk. Then he dropped the skirt and exited as a woman. Durang painted self-portraits of himself performing this routine that are part of the collection of the Historical Society of York County (PA). The paintings are reproduced in his memoir.

Both versions of those two routines were inspired by the Asuk Musuk dance traditionally performed by Turkish children.

Clowns with the Ringling Bros. Barnum & Bailey Circus have done lift ups. Christopher Hudert performed one where a Strongman transformed into a Bearded Lady. Another clown with that circus transformed from a woman into a mermaid.

Objects can be transformed. Transformations are frequently performed by magicians. Usually, they are just a demonstration of the magician's skill. However, they can be comedy bits if they are performed for a funny reason.

In one of my routines, I put three juggling balls into a tube. I ask if the audience would like to see me make them vanish. Then I lift the tube revealing that the balls had been transformed into a canister of Vanish bathroom cleanser.

In another of my routines, I held up a sign announcing "Balloon to Dove." I attached a balloon to the top of the sign. Suddenly the balloon burst revealing a bottle of Dove dish soap balanced on top of the sign.

When I was young, I remember seeing a transforming marionette. It started off as Cinderella wearing her rags, then it suddenly changed to Cinderella in a ball gown. The puppet had two torsos joined end to end at the waist. The dress was reversible and had a hoop sewn inside the hem. When the puppet made its entrance, the dress covered the ball gown torso. When the puppet flipped over, the dress slid down covering the ragged torso. When the clock began to strike midnight, the puppet was flipped over once again. The dress slid down over the body covering up the fancy torso.

Mark Anthony pioneered props carved out of foam rubber. He created ones that would transform when they turned inside out. In my collection, I have a rabbit that turned into a tortoise and a skunk that turned into a bouquet of flowers.

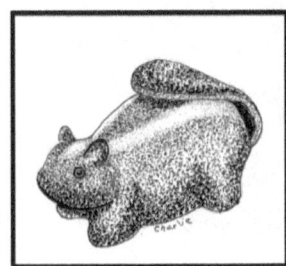 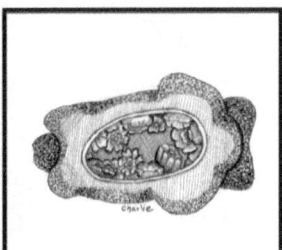 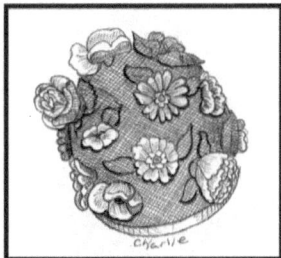

Mark also constructed a little brown moonshine jug that turned into a pink elephant, a little brown jug that turned into a kicking mule, a whale that turned into Jonah floating on a raft, and a moon rock that turned into a wedge of cheese.

Magic by Gosh manufactured and sold a red sponge ball that turned into a red sponge rabbit cut out shape when it was turned inside out. When I performed with that, I would start telling rabbit jokes. After the transformation, I said, "Don't I have nice red hare?" Then I produced a small grey rabbit that I had carved out of foam, and said, "Oh, no, I found a little grey hare."

Transformations are an important part of Chalk Talks /Trick Cartoons.

There are actually two types of Chalk Talks. In one, a picture is painted using pastel chalks. When the normal lighting is turned off and a black light is turned on, the picture suddenly transforms. For example, a bridge suddenly appears spanning a chasm. This type of Chalk Talk is usually performed for dramatic effect as part of a Gospel Ministry presentation.

In the other type of Chalk Talk, a drawing or a printed word is transformed, usually by adding additional lines. I refer to these as Trick Cartoons because lay people don't understand the term Chalk Talk. During the vaudeville era, these drawings were done on a large newsprint pad using a charcoal stick. Sometimes colored chalk was used. Contemporary Trick Cartoons are often done with markers or pens. When I do strolling entertainment, I carry a 3x5 notepad and a fine tip marker for doing the cartoons.

In some cases, you start with a word and then transform it into a related drawing. For example, turning the word "SPOT" into a drawing of a dog.

In some cases, you turn a drawing of one object into another. For example, a drawing of an apple transforms into a drawing of a serpent.

The final type of Trick Cartoon is an optical illusion. For example, a drawing of a greedy man transforms into a picture of a pig's face when the paper is turned so the picture is upside down.

Frequently, these transformations result in laughter when they are performed.

Ed Harris was known for creating Trick Cartoons. He wrote Trick Cartoons columns for *New Tops* and *Laugh-Makers* magazines. He published several books of his creations. Ralph Dewey and Randy Christensen have also self-published pamphlets of Trick Cartoons.

Dr. Harlan Tarbell is known mainly as a magician, but he also created Trick Cartoons. He wrote humorous poems to accompany some of his cartoons. For example, in "The Mouse and the Lady", he drew a picture of a mouse. Then as he recited a short poem about a mouse visiting a farmer's house, he added lines to turn it into a picture of a screaming woman.

Tarbell also combined magic effects and trick cartoons. He originated the effect where you draw a deck of cards on your pad of paper and then a drawing of a chosen card slowly rises up from the drawn deck. I perform one of his routines where you draw a picture of a sack of money. Then you say, "When you do trick cartoons, you can draw your own salary." You tear the paper and pull out a stack of dollar bills. Some of his trick cartoons are included in *The Tarbell Course in Magic Vol. 8.* Two books of his Chalk Talk creations were published.

VISUAL PUN PATTER

NOW YOU WILL create patter to go with your visual pun. Start with a list of things associated with each definition of the word. I'll use my Hot Dog as an example.

Here is a list of things associated with dog defined as an animal.

* Pure Bred
* Papers
* Police Dog
* Tail
* Buns
* Ears
* Collar
* Leash
* Bark

* ★ Dog Tags
* ★ Dog Races
* ★ Watch Dog
* ★ Shepherd
* ★ Poodle
* ★ Obedience School

Here is a list of things associated with dog defined as food.

* ★ Buns
* ★ Ketchup
* ★ Mustard
* ★ Relish
* ★ All Beef
* ★ Ballpark Frank
* ★ Bread
* ★ Napkin
* ★ Bratwurst or Brat
* ★ Sausage
* ★ Pickle

The next step is to look for things that the two lists have in common. The word Buns is on both lists. One list has papers while the other has napkin.

Then start looking for verbal puns, especially ones that link words from the two lists. For example, Not Cutting the Mustard means not meeting the requirements. That can be paired with the high demands for a Police Dog.

The two lists inspired this patter to go with my Hot Dog. "This is my dog, Frank. I bet you never sausage a dog, but doesn't he have nice buns. He is pure bred, all beef. Would you like to see his papers? (Pull out a napkin.) He flunked out of obedience school because he was a little brat that was always getting into a pickle. He wanted to be a police dog, but he couldn't cut the mustard. He tried to enter dog races, but he just couldn't ketchup. He thought about becoming a watch dog, but he didn't relish the hours."

☛ Look at the list for possible details that you could add to your prop. Often, I got a great second laugh when audience members noticed that Frank has a dog tag attached to his harness.

☛ Now select one of the visual puns from the previous exercise and use this method to write patter to go with it.

★ ★ ★

Hidden Element

A HIDDEN ELEMENT IS something the audience sees, but the character doesn't. It might be Clarabell the Clown sneaking up on Buffalo Bob with a seltzer bottle. It could be a puppet that peeks out when the performer turns away, and ducks out of sight when the performer looks back. W.C. Fields would doff his hat, and when he replaced it, it would end up on his cane which he was carrying over his shoulder. He couldn't find the hat even though it was in plain sight to the audience.

This is a good way to involve the audience. Children will yell at the performer about what they see. The performer can fail to find the hidden element as long as the audience response continues to build.

One of my first original circus routines was based on a Hidden Element. I would do a simple feat, and then take off my hat as I performed a sweeping bow. When I straightened up, I swung my arm to replace my hat. I released my hat so that it landed to my right. I continued moving my right arm up as if I was putting my hat on my head. When I felt my hair, I began patting around trying to find my hat. Then I looked up at my empty hand. At this point, kids would begin yelling that my hat was beside me. I would turn to my left and look down. This meant that my hat was now behind me. If the kids told me to turn around, I would quickly spin 360 degrees and look down at the same spot. If the kids told me that my hat was behind me, I would point in that direction. Then keeping my hand pointing in that direction, I would take one step in that direction while turning 180 degrees. That meant that I stepped over my hat so it was once again behind me. I could continue not seeing my hat for as long as audience response justified it.

A hidden element gag is especially effective if finding the element leads into the next gag. With my hat routine, when I thought audience response was peaking, I would take several steps towards the audience and shrug my shoulders. Now when the audience told me where my hat was, I turned and saw it. I took a couple of steps towards my hat, bent down to pick it up, and accidentally kicked it so it slid away from me. I would move towards it again, and once more kick it away just as I was reaching for it. I could chase my hat around the ring or across the ground.

Finally, I would sneak up on my hat. Sometimes I stomped on it to keep it from escaping. Sometimes I would get down on my hands and knees, crawl up to it, and then slap it flat. That led into another routine involving me not being able to figure out how to put my hat on properly.

I-Had-It-Right-Here

T HIS IS THE reverse of a Hidden Element. The audience can
see that something is gone, but the character doesn't know
that so they continue to act as if it is there.

In comedy chases, frequently somebody will crouch down
behind something to hide, and that object is moved away by
somebody else. The comic stays crouching out in the open thinking they are still hidden.

In the film "Safety Last", Harold Lloyd is late for work. He
tries to sneak into the department store where he is employed. He
sees somebody pushing a trash can down an aisle. He crouches
down and walks along beside the trash can. The person pushing
the trash can turns down another aisle, but Harold continues
walking straight ahead in his crouched position.

In another example, a clown carries out a trash can then turns
away to gather an arm load of trash. In the meantime, somebody

else has moved the can. When the clown returns, they drop all the trash on the floor where the can had been.

It is common for a clown to be sitting or leaning on something, move for some reason while the object is taken away, resume their original position, and then after a delay notice the object is gone and fall.

★ ★ ★

ENTERTAINMENT GUIDE

I CALL THIS FORMULA Joke an Entertainment Guide. It consists of a brief plot synopsis of a movie or TV series, followed by the title, which is a pun on a currently popular movie or TV series.

It is a type of joke that Johnny Carson performed frequently on "The Tonight Show." I remember one that he told in 1983 shortly after Barbara Streisand starred in "Yentl," a film about a young Jewish girl in Poland trying to pass as a boy because men had more opportunities. His joke was, "Barbara Streisand is starring in a new film about a Jewish bear. It is called 'Yentl Ben.'" (Gentle Ben was the name of a film and TV series about a bear.)

Here are four examples that I wrote in 1985.

* "The touching story of a farm boy who goes to the big city to make good, but fails. It is called "Back to the Futures".
* "A man who makes his living by romancing rich widows, titled Heir Wolf."
* "Pamela Sue Martin studies ice sculpture in a story called "The Fallon and the Snowman".
* "The incredible story of a faith healer who claims he can restore broken string. It is called, "Ripley's Believe It Or Knot."

People laugh at the familiar. A joke referring to a current hit will get more laughs than an obscure one from the past. Current audiences probably won't laugh at the examples I wrote in 1985. Here is why.

The "Back to the Future" film trilogy was very popular at the time. The first of the three films were released in 1985. They are frequently shown on cable TV so that joke might still be useable.

"Air Wolf" was an adventure television series broadcast for three seasons, 1984–1986. I haven't heard any references to it lately so most people will have forgotten it or never heard of it.

"The Falcon and the Snowman" was a 1985 adventure film based on a true story. I think that it is largely forgotten. Understanding this joke also requires remembering that Pamela Sue Martin played Fallon Carrington Colby on TV in "Dynasty" between 1981 and 1984. Few people would understand the joke today. Those who did understand it would have to expend so much energy figuring out the references that there wouldn't be any surprise. So, it is no longer a useable joke.

That demonstrates the key to using topical material. You have to wait until everyone is familiar with something, and then retire it before they have forgotten it.

> ☞ Write ten entries for an entertainment guide using titles of current movies and television shows. Start playing with the titles to see what puns you can form. The less you have to change the title, the cleverer the joke. Then write the plot synopsis to set up your pun.

★ ★ ★

REVELATION

THIS IS THE opposite of a hidden element. In this technique the audience sees something and they later discover it isn't what they thought it was.

Harold Lloyd liked using revelation to open his films. In the first scene of "Safety Last", Harold is standing behind bars. A noose is visible in the background. His girlfriend and a woman are in front of the bars weeping. An officer and a priest are talking to "The Boy." The two women leave the frame and reappear on the other side of the bars. They tearfully say goodbye. The group begins to move through an archway. Apparently, Harold is in prison about to be executed. The next scene is a reverse shot on the other side of the arch revealing that Harold is in a train station. A station master attaches some mail to the noose which is snagged by a man onboard an arriving train. Harold is going to the big city to seek his fame and fortune. In a title card, he tells the woman, who is his mother, "Mildred has promised to come to town and marry me just as soon as I make good."

Flying Wardrobe is a traditional revelation ending to an equestrian clown act in the circus. After the riders demonstrate a few tricks, an audience member enters the ring demanding a chance to ride the horse. They do everything wrong. When they fall off the horse, the riders demonstrate another trick. Then the audience member demands permission to make another attempt. Again, they fail. The riders and the audience member continue to alternate riding the horse. Finally, the audience member manages to remain standing on the horse's back while riding around the ring. They take off their coat. Then they take off a vest revealing another vest underneath. They continue shedding items of clothing as they ride around the ring. Eventually it is revealed that they are wearing tights matching those worn by the others in the act. They are not an actual audience member. They are the most skillful rider in the group. The act concluded with the clown performing the most difficult trick attempted during the act. Then the clown joins the rest of their group as they all take a bow.

A type of clown magic is based on revelation. The clown performs a magic trick, and then the method is accidentally revealed. For example, the clown might drape a foulard over an object, and then whip the fabric away revealing the object has vanished. When the clown turns to exit, the object is seen hanging from a piece of elastic pinned to their back.

This is different from doing a magic trick so ineptly its secret is revealed. First of all, the magic trick must be successfully completed to set up the surprise. Second, the method used by the clown should be so obvious when it is revealed that the audience would assume no true magician would use it. Third, it should be clear that the clown is impersonating a magician. It is especially effective when the clown is copying a trick done by a magician, and it is obvious the magician could not have used the same method. The audience can feel superior because they caught the clown cheating.

Sucker magic is also based on revelation. The audience thinks they see how the trick is done, and then it is revealed that they are wrong. Its disadvantage is that it can give the audience a feeling of inferiority, which is not a good feeling.

Revelation can he used in verbal routines by incorporating an offstage character. On the Fibber McGee and Molly radio program, whenever Fibber made a phone call, he would start off by saying, "Hello, operator, give me... Oh, hello Mert! How is everything?"

Then he would have a conversation with Mert, the phone operator. Only Fibber's half of the conversation was heard. Based on his comments, Molly assumed that something terrible had happened. Then he would reveal that it really wasn't serious at all.

On the March 5, 1940 episode, Fibber said on the phone, "Your Uncle Gomer. They haven't found the body yet!"

Molly responded, "Oh, dear!"

Then Fibber explained to Molly, "Everything is okay. He drove his car off a cliff and had to walk home. They found the chassis in a tree, but they haven't found the body yet."

★　★　★

CARTOON INSPIRATION

CARTOONS CAN BE a source of inspiration. The copyright law covers the expression of an idea, not the idea itself. However, you cannot copy a character from a comic strip because they are protected by the trademark law.

You can use the basic idea of a comic strip.

For example, in a 1992 "Sibling Revelry" comic strip by Man Martin, Stu tells his sister that he is proud that it only took him three days to finish a jigsaw puzzle. When she asks him why he is so excited, he explains, "On the box it says three to four years."

Lee "Juggles" Mullally turned that into a clown skit that he performed at the 1992 World Clown Association convention.

He entered the stage with three large pieces of a jig saw puzzle. (The pieces were cut out of foam core.) He asked the emcee to time how long it took him to put the puzzle together. He fumbled around a little bit. Finally, he got the pieces arranged so they formed a picture of the WCA logo. The emcee announced that it took him 96 seconds. Lee exclaimed, "That's Great! On the box it says three to four years." Then he joyfully made his exit.

Chad Carpenter repeated a gag twice in his Tundra comic strip. On June 14, 2020 and June 29, 2017, he depicted an old man sitting in a rocking chair on a porch. A faint outline of a hunched over rooster in front of him is saying, "Cock-a-doo-dle BOOOOOOOOO!" The faint outline of chicken behind a chair has thrown an egg which breaks on the back corner of the chair. A chicken in midair has a sheet over its top half. The old man thinks, "Lousy Poultrygeists."

I turned that into a sight gag using a rubber chicken. I put a cotton handkerchief over the head of the chicken. I put a rubber band around the chicken's neck. Then I used a permanent marker to draw black circles representing eye holes on each side of the chicken's head. I used the prop just before Halloween explaining that my chicken was going trick or treating costumed as a poultrygeist.

Actually, comic strip artists sometimes use clown routines as their inspiration. Early in the twentieth century, Footit and Chocolat performed this routine in European circuses.

FOOTIT: Chocolat, come here. I have a riddle for you. My parents had a child, it wasn't my brother or my sister. Who was it?

CHOCOLAT: I don't know.

FOOTIT: It was me.

CHOCOLAT: Oh, that is a great joke. Mr. Ringmaster, come here. I have a riddle for you. My parents had a child, it wasn't my brother or my sister. Who was it?

RINGMASTER: It was you.

CHOCOLAT: No, it was Footit.

Jerry Bittle used the Footit and Chocolat routine in a 1985 Sunday "Geech" comic strip. Artie, Geech, and, Mel are sitting at the counter in a dinner. Artie does Footit's lines. Geech does Chocolat's lines. Mel plays the role of the Ringmaster.

When I was touring with Circus Kirk in 1976, one of the other clowns performed a traditional clown walkaround gag. He would get somebody in the audience to pose while he drew their picture. He would frequently hold up his thumb to measure proportions. When he finished the sketch, he turned his sketch

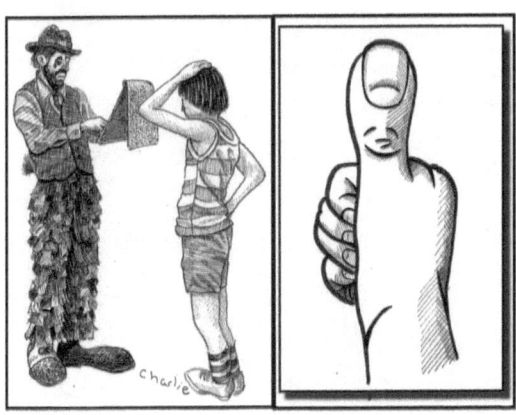

pad around to reveal to the audience that he had drawn a picture of his thumb. I used that idea myself for over twenty years. Eventually Tom Wilson depicted that gag in one of his Ziggy comic panels.

The same approach can be used with animated cartoons. I remember seeing a Betty Boop cartoon where she visited a fair pavilion with a sign announcing inventions of the future. One of the machines was labelled "Spot Remover". Betty placed some soiled clothes in the machine. When she removed them, there was a hole everyplace there had been a spot. I turned that into a magic routine. I displayed a handkerchief with a hand print and several splotches on it. (I painted them on with acrylic paint.) I used a bottle labelled "Spot Remover" to spray water on the handkerchief. I placed the handkerchief into a drawstring change bag. I twirled the bag around announcing that I was spin drying the handkerchief. When I removed the handkerchief, there were holes that matched the previous spots.

☞ Look at the comic strips that you have collected. Can you act any of them out as the basis for a clown skit? Can you create a sight gag inspired by any of the strips? Can you invent a magic effect based on one of the strips? In addition to those comic strips that you have collected, do you remember any animated cartoons that can be turned into a routine?

☞ Continue reading comic strips. Look for ideas that can inspire new routines for you. Clip out your favorite strips and panels to add to your collection.

SELF-DEPRECATION

THIS MEANS THE entertainer allows some of the jokes to be at their expense. Instead of maintaining a perch on a pedestal, they come down to the audience's level. It makes the entertainer approachable and likable. People like somebody who can laugh at themselves.

David Ginn was the emcee for an Open Mike Session one year at Clown Camp. After one of the acts finished, I followed David on stage. I had a pad of paper and a pen. I said, "David, David, may I have your autograph." He graciously agreed to sign the pad of paper. When he was finished, he gave it back to me. I started to leave the stage, looking at the signature as I took a couple of steps. Suddenly I stopped, and turned back to look at David. I asked him, "Is your name David Gin?" (I mispronounced his last name on purpose.) When he nodded, I said, "Oh, I thought you were that Copperfield guy." While everyone laughed, I tore up his signature and exited the stage. Afterwards several people told me that couldn't believe that I would do that to David. Actually, it was David's self-deprecating joke that he asked me to perform with him. I was his audience stooge.

Jack Benny's first radio appearance was as a guest on a variety show. He started his act by saying, "Hello. My name is Jack Benny. There will be a short pause while everyone says, 'Who cares?'"

Here is an introduction that I have used sometimes, "If you are truly great you can be identified by one name. In country music, there is Reba. In rock and roll, there was Elvis. Now, here in clowning is Bruce Charlie Johnson."

Early during the 2020 pandemic, our local grocery store restricted access during the first two hours to senior citizens and others at high risk. I told my grandchildren that I had gotten up early to shop and was disappointed that nobody asked for my ID to prove that I was old enough to enter.

Self-deprecation is like yeast. A little goes a long way. If you overdo it, you can seem insincere and alienate the audience, or make them believe you and see you as an inferior performer.

Jack Benny made fun of his 1945 film "The Horn Blows at Midnight". I think that too many people believed the jokes and it does not receive the respect that it deserves.

★ ★ ★

SELF-DEPRECATION

☞ Write at least ten self-deprecating comments that you could use in your performances.

GAG FILE

𝕬 GAG FILE IS a collection of jokes that you can use to create routines. Many comedians keep a gag file. When Ed Wynn first began performing on the radio, his gag file had an estimated eighty thousand to a hundred thousand jokes. Working with a collaborator, he would go to his file and pull-out potential jokes related to a topic he wanted to cover on his program. Each joke was placed on a file card and posted on the wall. Then Wynn walked back and forth taking down jokes in an order that seemed to work out best.

By collecting comic strips and verbal jokes that you like as part of these exercises, you have already started your personal gag file.

It is not enough to collect jokes. Steve Allen wrote, "For a while I filed jokes away like a beaver—and then came the day when I began having trouble finding particular jokes in the stack. I had created not a gag-file but a gag graveyard. Jokes went in, but they hardly ever came out again."

Magician Ralph Huntzinger once said, "If you can't find it, you don't have it."

To be useful a gag file has to be organized.

When I collected comic strips that I liked, I put them in envelopes. Each envelope had a topic on it.

Some people create idea journals with a different page for each topic.

I know one person who organized their gag file by months of the year. For example, he put patriotic jokes, picnic jokes, and Independence Day jokes on a page for July. He put school jokes on a page for September.

Some people enter their gag files into a computer. It can be easy to search for a specific word or topic. However, you only find what you look for. Serendipity is making a valuable discovery when you are looking for something else. Having a gag file in a paper format you can flip through at random will sometimes present you with surprising juxtapositions.

Jokes that you write should go into your gag file for future use.

You can purchase joke files. Robert Orben was a magician and a prolific comedy writer. He published a newsletter of material for comedians that was called *Robert Orben's Current Comedy*. He published many collections of jokes. One of them, *Magicdotes – A Book of Anecdotes and Stories about Magic, Magicians, and Mentalists*, has material specifically tailored for magicians. I know many variety artists who have used jokes published by Robert Orben.

Bennett Cerf is another prolific author of joke collections. Some of his jokes may seem dated now, but they are great sources of inspiration for writing new jokes.

Henny Youngman, Milton Berle, and Steve Allen are among the famous entertainers who have published a book of jokes from their personal gag files.

I recently discovered a small book originally published in 1922 that is a collection of Tramp Jokes and Monologues. There are some jokes in that book that I would never use, but there are surprisingly many that seem relevant today and would entertain modern audiences. Others are great sources of inspiration for new jokes.

One advantage to looking for historical sources is that others are not doing it. That means you can discover a treasure trove of ideas that will make you unique. One of the gags that I perform in my juggling act is spinning a plate on a zig zag stick which is balanced on the tip of another stick. That is an idea I found in *The Juggler's Bulletin*, a newsletter for jugglers that was published by Roger Montandon in the 1930's and 1940's. Because it is an idea that everyone else has forgotten, I am sometimes credited with originating it.

The copyright law does not protect individual jokes. However, what is legal is not always ethical. It is considered unethical to copy a joke that is unique to an entertainer's act, especially if it is something that they have become known for.

Ideas, and how they are expressed, is known as intellectual property. Like other types of property, they have value. They can be sold, given to somebody, or kept as personal property. The code of ethics of magic organizations calls for respecting and honoring the intellectual property of others. As far as I know, no clown organization has taken that step yet. Respecting intellectual property is important. Other people deserve to benefit from the effort and expense they have invested in creating material. Respecting intellectual property also ensures that variety arts move forward. If people are afraid their ideas will be stolen, they become secretive. Then we lose all the additional ideas that would have been inspired by those ideas.

However, there are many jokes that are considered part of the public domain. Those are jokes that are so old or that have been used by so many people that they are no longer associated with a specific person. You are free to use public domain ideas.

Organize your gag file. What format will work for you? Group your favorite comic strips and verbal jokes by topic. You should also include some of your responses to exercises in this book. Your gag file doesn't have to include every exercise response. However, it should include those that you particularly like or think that you might potentially add to your repertoire.

★   ★   ★

Doctor Routine Setting

Appendix B is a sample Doctor Gag file. In the next few exercises, you will work with that file to create your own doctor routine.

The first step is to decide where the routine will take place. Setting it in a doctor's office is a cliché. That is an acceptable choice. In *Dream It, Do It*, Marty Sklar quotes George Lucas saying, "Don't avoid cliches—they are cliches because they work."

Clowns, and other variety artists, often use a cliché to be sure the audience understands what is happening. If audience members are confused, they can't pay attention to your humor and enjoy it.

However, a change of setting or characters can have a dramatic effect. I was participating in a class where the instructor asked us to find a partner. Then she handed out short scripts. I think there were four different scripts so each one was performed by more than one pair of participants. The one my partner and I received was a scene between a male character and a female character. The final two lines were:

MALE: I will love you until I die.
FEMALE: How soon will that be?

Most of the other couples performed it as two people meeting on a first date or two people who had been married for a long time. The women said the last line with a lot of aggression as if they hoped he would die quickly. There was some laughter, but I don't think anyone in the audience really liked either character in the scene.

We didn't have time to rehearse. We were reading the scripts cold. My partner and I were the last to be called up. Just as we were nearing the performance area, I asked her if she could play a little girl. She quickly agreed. When we started our scene, she skipped in and was seated in a chair. I slowly followed her walking like an elderly man. We slipped into an old man and his granddaughter relationship. We got laughs with our first lines. She played them perfectly fiddling with her clothing and not really paying attention to me. I put my hand on her shoulder, and tenderly said my last line. She suddenly stopped fidgeting. She turned and looked at me a moment, and then with a tremble in her voice, she said her last line. In unison, the audience took a sharp breath and then everyone went "awe." Our change allowed us to touch them emotionally. The fact that I was lucky to be paired with a talented entertainer also had a lot to do with the reaction.

When I have used this Doctor Gag exercise in classes, the majority of students set their routine in a doctor's office.

However, a doctor's office is not the only choice. Another cliché is that people at a party, hoping to get free medical advice, will ask questions of a doctor.

I once had two students surprise me with what I thought was a brilliant choice. They set their routine on a golf course. A doctor was going to tee off. Just as he started his swing, his opponent would interrupt him with a question about his medical practice. The doctor got increasingly frustrated by this attempt to break his concentration.

There are other choices for where a doctor routine might take place.

☛ Where will your doctor encounter their patient?

PERFORMER-IN-TROUBLE SYNDROME

SOMETIMES THIS IS referred to simply as the PITS. Just as the title suggests, the performer gets into some kind of difficulty. It may me closing the lid of a box on their hand, or getting a finger caught in a bottle, or constantly dropping a juggling prop, or having a magic trick go wrong.

Children delight in seeing an adult in trouble, another example of reversal. However, the performer should be able to somehow eventually triumph over the trouble.

A whole type of take-a-card magic tricks is based on this technique. The performer ties to reveal the identity of a chosen card, and fails. Then they accidentally succeed. They might pull a handkerchief from their pocket to wipe their brow and discover a picture of the card printed on the handkerchief. They might open an insurance policy to check its terms and discover a picture of the card inside. They might magically get out of trouble by visibly changing the wrong card into the correct one. They might ask the volunteer to place a phone call to another magician, and without the performer going near the phone, the other magician reveals the chosen card. Most of these PITS card tricks are based on being able to control which card will be selected. Magicians refer to this as a Force.

Shane Cobalt advised magicians, "Build 'accidents' into your routine. It lets people think something might go wrong. If you can recover from a mistake, the audience thinks you can do anything. If you are too perfect it seems unnatural. If you are too perfect it is sterile."

I took my parents to the Hollywood Magic Castle. The magician appearing in the Close-Up Room was known for performing a Faro Shuffle. That is a shuffle in which the cards are perfectly interlaced. It allows you to preset your cards in a specific order so you know they will be in the order you desire after doing a certain number of shuffles. My mother did not know what the magician was doing, but she knew that his actions were too perfect to be natural. She whispered to me, "I would like to see him do that the way I shuffle."

I saw David Copperfield performing live. He had just finished a very impressive large illusion. As he started to leave the stage to pick an audience volunteer, he stumbled a little bit. He muttered a quick remark about his clumsiness. That little bit humanized him. I realized that the stumble was part of the act's choreography. There was a song that usually played as soon as he started towards the edge of the stage to pick a volunteer. However, this time, the song didn't begin until after he had stumbled.

In one of my routines, I display a message printed on a strip of paper. The words are printed in the wrong order. I rip up the paper and squeeze the pieces together. When I begin to unfold the strip of paper, a packet of paper falls to the floor. I pause in surprise, and cover that packet of paper with my foot. I continue unfolding the paper that I am holding demonstrating that it is now a restored strip of paper with the words in the proper order. The audience calls my attention to the paper under my foot. They assume that it is the torn pieces. I pick it up revealing that it is a complete strip of paper with a related message printed on it. I use one version of this routine in performances for church groups. Frequently, my contact person has said, "When you dropped those pieces of paper, I began praying that somehow you would be able to succeed."

The reason that they believed I had made an actual mistake is because I found a method for the "accident" to happen automatically. There is a difference between a piece of paper falling on its own and a piece of paper being deliberately dropped. Because the paper falls automatically, I don't think about dropping it. Your thoughts are communicated to your audience through unconscious facial expressions and body language. Also, because the paper falls automatically, I don't know for sure exactly when it will fall. That means I am actually surprised by when it falls. That real surprise is perceived by the audience.

★ ★ ★

Doctor Routine Body

Turn to Appendix B and select some doctor jokes that you like.

Next put them into an order that makes sense to you. Rewrite them if that is required to give your routine a greater flow.

When I use this as a class exercise, I pair up participants. Each team selects three jokes, puts them in order, and practices their short routine. Then each pair performs their skit and I give them feedback. I use three jokes in that setting because that fits the available time during most class periods. Also, three is the minimum that works for creating a routine with jokes that flow from one to another.

☞ For this exercise, I am not assigning you a quota. Choose as many jokes as you like from the gag file. You may also add other doctor jokes that you know.

★ ★ ★

PRACTICAL JOKE

A PRACTICAL JOKE IS a trick pulled on a victim. The Candid Camera TV program was built upon Practical Jokes. Some of them were quite elaborate. I remember one in which the motor was removed from a car. Then the car was pushed so it would coast into a service station. The female driver would ask a mechanic for assistance. Explaining that the car didn't seem to work anymore, she asked him to check it out for her. When he opened the hood of the car, he was shocked that the motor was missing. The hidden cameras recorded him trying to explain to the woman why the car didn't work. When he said the motor was gone, she demanded to know what he had done with it because she was sure she had it when she left home.

Magic and gag shops sell many practical joke products. For example, you can purchase a finger nail polish bottle with a hardened pool of polish attached to it. You lay it on the carpet in a friend's house and watch their reaction to the damage they assumed had been done by accident.

Many people are wary of being the victim of a clown's practical joke. When I first started clowning, a small plastic camera that squirted water was popular in joke shops. It was so common that most people recognized it. When they saw a clown with one, they would move away.

Clowns are sometimes referred as Tricksters. Some performers believe that means a clown is supposed to pull tricks on their audience. However, making an audience member the victim of a trick can backfire. A comedy magician was performing a banquet show in a hotel. He asked one of my friends, who was seated next to me, to join him on stage. The magician stuck a funnel in his waistband. Then he leaned his head back and placed a quarter on his forehead. He straightened his head so the quarter fell landing in the funnel. The magician challenged my friend to perform the same stunt. Reluctantly, my friend stuck the funnel in his waistband. When my friend tilted his head back, the magician grabbed a pitcher of ice water supplied by the hotel and poured the contents into the funnel. My friend gave the magician a disgusted look and marched back to our table. He sat there cold and wet for the rest of the banquet. Everyone seated at our table could tell how miserable he was. We all resented the way the magician had treated him. Nobody at our table laughed during the rest of the magician's act even though he did some truly funny material. His practical joke was based on a traditional clown act known as Niagara Falls. His mistake was making a member of the audience his victim.

It is best to pull a practical joke on another entertainer in your show. Here is how Niagara Falls is normally performed.

The Whiteface Clown challenges Auguste to perform a stunt. He demonstrates it by placing a funnel in the waistband of his pants, tilting his head back, balancing a coin on his forehead, and then tipping his head forward, catching the coin in the funnel.

When the Auguste tries to do it, the Whiteface pours a glass of water into the funnel as soon as the Auguste tips his head back. Of course, the Auguste gets mad, but the Whiteface urges him to be a good sport and pull the joke on somebody else.

Another Whiteface Clown enters. The Auguste challenges him to perform the stunt. When the Auguste demonstrates the stunt, the Whiteface clown, pours another glass of water into the funnel. The two Whiteface clowns urge him to try it once again.

A Tramp clown enters. The Auguste challenges him to perform the stunt. The Auguste starts to demonstrate what he wants the Tramp to do, but then he remembers what happened before. So, he just describes the stunt. When the Tramp tips his head back, the Auguste pours a glass of water into the funnel. The Tramp doesn't react. Instead, he successfully catches the coin in the funnel. The Auguste challenges him to do it two out of three times. The Tramp tips his head back, and the Auguste pours another glass of water into the funnel. Again, the Tramp doesn't react. The Auguste dares him to do it one more time. Now, the Auguste pours an entire pitcher of water into the funnel. There is still no reaction from the Tramp. The Auguste leaves in disgrace. The Tramp reaches into his waist band and pulls out a hot water bottle. He tells the audience, "I will never fall for that trick because I am the one who invented it."

Going back to the 1600's in Europe, and even longer in other cultures, there tended to be pairs of clown characters. One would be a clever rogue while the other would be the less intelligent assistant in their schemes and victim of their practical jokes.

Reversal and Delayed Anticipated Action are often used with a practical joke performance. For example, the Joker sets up a pail of water over a door. Their intended victim walks through the doorway, but the bucket doesn't fall. The Joker cautiously opens the door, and the bucket doesn't fall. The Joker stands under the bucket inspecting it. He looks at the audience, shrugs, and then the bucket tips dowsing him. This structure was used frequently in the Road Runner cartoons.

Sometimes clowns try to blame an audience member for a practical joke. I saw Bill Irwin perform "Scapin" in Seattle. At one point in the play, he convinced another character to hide by climbing into a cloth bag. He began hitting the bag with a club. After he was done, he handed the club to somebody sitting in the front row. He told the other character that it was safe to get out of hiding. After the character exited the bag, Irwin pointed to the audience member holding the club.

What if you are a solo performer? You can still perform practical jokes by reversing it so you are your own victim. I call this being an Impractical Joker. One of my first clown routines involved the use of a Joy Buzzer. A Joy Buzzer is a spring-loaded device with a button. When the button was pressed, the spring would be released and spin around inside the buzzer's housing. That created a sound and a faint vibration. A ring on the back of the buzzer would fit onto your index finger is such a way that the buzzer was hidden against your palm. You would put the buzzer on and wind it up. When you shook hands with someone, their palm would push the button setting off the device. The unexpected sound and feeling would startle them.

I would wind up a Joy Buzzer, and wear it on my left palm. Using my right hand, I would shake hands with a child. I would act surprised when nothing happened. I would bring my hands together setting off the Joy Buzzer. I would jump in surprise by being caught in my own trap. I would transfer the buzzer to my other hand and get the child to shake hands with me again. Since the buzzer had not been wound up, nothing happened. Frequently, kids would tell me that the buzzer had to be wound up. I would wind it up. I tested it by pushing the button. I would react in surprise, but make sure that it ran all the way down. Then I would shake hands with the child, and nothing would happen. I would wind up the buzzer and give it to the child. They would put it on, and when they shook hands with me, I would get caught the third and final time.

☛ How would you use a practical joke in your performances?

☛ If you work with a partner, who would play the practical joke? Who would be the victim? What type of joke would be played? How might you incorporate delayed anticipated action? How might you incorporate reversal? Would you try to blame a fall guy? Who would that be? How would you frame them?

☛ If you are part of a group, what role would each person play? How might you fool the original victim into being victimized again when they try to pull the joke on a third character? How might the third character cheat to avoid becoming the victim?

☛ If you are a solo performer, how would you use reversal so that you are the victim of your own joke?

$\star \quad \star \quad \star$

EXERCISE

Doctor Routine Transitions

TRANSITIONS ARE IMPORTANT in creating an act or a show. People who enter skit competitions at clown conventions are often limited to five minutes of performance time. They are sometimes given two to three minutes for set up and another two to three minutes for clearing the stage. That extra time at that venue is unimportant because the judges are filling out the score sheets so the next act can't begin anyway. I have been at other events where competition winners are invited to perform a thirty-minute show. They usually do a five-minute routine. Then they spend five minutes or more switching their props and sometimes leave the stage to do a costume change. They do another five-minute routine before there is another five-minute break in the show. Frequently, they finish by doing another five-minute routine. So, they actually spend only half of the time during their show entertaining the audience. That is all they know to do because entering competitions only teaches you how to enter competitions.

At the same event, when somebody else with actual entertainment experience is invited to perform a thirty-minute show, they start by performing one routine. As soon as it ends, they begin another routine. They continue performing one routine after another. They spend their entire time period entertaining the audience. That is because they have learned how to make a transition between routines.

During the 1980 season with the Carson & Barnes Circus, I was challenged with creating transitions. At the start of the season, the show had just three clowns. Bubba was an obese man with limited talent. We cast him as the nurse for our doctor routine. We knew that he would get his largest laugh when he made his first appearance because he looked ridiculous wearing a nurse uniform with a tiny hat on top of his head. That meant we had to highlight that moment. In order to do that, I entered first. Then Kaddee, who played the doctor, entered. Kaddee and I would look at the performer's entrance and she yelled for a nurse. That focused everyone's attention on that entrance. Bubba would burst through the curtain, and strike a pose as the audience roared with laughter.

At the beginning of the season, the Ringmaster introduced me. I entered and began juggling three balls. After a moment, I would throw one ball high and let it hit me on top of my head.

I would collapse on the ground. The Ringmaster would ask, "Is there a doctor in the house?" Then Kaddee made her entrance.

During a long circus season, acts come and go. Some acts join the show during the season after their contract with a different show runs out. Some acts leave during the season because they are unhappy. Some acts leave before the end of the season because they have a contract with an indoor winter show. New acts are hired to replace those that leave.

After we had been on the road for about a month, a family from Mexico joined the show. The acts that they performed included a flying trapeze act. Ernesto, their teenage cousin, was traveling with them to learn to perform as a flyer in their act. D.R. Miller, the owner of the Carson & Barnes Circus, decided that Ernesto needed something to do during the show. So, he declared that Ernesto had to become a clown. I created a new routine to perform with him that transitioned into the doctor routine. I don't remember the details any longer. However, Ernesto turned out to have great instincts for clowning. We developed a slapstick routine that ended with him accidentally knocking me out. He took my hat and began fanning me off trying to wake me up. Then the Ringmaster asked if there was a doctor in the house.

Maddie Lou "Flip" Flippen Bayliss joined the Carson & Barnes Circus at the beginning of the summer. Flip had been the first woman to enroll in the Ringling Bros. and Barnum & Bailey Circus Clown College. She and Peggy Williams both graduated the following year, making both of them the first women to complete the training and be hired by the RBB&B Circus. In 1980, Flip's mother and her sister, Eddie, were travelling with her. So, Flip taught them how to assist her in clown routines.

There were three cast changes in the fall that affected the doctor act. Ernesto's cousins left for an indoor show, and he went with them. Flip left to enroll in a trade school studying to become an electrician. Eddie decided to stay with the circus. A dog act that had been touring with another circus with a shorter season joined our show. A young man was travelling with the act as an assistant. D.R. decided that the assistant had to do something else in the show. D.R. declared that Eddie and the dog act assistant had to be added to the doctor act.

That meant I had to create a new routine that would transition into the doctor act. The dog act assistant refused to apply clown makeup. So, I created a park scene. I was going for a walk in the park with Eddie, who played my wife. The assistant, wearing a bandanna across his face, jumped out at us. I stepped in front of Eddie to protect her. However, I became frightened when he pulled out a large knife. I covered my eyes and shivered all over. Eddie jumped in front of me and pulled a large rolling pin out of her purse. When she raised the rolling pin over her shoulder getting ready to hit the crook, she accidentally hit me on the head knocking me out. (The rolling pin was made out of foam rubber.) She chased the mugger away. She returned and tried to wake me up. Then the Ringmaster called for the doctor.

In all three versions of the act, the doctor portion ended with me seated in a chair. Then we made a transition to another traditional clown routine. Kaddee waved a prop skunk under my nose causing me to pass out and slowly slip out of the chair. I ended up lying on the ground in the opening position for an act called Dead and Alive. She sent the other clowns out to get a stretcher. Then she and I performed the Dead and Alive routine.

In a verbal routine, you can use a joke to transition to a different topic. For example, a possible doctor act transition is, "I don 't understand doctors. They tell you to rest and take it easy, then give you a bill that will keep your nose to the grindstone for six months." That could lead to jokes about earning a living, or about the high cost of everything today.

> ☛ Now look at the doctor routine that you created in the previous exercise. Prepare a transition to that routine. It can either be something that causes the patient to consult the doctor or something that happens after the patient has seen the doctor. What would happen in general in that other routine? The main thing is to decide on a transition. However, if you want, you can write the entire other routine.

I have used clown acts as my examples, because that is my experience. Other variety artists can incorporate doctor jokes. In the film, "Look Who's Laughing", Edgar Bergen, Charlie McCarthy, and Lucille Ball perform a doctor routine. (In the film, Edgar plays himself in his role of an entertainer appearing on radio.)

> ☛ On a few occasions, I have seen magicians play the role of a doctor. If you are a magician, how might you transition from a magic illusion into doctor jokes? How might you transition from some doctor jokes into performing an illusion?

PLAUSIBLE IMPOSSIBLE

I FIRST ENCOUNTERED THIS term in reference to animated cartoons, especially those produced by the Warner Bros. Studio. This means that something is impossible, but within the rules of the story it is plausible. An example is a cartoon character walking off the edge of a cliff. They don't realize that there is no longer any ground underneath them so they keep walking. When they realize where they are, they panic. They turn around. Their legs move frantically as they scramble to get back to solid ground. Finally, they make it back to safety. Clearly this is impossible. However, it is plausible if you assume the law of gravity takes effect only when you are aware of it, and assume that their legs compressed air molecules to support them long enough to return to the cliff.

I used this in one of my circus routines that I performed during the Come In (pre-show) with Maddie Lou "Flip" Flippen

Bayliss when we both toured with the Carson & Barnes Circus in 1980. Playing the role of a janitor, I carried a mop and bucket. I leaned my mop against a tent pole. Then turned my empty bucket upside down, placed it on the ground, and sat on top of it. I began waving to members of the audience. Flip came along, and noticed me. She pulled the bucket out from beneath me and sat on it herself. I stayed sitting in midair. When she began to talk to me, I turned towards her. Noticing that she was sitting on a bucket, I wondered where she got it. Then I looked down. Realizing that I was sitting on nothing, I fell backwards. I got up, and pulled the bucket out from under her. She fell backwards as I decisively put the bucket back where I wanted it. That led into a fight over the bucket.

I have seen puppeteers use the plausible impossible with a Rabbit in Hat glove puppet. The performer uses his left hand to hold a hat. A rabbit pops up as if it is standing inside the hat. (The puppeteer's right hand enters the back of the hat to operate the puppet.) The puppeteer has to get a prop that is on a nearby table. So, the puppeteer tells the rabbit to hold onto its hat. The rabbit grabs the brim of the hat. The puppeteer lets go of the hat and reaches for the prop. The rabbit is apparently holding the hat in midair.

My favorite Plausible Impossible gag is part of the 1952 film "Son of Paleface". Bob Hope is driving his car while Roy Rogers rides Trigger. While they are racing down the road, the front driver's side wheel comes off Bob's car. Roy lassos the axle and holds the car up as it continues moving forward. Then he hands the rope to Bob. Bob keeps the car from teetering over while Roy races off to catch the rolling wheel. Breaking the Fourth

Wall, Bob yells, "Hurry Up! This is impossible!" Roy grabs the wheel, rides back, and sticks it back into position on Bob's car.

In a famous scene from the "Job Switching" episode of "I Love Lucy" (S2 Ep 1, 1952), Lucy and Ethel are assigned to wrap chocolates passing on a conveyor belt. The conveyor belt starts moving slow enough that the two women could be realistically expected to finish the task. Then the belt gradually began moving faster causing them to have problems. They hide their difficulty so their supervisor believed they were coping. The supervisor ordered that the belt be speeded up a little. Now it was moving much too fast for them to be able to cope. Their attempt is hilarious. If the conveyor had started off at the highest rate, the audience would not believe that the girls could be expected to succeed. The audience wouldn't believe that the women would even attempt to keep up at that point.

According to Jess Openheimer, head writer of the show, "I always insisted that every "I Love Lucy" show have a logical foundation. I wanted there to be a sound reason for everything in the script, because I knew from experience that if you start with a believable premise and take the audience one step at a time, and they know why they're being taken there, you can go to the heights of slapstick and outlandish situations."

I use the same approach in some of my magic routines. For example, in my Floating Balloon Swan routine, I take off my hat and put it on my magic table. (At the same time, I am attaching to the table a fine thread from an Invisible Thread Reel pinned inside my vest.) Then using my right hand, I rub the balloon on my hair as if I am trying to build up static electricity. Then I secretly hook the neck of the swan over the thread. I touch the tip of my left forefinger to the top of the balloon. I let go of the balloon with my right hand and it seems to be clinging to my left finger. I touch the balloon with the tip of my right forefinger, and move my left hand away. Now the balloon is clinging to my right hand. I look at the audience, and without thinking about it move my right hand away from the balloon in order to shrug. At first, I don't notice that my finger is no longer touching the balloon. When I realize that the balloon is floating in midair, I wave my hands above and below it trying to find what is supporting it. I grab the balloon with my left hand. I take my hat off the table, dislodging the thread, and put the hat back on my head. Then I give the balloon to somebody in the audience as a souvenir.

It is amazing how convincing starting off with a plausible explanation can be. I performed my Floating Balloon Swan routine in the first half of a variety show. There were many other entertainers in the audience. As the intermission was ending, the theater manager came backstage to tell me that the lobby was full of people who had twisted balloon swans and were rubbing them on their hair trying to create enough of a static charge to recreate my routine.

The plausibility test is one that I think many marketed magic tricks fail. I read the descriptions in advertisements and my first reaction is if you really could do magic why would you waste your time and efforts doing that. My second thought is why would an audience member care that you have done that.

Disney's 1997 film "Flubber", starring Robin Williams, also failed the plausibility test. I found it impossible to care about Professor Philip Brainard's efforts to invent a flying car when he already had a flying robot. The original 1961 version, "The Absent Minded Professor", starring Fred McMurry, was much more satisfying because he had nothing that was capable of flying.

★　　★　　★

DOCTOR ROUTINE ENDING

I F YOUR DOCTOR routine does not transition to another routine, if needs a definite conclusion. You don't want the audience to wonder if the routine is over. That confusion causes sporadic laugher or applause. You want the audience to either applaud or laugh in unison when the routine ends.

You can use a joke that serves as a conclusion. Here is how Smith and Dale finished their famous doctor routine.

"How much do I owe you?"
"I'll make that cheap, ten dollars. "
"For what?"

"For my advice. "

"Ten dollars for your advice. Well, doctor, here's two dollars. Take it. That's my advice. "

"You come here and waste my time. "

"One more word from you and you only get a dollar. "

"You.."

"That's the word. (Grabs back a dollar and exits.)

☞ Write a definite ending to your doctor routine. You can adapt one of the traditional circus endings from Appendix B or you can create your own ending.

IRONY

IRONY IS A twist of fate. It involves a circumstance that seems inappropriate. For example, the legend of the clown whose big smile hides a broken heart, or the bag lady who dies leaving a fortune she has been saving for a rainy day.

Charlie Chaplin (1889–1977) developed his physical comedy skill while performing with the Karno Pantomime troupe. It is important to realize that the word Pantomime in the group's name does not have the modern American definition of silent acting. The Karno troupe was from England where Pantomime was a specific type of stage show that was a fast-paced spectacle with knock-about comedy, verbal humor,

charlie

songs, and topical gags. According to Glenn Mitchell, "He (Karno) was also responsible, at least in part, for Chaplin's blend of laughter and pathos, exhorting his comics to 'keep it *wistful...* we want sympathy with the laughter.'"

An ironic ending to a comic routine can touch the audience emotionally. Charlie Chaplin did this in "City Lights", a 1931 film. Charlie befriends a blind flower girl, who mistakenly thinks he is rich. Afraid of losing her love, Charlie gets a job so he can maintain the impersonation. He discovers an operation could restore her sight, and arranges for her to receive it. The operation is a success. When she sees that Charlie is a tramp, she laughs at him. When she learns who he is, she is visually crushed. The film ends with him holding a flower while looking at her hopefully.

I don't normally use irony in my performances. However, my final project for a college mime class was to create a solo act with an ironic ending. In my act, which was well received by the other students, I alternated between playing a marionette and a puppeteer. I established through my movement that I was a marionette, and then I transitioned to his master who enjoyed controlling him. I switched back to playing the puppet, who resented being controlled by someone else. He decided to cut his strings. He found a pair of scissors. He cut the string to his left hand. Now his left arm just flopped by his side. Using his right hand, he lifted up his left hand. When he let go of it, his left arm fell again swinging back and forth slightly. I switched to playing the puppeteer again. He was enjoying watching the distress of his puppet. I switched back to being the marionette again. By twisting his torso, he was able to get the arm to swing further. However, he couldn't control its movement. Giving up, he held up the end of the string attached to his left hand so the puppeteer could tie it back together. Now he was under his master's complete control again. I switched back to playing the puppeteer. Satisfied with the outcome, he hung up the control rod for his puppet. He started to leave, when suddenly he was pulled back to center stage. I repeated my initial movements. The marionette's master had thought he was in control, but he was actually just another puppet being controlled by somebody else.

SATIRE

SATIRE IS USING comedy to hold up human vices and follies and abuses to ridicule or scorn. The goal is to shame individuals, groups, or society itself into improvement.

It is not a technique that I have used personally, but it has a long history.

The role of the clowns of many indigenous cultures is to police society and correct those who were doing wrong. In America, the clowns of the Hopi Nation tried to use humor to combat what they felt were the negative influences of the Europeans. For example, Europeans introduced alcoholic drinks to the indigenous people causing a crisis. The clowns would counter that by portraying a drunk man. The public ridicule would sometimes be enough to cause members of their nation to change their behavior.

In medieval morality plays, clowns also used satire. The clowns would portray people comically breaking the Ten Commandments and other religious guidelines. Then they would be carried off through the mouth of hell that was represented on the side of the stage.

Satire is frequently used in literature. For example, *Gulliver's Travels*, by Jonathan Swift is a famous satire of the politics of his day.

Personally, my favorite series of satirical novels were the stories by Leonard Wibberley about the Duchy of Grand Fenwick. The first novel was *The Mouse that Roared.* The tiny country decided to declare war upon the United States in order to receive the aid that America provided to its defeated enemies. Through a series of comic events, the Duchy accidentally defeats the U.S. They discover that the money they receive from America is causing problems. So, in *The Mouse on Wall Street*, they invest in stocks hoping to lose the money. A series of unforeseen events results in their investment paying great dividends. In *The Mouse on the Moon*, the Duchy decides to update the plumbing in the castle. To receive the aid they want, they describe the water tanks and pipes they request as parts for building a missile. The U.S. wouldn't provide plumbing supplies, but it would help them build weapons. One of the members of the Duchy's government insists that if they described the shipment as missile parts, they have to build a missile. Their missile works and they win the space race by being the first to land on the moon.

Famous satirical anti-war films include "M*A*S*H" and "Dr. Strangelove or: How I Learned to Stop Worrying and Love the Bomb."

Satire can be hard to handle because if it is too subtle its meaning is missed, or if it is too heavy it might seem crude and in poor taste.

EXERCISE

#

H ERE IS ANOTHER formula joke.

* What do you get if you cross an elephant with a couple of gold fish? A pair of swimming trunks.
* What do you get if you cross an owl with a goat? A hootin' nanny.
* What do you get if you cross a rooster with a Poodle – Doberman mix? A Cock-a-poodle-do
* What do you get if you cross a toy Poodle with a man crossing the street? A mini-pede.
* What do you get if you cross a groundhog with a catcher's mitt? Six more weeks of baseball.

☛ Write at least fifteen crossing jokes.

SARCASM

S ARCASM IS MAKING a statement that is the opposite of what is true. It is often used to say something that you really don't feel. For example, after somebody watches you struggle to carry a stack of packages across the room, you turn to them and say, "Thanks for your help."

Another example is when somebody tells you something happened to them that you had predicted, you respond by saying, "Well, what a surprise."

Sarcasm is used frequently on the television series "Young Sheldon". Missy and Sheldon are twins. She is a normal girl in elementary school. Sheldon is a genius attending high school. He is very accomplished at math and science, but lacking in social skills. When Missy thinks Sheldon has a ridiculous idea, she tells him that she thinks it is a good one. When he thanks her for her compliment, she replies, "You don't understand sarcasm at all."

Because tone of voice is important in conveying that you don't believe what you are saying, sarcasm is mainly a verbal from of comedy.

EXERCISE

YOU MIGHT BE

HERE IS ANOTHER formula joke.

The set up is "You might be _____ if..."

Then there is a list of punchlines.

Jeff Foxworthy became very well known for his "You might be a redneck if..." series of jokes.

I grew up attending Lutheran churches. So, for examples here, I decided to use "You Might be a Lutheran if..."

The internet had many long "You might be a Lutheran if..." lists. None of the jokes are credited to a person or source. Many of the same jokes were included on several different sites so I won't try to credit one site as the source for these examples.

Some of the responses have been around for a long time. I heard this one in the 1970's. "You might be a Lutheran if in response to somebody jumping up and shouting 'Praise the Lord', you politely remind them that we don't do that around here."

"You might be a Lutheran if you automatically sing 'amen' at the end of every song you sing." That to me is very funny because I recognize that was true during my childhood. Younger people who attend churches where praise choruses are sung would not understand it at all. It would be an inappropriate joke for them.

One of the responses is "… you laugh out loud while reading this list, and relive your childhood at the same time." I shared a long list with a friend who grew up attending a Lutheran Church and is about my age. She said that she did laugh out loud, and that it reminded her of her childhood.

Some of the responses could be easily applied to other groups. For example, "… It's time to change the lightbulb and the left side of the aisle begins a debate on 'change,' while the right side musters five volunteers—one to hold the light bulb, and four to turn the ladder."

Here are some of my other favorite responses.
"You might be a Lutheran if…

* … during the entire service you hold your hymnal open but never look down at it."
* … the pastor skips the last hymn to make sure the service lasts exactly 60 minutes."
* … you hesitate to clap for the church choir or special music because 'it just wasn't done that way in the old days.'"
* … you feel guilty about not feeling guilty."
* … the third service each Sunday is coffee hour."

You have to use what you know when you are creating humor. The above responses could not have been written by someone who was not familiar with Lutheran church services.

You also have to know your audience. "You might be a Lutheran if..." would not be understood or appreciated if I performed it for members of a Baptist congregation.

☛ Fill the blank in the set up line with something that you are familiar with. It could be a profession, like plumber. It could be a role in life, like grandfather. It could be a hobby, like Pickle Ball player.

☛ Then write as many responses as you can. Don't worry about each one being a good response. They won't be. The more responses that you write, the more useable ones you will end up with.

BREAKING THE FOURTH WALL

T HE FOURTH WALL is a theatrical term for an imaginary wall between the stage and the audience. The audience can see through the wall, but it is opaque to the actors. The performers act as if they don't know the audience is there.

In breaking the fourth wall the audience's presence is acknowledged, and the artificialness of the medium is referred to.

In an episode of the Fibber McGee and Molly radio program, Fibber announced he was going to go to the hardware store. The director said, "You had better hurry, we 're running late. "

Fibber replied, "In that case, here's the hardware store. Who said radio isn't a flexible medium?"

Bob Hope made breaking the fourth wall a part of his screen personality. "The Princess and the Pirate" is a 1944 film produced by Samuel Goldwyn. At the conclusion, Virginia Mayo, Bob's leading lady, abandoned Bob to run to the arms of Bing

Crosby who is making a cameo appearance. Bob complains to the audience, "How do you like that? I knock myself out for nine reels and some bit player from Paramount comes over and gets the girl! Boy, That's the last picture I do for Goldwyn."

Breaking the fourth wall is often used by ventriloquists. I have frequently seen a vent figure comment, "They can see your lips moving."

My wife, Carole, would take a rabbit puppet or a sheep dog puppet when visiting nursing homes as a clown. The puppets were realistic looking and she did a great job manipulating them. When residents asked if the puppet was real, she would respond, "Shhh, he thinks he is real."

Some boys around eight and ten years old will often try to announce how every magic trick is done. They don't care if they are correct. They are just trying to prove that they are intelligent enough to know that magic isn't real. If I am doing closeup magic and somebody announces that they know I have a coin hidden in my hand, I say, "Of course I do. What do you think I am, a real magician?"

That always gets a laugh. It also defuses the adversarial relationship. I have just acknowledged their intelligence. I have also proven that I don't care that they know how something is done so there is no motivation to keep challenging me. Then I usually follow up with an effect that I know will definitely fool them. My goal is to win back their respect. More than once I have had a boy exclaim, "I know there is no such thing as real magic, but that is magic."

Children who challenge magicians, will also challenge clowns. They will tell an entertainer, "You aren't a real clown."

Some clowns are very concerned about maintaining the fourth wall and have devised elaborate arguments trying to prove that they are real clowns. I have never seen them convince a child. The child is not displaying disapproval of the performer. They are demonstrating that they are intelligent enough to know the difference between fantasy and reality. They know that an actual person is portraying a clown. Breaking the fourth wall is a much more effective way to handle the situation. When he was challenged, Richard Snowberg's response was, "You're right. But I heard that there is going to be a clown here today. I love clowns. So, when you see the clown be sure to let me know." The reaction was always laughter followed by the kids announcing that he is the clown.

About thirty years ago, clowns doing makeup demonstrations was debated. Like many clowns, I would sometimes do a makeup demonstration prior to a performance at a preschool to prevent the children from being frightened by my fantasy character. Some clowns criticised that approach because it broke the fourth wall. The critics said, "you are showing the children that clowns weren't real".

I found that even though they had seen the transformation, the kids reacted as if my clown character was real. They were just as enthusiastic about my performance as kids at other performances. The reason is "suspension of belief." Audience members know that what is happening is not real, but they willingly pretend that it is real.

Breaking the fourth wall is a standard part of Gospel Magic Ministry. Because members of a church believe in a spiritual world, they are more likely to believe a magician has special powers. There may be resistance to a magic performance. So, people involved in using illusion as an object lesson teaching spiritual lessons clearly state that they don't have any special power. When I do clown ministry performances, I explain, "I do illusions for two reasons, one is to have fun. As Christians, it is okay to have fun. The second reason I use illusions is to give you something you can see to help you remember something that you can't see." Sometimes I turn it into a joke. For example, I say, "I have been using this magic wand. It really doesn't have any special powers. It is just a stick that has been painted black and has white tips." That generally gets a laugh, especially if any children appear disappointed that it is so ordinary.

☞ How can you break the fourth wall? What are the conventions of the medium in which you work? How can you poke fun at them? How can you use breaking the fourth wall to handle a potential problem? When would you want to break the fourth wall for a serious reason?

EXERCISE

Counting Sheep

COUNTING SHEEP IS an extremely popular comedy topic. It is a great example of comedy based on character.

Here is just a small sample of my collection of counting sheep comic strips.

* In Donald Duck, both Donald and Uncle Scrooge are dreaming of sheep. In Donald's dream, the sheep are simply jumping over a fence. In Uncle Scrooge's dream, a man is purchasing the sheep so he is paid for each sheep that he counts.
* In The Family Circus (October 12, 2003, by Bil Keane, the father falls asleep counting sheep while the mother falls asleep counting her kids arriving home safely.

* In "Hagar the Horrible" (August 31, 2002), by Chris Browne, when Hagar is told to count sheep, he counts "Leg of Lamb, Lamb Chops, Curried Lamb, Lamb Patties...".
* In the "Wizard of Id" (April 15, 2010), by Parker and Hart, the King falls asleep counting citizens jumping over a fence to pay their taxes.
* A cartoon by JIMRO5, printed in the March 2006 issue of *The Linking Ring*, a magician falls asleep counting rabbits hopping out of a top hat.
* In Blondie (October 7, 2012) by Dean Young and John Marshall, Dagwood complains that he hasn't been able to get to sleep even though he has tried counting sheep and various types of his favorite foods. Blondie suggests that he count office chairs like the one that he has at work. He immediately falls asleep. Blondie concludes, "Once you figure out which buttons to push, it's easy."
* In the Wizard of Id, (September 16, 2019), by Brent Parker, the Wizard complains that he can't get to sleep. His wife suggests that he count sheep. In the last panel, a farmer discovers the Wizard sleeping on the fence surrounding his sheep fold because he took his wife's suggestion literally.
* In the "Wizard of Id" (March 24, 2013), by Parker and Hart, the King is counting sheep jumping over his bed. He falls asleep when he reaches one hundred two. The last panel reveals that the sheep was actually a single citizen using a mini-trampoline to jump over the bed while wearing a sheep costume

★ In 1996, the Ringling Bros. Barnum & Bailey Circus Blue Unit had a story line involving a clown family. Tommy and Tammy Parish played the parents and a Little Person played their Baby. In the Chiavari act, Baby was put to bed, but he had trouble getting to sleep. His bed was actually the top of a gym hurdle. Then the other clowns, in sheep costumes, used a mini-trampoline to jump and summersault over the bed. The act ended with someone in a wolf costume entering and chasing away the sheep.

When Kenny Ahern told me that he was working on a sleep walking character, I suggested that he do a counting sheep gag. He got three soft sculpture sheep and weighted them with bean bags. Then he juggled them as he counted them.

☛ Write at least ten counting sheep jokes. What would happen to the sheep after they were counted? Who would count something other than sheep? What would they count? What other activity requires counting that might cause someone to fall asleep at an inappropriate time? What would happen if somebody took the advice to count sheep literally?

☛ How might you use the counting sheep concept in your performances?

☛ What other activity has a cliched response? How would you approach that activity?

PARODY

A PARODY IS AN imitation or burlesque of a general genre or of a specific work. It is a useful technique, because it gives you a springboard for ideas. Provided the original is well known to your audience, some of your jokes will already be set up for you.

Jack Benny would perform parodies of specific movies on his radio program. One of my favorites was his parody of "Lost Weekend", a 1945 film starring Ray Milland.

Parodies were popular on television variety shows. Mel Brooks produced movies that are parodies of a genre.

Properly done a parody doesn't ridicule the original, but copies its style and has fun with its conventions. The fans of the original enjoy a parody. You will be most successful parodying something you like. It is something that you have to be very familiar with. Part of your audience will be very knowledgeable and critical. Fans love a parody, but only an accurate one.

Herb Camburn, one of my college instructors, frequently said, "You cannot fake it when you are faking it." By that he meant that when imitating or parodying something you have to know what the real thing is like.

In the "Job Switching" episode of "I Love Lucy", Lucille Ball was required to parody someone dipping chocolates. In preparation, she spent a week working in a real Sees chocolate factory learning how to actually dip chocolates. Once she knew how to do it correctly, she understood what changes to make in order to entertainingly do it wrong.

The more you know about your topic, the greater your resource is for ideas. The theme for the 1981 Carson & Barnes Circus Spec was Cowboys and Indians. I got permission to design my own cowboy costume. In researching cowboy films, I discovered that there are two types of chaps, shotgun, which are tight fighting, and batwing, which have a flap. I discovered that the heroes usually wore shotgun chaps while the comic sidekicks usually wore batwing chaps. So, I created a pair of batwing chaps for my costume. When I arrived at Winter Quarters, I discovered that all the other cowboy costumes had shotgun chaps which made me stand out as a clown. I also found that the batwing style accentuated my leg movements making it ideal for physical comedy.

In the film, "Gone With The Wind", (1939) Scarlet O'Hara learns that Rhett Butler is coming to visit following the end of the Civil War. She does not have any good clothing. So, she takes down a curtain and sews a new dress from the drapery material. It was parodied on "The Carol Burnett Show" in a sketch titled "Went with the Wind". (S 10, ep. 8, November 13, 1976). Bob Mackie, the series costume designer, created a famous curtain dress. When Carol Burnett descended the stairs, she had the curtain rod balanced on her shoulders.

Parodies parrot or twist as many cliches of the genre as possible. The names of the characters are often puns of names in the original. In one edition, The Ice Capades did a parody of James Bond films with Jane Blond, a female skater, fighting Cold Finger.

Early in my career, I created a detective parody routine. I carried a brief case that identified me as Sir Lock Homes, Private Defective.

The Ringling Brothers and Barnum & Bailey Circus clowns often performed parodies. For example, the 1988 RBB&B Blue Unit included a parody of Tarzan movies with Tammy Parish playing a female explorer. Michu appeared as a miniature version of Tarzan swinging in on a vine to protect her from someone wearing a gorilla costume..

Artwork can be parodied. Norman Rockwell created Triple Self Portrait depicting him seated on a stool looking at himself in a mirror while working on his portrait. That painting has been widely parodied. In one version, Walt Disney is working on his self-portrait which is a picture of Mickey Mouse. Twice I have created versions where Charlie is doing his self-portrait.

Charlie

★　　★　　★

EXERCISE
_____

MY HOMETOWN
WAS...

M Y HOMETOWN WAS so small...
How small was it?
My hometown was so small that I fell on the playground and
skinned my knee. By the time I walked home the doctor had
arrived, a neighbor had delivered a bowl of chicken soup, and
I had received a dozen get well cards.

☛ Did you grow up in a small town or a large city?
Choose the one that best fits your experience. Then
write at least fifteen jokes fitting this formula about
either how small your town was or how large it was.

SHOP TALK

PARODY IS HAVING fun with the conventions of a genre. Shop Talking is having fun with the conventions of an occupation or organization. You use phrases they would use and transfer them to another situation, take them literally, or switch them. Audiences are very flattered that you have taken the time to learn about them. A mildly funny shop talk joke often gets a better reception than a hilarious joke of another type.

Bob Hope played Larry Lawrence In "Ghost Breakers", a 1940 film. Larry Lawrence and Mary Carter investigate an isolated castle that Mary inherited on a small island off Cuba. The castle is rumored to be haunted. After they think they see a ghost, Larry asks, "Where's the money?

Mary responded, "What money?"

Larry says, "Isn't there always money when the ghost walks."

That is circus Shop Talk. Circus people are more likely to be the victims of a crime that its perpetrator. To prevent local thieves from knowing that the people with the show have just received their pay, a code is used to announce that payroll is being distributed. When word is passed around the lot that the Ghost is Walking, circus employees know they can report to the office wagon to be paid.

Sheldon Leonard played a race track tout as a recurring radio character on "The Jack Benny Show". He would always give Jack advice whenever Jack was making a choice. He always expressed it in terms used in gambling on horse races. For example, on the December 13, 1953 episode, Jack was thinking about getting a pair of silk pajamas as a gift for Florence, his sister. The Tout advised him to get a nightgown instead because "nightgown is a sleeper..." "but with pajamas when they are off the legs will fold." "When you make your selections, you've got to consider the (pajama) strings, they're okay going around the backstretch but when it comes out in front it gets tied up in a knot."

Shop talk was also frequently used on the "Life of Riley" radio program. Riley would frequently encounter Digger O'Dell, an undertaker. No matter what they discussed, Digger would use expressions that an undertaker might say. The routine always ended with Digger saying, "Well, I will be shoveling off now."

Entertainers who do motivational speaking can use business phrases as the basis for routines. For example, "I just got a job with a tree trimming company! I'm the new branch manager. My brother just got a job with a bicycle manufacturer. He's their spokesman. My sister got a job with a janitorial company. She's their floor manager."

I know a high school chemistry teacher who tells his students jokes where the punchline is a chemical element. For example, "What do they do when a chemist dies? They barium."

Here is another chemistry teacher shop talk joke. "For chemists, alcohol is not a problem. It's a solution."

★   ★   ★

Shop Talk

WHAT SHOP TALK phrases or words are used by a group that you belong to or by a group you may be entertaining? Write at least ten jokes based on them.

☞ Does your performance character belong to any particular groups? What Shop Talk words or phrases do those groups use? How can you use them as a joke?

Popular Phrase

Ⓣ HIS IS SIMILAR to shop talking. However, instead of using phrases known by a specific group, you use phrases known by the majority of the population.

When you use a popular phrase, you have built in audience appeal. You know people like the phrase. The problem is identifying popular phrases early on, and knowing when to drop them before people get tired of them.

In the early 1990's, a group of teenagers were participants at Clown Camp. Many of them had not met before, but they performed a new skit during the Open Mike session every night. The first night, one of the boys entered doing a gorilla impersonation. He climbed up onto a chair. The other teens entered carrying paper airplanes. They used the airplanes to attach the boy that the audience identified as King Kong. Finally, he clutched his heart, and fell off the chair. While lying on the stage floor, he lifted his head and shouted, "Help, I've fallen and I can't get up."

That phrase was from a series of commercials for Lifeline, an emergency call service. Those commercials appeared frequently on television at that time. Every night that week the teens came up with a different skit that used "Help, I've fallen and I can't get up" as the punchline. Everyone looked forward to their appearances because we were curious about what idea they had been able to come up with.

A currently popular business phrase is "Thinking outside the box." Actually, it has been too popular and overused. A recent survey revealed that many people are turned off by the phrase. The phrase is meant to encourage creativity. However, it is such a cliché that using it demonstrates the speaker's lack of creativity. It is appropriate to use it as comic inspiration although its lifetime may be coming to an end. I recently drove past a nursery whose reader board said, "Think Outside—No Box Needed."

Newly popular phrases can be topical with limited durability. Also, only a certain segment of the population may be aware of them.

However, some popular phrases have been passed down through generations. They are widely known throughout society. They are sometimes referred to as proverbs.

According to one proverb, "if at first, you don't succeed, try, try, try again."

W. C. Fields turned it into a joke by adding to the line. He said, "If at first, you don't succeed, try, try, try again, and then give up. There is no sense making a fool of yourself."

Another joke inspired by the same proverb is "if at first you don't succeed, try playing second base."

★ ★ ★

More Fractured Proverbs

Add some currently popular phrases to the list in Appendix A. Continue to add to this resource as you continue writing comedy.

In an earlier Fractured Proverbs exercise, you were given the first portion of a popular phrase to complete.

☞ Write at least 25 new Fractured Proverbs using phrases that you have selected. They can be based on phrases in Appendix A or on other phrases that you know are currently popular.

SWITCHING

WITCHING IS CREATING a new joke based on an existing one. It is taking an existing idea and updating it or expressing it in a new way. It can be done by changing the setup, punchline, or both. It is possible because the copyright law protects the specific expression of an idea, but not the idea itself.

You have already been switching individual jokes when you have completed exercises involving formula jokes.

Entire routines can be switched by copying the basic structure or premise.

The 1939 movie "Never Say Die", was written by Don Hartman, Frank Butler, and Preston Sturges. In it, Bob Hope is forced into a duel which he is certain to lose. Martha Raye is in love with him and bribes the judge to load one of the pistols with a blank. Bob is told, "There's a cross on the muzzle of the pistol with the bullet, and a nick on the handle of the pistol with the blank. " His opponent learns of the plan. As they approach to choose their weapons, they both recite the line over and over again trying to remember it, and get it all jumbled up. Many of their mistaken versions are spoonerisms. Bob chooses the wrong pistol, but he is saved anyway

The 1955 movie "The Court Jester", was written by Norman Panama and Melvin Frank. In it, Danny Kaye is forced into a joust which he is certain to lose. Princess Gwendolyn is in love with him and orders a witch to poison one of the cups that will be used for the pre-joust toast. Danny is told, "The pellet with the poison is in the vessel with the pestle, and the chalice from the palace has the brew that is true. " He begins repeating it to remember it and gets it jumbled. Just as he gets it straightened out, he is told they broke the chalice from the palace. Now he must remember, "the pellet with the poison is in the flagon with the dragon, the vessel with the pestle has the brew that is true." His opponent learns of the plan. As they approach to drink the toast, they both recite the line over and over again trying to remember it, and get it all jumbled up. Many of their mistaken versions are spoonerisms. Danny chooses the wrong cup, but the toast is skipped, and he is saved anyway.

Abbott and Costello performed a famous baseball sketch. The premise was that the players on the team had unusual names. Who was on first. What was on second. I Don't Know was on third. It went something like this:

COSTELLO: Tell me the name of the first baseman.

ABBOTT: Who.

COSTELLO: The first baseman

ABBOTT: Yes.

COSTELLO: Who is on first?

ABBOTT: Certainly.

COSTELLO: Listen, all I want to know is what is the name of the player on first?

ABBOTT: No, What is the name of the player on second.

COSTELLO: I don't know.

ABBOTT: Oh, he's playing third base.

Abbott and Costello would do a switch on their own routine. When Bob Feller was a famous pitcher, they did lines about him, like this:

ABBOTT: Say, is Feller pitching?

COSTELLO: Of, course there's a fella pitching.

ABBOTT: No, I meant Feller. There's only one Feller on the team.

COSTELLO: He must be pretty good if he don't need any other players.

ABBOTT: No, there's lots of fellas but only one feller.

COSTELLO: There's lots of fellas but only one feller. Let me smell your breath. You mean if the coach yells, "Hey fella come here, " this fella knows he means him.

Johnny Carson did a switch on the Who's On First routine on "The Tonight Show." The premise was that Johnny played Ronald Reagan being briefed by James Bacon for a press conference. James Watt was the Secretary of the Interior. The routine had lines like:

> **REAGAN:** They'll ask me about the Secretary of the Interior.
> **BACON:** Watt.
> **REAGAN:** I just told you they will ask about the Secretary of the Interior.
>
> **REAGAN:** I 'll need the first name of the head of the PLO, that Arafat fellow?
> **BACON:** Yasser.
> **REGAN:** I appreciate you being polite, but would you just tell me his name?

Switching can give an act coherence. You can take ideas with many different settings and switch them so they fit one theme. As an example, here is another Abbott and Costello routine.

> **COSTELLO:** I went to the farm and boy did they have a big bunch of cows.
> **ABBOTT:** Herd!
> **COSTELLO:** Herd what?
> **ABBOTT:** A herd of cows.
> **COSTELLO:** Of course, I have heard of cows. Do I look stupid or something?

The routine can be easily switched to any animal that is referred to as being part of a herd. Two of my students switched it to being elephants. One was creating a safari themed show. The other was creating a circus themed show.

To be able to switch material, you must study or observe enough material to have something available to change. I listen to a lot of classic radio comedy programs. Here is how I switched two jokes from the Jack Benny radio program when I was appearing as Santa Claus.

Jack Benny loved outrageous puns based upon names. For a radio show near Christmas, he asked his guest star, Barbara Stanwick, "Do you believe in Santa, Barbara?" Since Santa Barbara is a resort town 50 miles north of Los Angeles, this joke cracked up his studio audience.

I was appearing as Santa in a mall about five miles from the town of Santa Monica, CA. A ten-year-old-girl told me that her name was Monica. So, I asked her, "Do you love Santa, Monica?"

On another Jack Benny radio show, director/producer Gregory Ratoff and Vincent Price were Benny's guest stars. Jack tried to convince Gregory to cast him instead of Vincent in a movie he was producing. Benny said, "I'm a good actor. I have box office appeal and I'll work cheap. I'll beat Vincent's Price."

I was appearing as Santa in a mall where Polaroid photos with Santa sold for $6.35. When I was near the front counter, a boy told me his name was Vincent. At the same time, the cashier told his parents the price of the picture. I asked, "Six thirty-five, is that Vincent's Price?" His parents thought that was hilarious.

This process is not limited to dialogue. It can be used with any routine, for example, the Give Away Flower. The way the routine normally is done is to take straws and slip them over the stems of artificial flowers. You offer somebody a flower. Naturally they grasp the straw, and you pull up on the flower leaving them with only the straw.

The villain in Walt Disney's 1961 version of "Babes in Toyland" was named Barnaby Barnacle. One of his henchmen was Roderigo, played by Gene Sheldon. In one scene, Roderigo offers some children a lollipop. When they take hold of the handle, he pulls upwards with the candy so they are left holding only a hollow tube that had covered the handle.

Early in my career, I was frequently hired to hand out helium balloons. I wanted to try to make it entertaining, so I came up with many different routines using the balloons. One was a switch on the Give Away Flower. I would cut the string of one balloon in half. Then I held the cut ends overlapping in my hand. When I offered the balloon to somebody, they naturally grasped the string below my hand. I would open my hand, and the balloon would float away. I would sadly wave good bye to it as it drifted upwards. I always had another balloon available to replace the escaped one. I would tie its string to the short piece they were holding. I hoped they would consider an extra-long string as being compensation for having a joke played upon them.

Switching can be a solution to when you have objections to a particular routine. In the Candy Store skit, one clown plays the clerk of a Candy Store, and another clown plays their customer making a phone order. When they answer the phone, the Clerk has trouble hearing the customer. Deciding that they must have a bad connection, the clerk brings an audience member on stage to hold up the telephone wire. This is repeated several times until there is a line of audience members on the stage. Finally, the clerk can hear the customer. Every time the customer mentions a type of candy, the clerk informs then that they are out of that particular type. In exasperation, the customer demands to know what candy is in stock. The clerk points to the audience members and announces, "All that I have is this long line of suckers."

Dorothy Beyers was an older woman with diabetes. She performed as Hopi the Sugar Free Clown. She hoped to be able to do school shows promoting good nutrition. She liked the Candy Store skit, but didn't want to perform anything dealing with candy. I helped her switch the routine to a Pet Store. The new punchline was, "All I have is this bunch of cuckoos."

Busy Bee is a practical joke skit where characters spray water out of their mouth on each other. Lorle "Sweetheart" Buehl and Don "Dee Gee" Gonsalves liked the idea of the skit. They thought that Sweetheart would never spit on anyone and Dee Gee was too much of a gentleman to spit on a lady. They asked me for my suggestion. I helped them create a squirt flower bouquet that could be used for the practical joke. It had the additional benefit that it could be turned backwards so the jokester squirted themselves. They liked using that reversal as the punchline better than the original ending of the skit. Their new version was published in the November 1991 issue of Clowning Around and reprinted in *The Best of Clowning Around*, published by the World Clown Association.

Chalk "Talkies" "A New Kind of Fun", a pamphlet written and published by Harry C. Bjorklund in 1929, contains a trick cartoon titled the English Count. You begin by printing the numbers Zero through Nine. Then by adding a few extra lines, you turn it into a drawing of a man smoking a cigarette. I learned how to do it because I liked the idea. I changed it a little bit. In the original version, the man is bald except for a few whisps of hair. I drew it as a man wearing a bowler hat. However, I didn't want to do anything that promoted smoking.

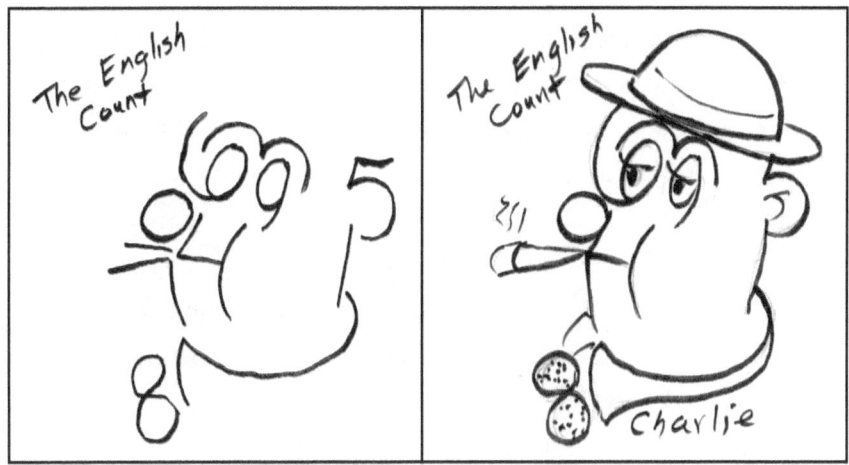

So, when I was appearing at Raging Waters, I switched it to a drawing of somebody using a bubble pipe to blow soap bubbles. That solved my objection, but I still wasn't satisfied with it.

When I began doing birthday parties, I discovered a switch that worked very well for me. I printed the numbers one through ten. Then I turned them into a picture of the guest of honor blowing out a candle on a slice of birthday cake. I would try to make the drawing look like the guest of honor, and then I gave it to them as a souvenir.

Sometimes switching can be the solution to a routine not working to your satisfaction. I had an idea where I would start by holding a book upside down while trying to read it. When I was working in a circus, I would take someone's program and open it upside down to read it. When they told me that it was upside down, I would turn it the wrong direction. I figured out a series of moves so that no matter what instruction they gave me it would never be held the proper way for me to read it. The problem with the routine was that very rarely did anybody tell me that I was holding the book wrong. It might be that they simply didn't care that I was doing it wrong. The fact that the book was upside down didn't impact them. It could be that they didn't believe what I was doing. They thought that I already knew it was upside down so they didn't need to tell me.

Then I switched the routine to using a sign that the audience was supposed to read. The front of the sign was yellow with black letters, which according to traffic engineers is the easiest color combination to read. The back of the sign is solid black except for a small symbol at the top which identifies which sign it is and which way is up for the start of the routine. I pull the sign out of my prop trunk without looking at the front. I begin displaying it to the audience sweeping it from one side to the other. I am concentrating on displaying the sign, so, it being upside down is not part of my silent script. The audience believes that I don't know it is upside down. Because they want to be able to read it easily, somebody always tells me that I am holding it upside down. When they do that, I flip it over horizontally so it is right side up, but backward. I continue trying to follow instructions from audience members, but misunderstand so I always turn the sign the wrong direction. Eventually, I accidentally turn it the right way.

☞ How can you update old routines by switching them with current references?

☞ How can you be inspired but not copy a routine by switching it? What can you substitute in an old routine to make it a better fit for your performance style and your audience?

☞ What do you dislike about a frequently performed routine? How can you switch it to eliminate your perceived flaws?

☞ If a routine does not get the response you expect, how can you switch the set up?

EXERCISE

SWITCHING THE LITTLE MEXICAN

CREATE YOUR OWN switch of this joke from the Jack Benny radio and television programs. Mel Blanc appeared many times as a character referred to as the Little Mexican. The appearances were always similar. Here is an example:

> **DON WILSON:** Jack, the next act auditioning is a brother magic act.
> **JACK BENNY:** So you do a magic act?
> **MEL BLANC:** Si.
> **BENNY:** With your brother?
> **BLANC:** Si.
> **BENNY:** What's your brother's name?

BLANC: Sy

BENNY: Sy?

BLANC: Si.

BENNY: What do you do?

BLANC: Saw

BENNY: Saw?

BLANC: Si

BENNY: What do you saw?

BLANC: Sy

BENNY: Sy?

BLANC: Si

BENNY: Who thought this up?

BLANC: Me

BENNY: Now cut that out!

On "The Tonight Show", Johnny Carson did a switch on this routine as a Russian Spy being interrogated by CIA agents.

Now you will create your own switch.

The first step is to analyze the original routine. Alliteration and repetition are important parts of this routine. The Little Mexican answers every question with one syllable. Jack repeats the answer as a question, and the Little Mexican responds with a one syllable form of yes. Then Jack asks the next question. The routine almost always concluded with Jack shouting, "Now cut that out! "

The little character could be any nationality with a one syllable form of yes, such as Russian (Da), German (Ya) , or French (oui). The character could be a farmer or hillbilly who says "yup. The character could be a lazy teen-age American who 'says, "Yah."

☞ Who would be questioned in your new version?

☞ Who will be asking the questions? In the case of a Little Hillbilly the questioner might be a City Slicker asking directions, a Census Taker, or a Revenuer.

☞ Once you have decided upon the characters, select a setting and motivation for the questions.

☞ Now write your version of the routine. If possible, learn it and perform it before an audience. How did the audience respond? Rewrite any weak spots, and perform it again.

☞ After writing a switch of this routine, choose a different routine that is one of your favorites. Then write your own switch of that routine.

TOPICAL

A Topical joke is one about something that is currently happening. It makes a routine seem fresh. The audience knows they aren't seeing old jokes, although it might really be an old joke switched to make it relevant to a new situation.

An old clown gag was a parody of the Sword Box magic Illusion. One clown would be placed into a cabinet. Swords were thrust through holes in the sides of the cabinet making it seem impossible for there to be room for the clown inside to escape injury. Then the swords were removed. After the clown exited the cabinet, they took a drink of water. Suddenly water squirted out from several spots on their costume. You can see this performed on a DVD of "Super Circus" highlights.

In 1976, there was a lot of debate about the value of acupuncture. Some customers wanted their insurance companies to pay for acupuncture treatments. Most policies excluded those treatments. Kenny Dodd produced an acupuncture act for the

1976 Clyde Beatty – Cole Bros Circus. After the patient had been treated with many oversized needles, they were given a glass of water. When they drank, water suddenly squirted out from several spots on their costume. Kenny had taken the traditional Sword Box routine and made it topical by changing the appearance of the props.

Paul Jung worked with Little People in some of his routines. He had created an act where a tall clown was placed into a steam cabinet with his head sticking out the top. Steam would come out of the cabinet. The clown's head would disappear. Then the front door opened and a miniature version of the first clown exited.

When there was a lot of commentary in newspapers about splitting the atom, Paul Jung decided to use that as the basis of a routine. He figured that a child hearing the phrase "atom smashing" might mistakenly think it was "Adam smashing." So, Paul added a pile driver to the top of his Steam Cabinet prop. A group of clown scientists grabbed a tall clown identified as Adam and shoved him into the Adam Smashing cabinet. Adam stuck his head up through the hole in the top of the cabinet. The weight descended upon him forcing him back into the cabinet. Doors on each side of the cabinet popped open and four Little People costumed as Adam exited. The four little Adams ran off in different directions. In his autobiography, Emmett Kelly said this topical Adam Smasher routine generated the most laughter he had ever heard during a circus performance.

When I was appearing at Raging Waters, in San Dimas, CA, I frequently used a shark puppet. One morning, it was announced that Shamu, a famous Orca at Sea World, in San Diego, CA, had passed away. I wrapped some black tape around one fin of my shark puppet. When I used it that day, several people commented how nice they thought it was that my shark was mourning the death of Shamu by wearing an arm band.

If there is something on everyone's mind, you have to get it off their mind and get them thinking about the topic that you want. Phyllis Diller broke her arm before an appearance in Las Vegas. She knew everybody would be wondering about it, so she asked a comedy writer to write a joke about it. *The Joy of Sex* had just been published. So, she started her act by gesturing to her cast, and commenting that there was a typographical error on page ## in *The Joy of Sex*. People laughed at that, forgot they were curious about how she had actually been injured, and paid attention to the rest of her material.

I was attending a clown conference where there was a cash prize for skit competition. The prizes were $100 for first, $75 for second, and $50 for third. There was a tie for first place. The director announced that the two top winners would split the $175 since it was a tie. Later that day, Gene Cordova was scheduled to perform his ventriloquist act with Bongo, his monkey puppet. Just before introducing Gene, the conference director announced that an anonymous donor gave the conference $25 so both first place winners would receive $100. Gene usually started his act by asking the monkey his name. The monkey would always respond, "my name is Bongo." This time, the monkey's response was, "my name is Anonymous Donor." I think that was greeted with the loudest laugh in his entire act.

The ability to do topical material requires the ability to create humor rapidly. The way to develop that ability is to work at creating comedy a little every day, and read comedy to discover formulas. It will start to become easier, and will become a habit. To write that much material you will naturally start turning to current events for inspiration. Topical material will automatically become part of your method of working.

★ ★ ★

TESTIMONIAL TIME

WHEN I WAS in Boy Scouts each verse of one of our favorite campfire songs ended with "Testimonial Time."

Then one of the scouts would testify to the current conditions. For example,
The scout would say, "Our town just poured all the beer in the lake."
Everyone would boo.
The scout would say, "But that is where we get all of our water."
Everyone would cheer.

After the next verse, a different scout would testify.
"My school backpack weighs one hundred pounds."
Boo!

"So, my parents gave me a pony to carry it."
Hurray!

☛ Write at least twenty testimonies that have a first line that sounds like bad news, and a second line that turns it into good news.

SLICE OF LIFE

A SLICE OF LIFE is based upon true experiences instead of manipulation of sounds and images. A Slice Of Life aims not at a few big laughs, but at a continual chuckle. It appeals not so much to the intellect as to the emotions. Because it reminds the audience of similar experiences, it is a good way of connecting with them and getting them involved. Afterwards audience members will tell each other of their own related experiences. A successful Slice of Life joke results in audience members saying, "Isn't that the truth?"

For example, in a Family Circus comic panel, Bil Keane drew the family wearing swimming suits digging in the sand of a beach. The caption is "Keep looking, everybody. We've got to find the car keys."

Here is one of my observations, "Did you ever notice that furniture polish and dish soap is made with real lemon juice, but lemon pie filling and lemonade are made with artificial lemon flavor?" That slice of life joke was inspired when I was getting something to drink from a self-serve soda fountain and the spigot for the lemonade was labeled, "contains 0% fruit juice." Just the night before, I had seen several TV commercials stressing that cleaning products had real lemon juice.

One of my friends had cataract surgery. She said that she was disappointed by the results. For the first time in years, she could see her reflection in a mirror clearly. She was shocked by how lined her face had become making her look much older. That was part of the inspiration of the story that I tell while twisting a balloon swan. A description of that routine is included in the section on Storytelling.

A Slice of Life joke is based on observation. One of my favorite observation jokes is, "Did you ever notice on the old black and white Superman television series, he stood there letting the bullets bounce off his chest, but when they threw the empty gun at him, he ducked?" No amount of word manipulation can produce that. It is simply the result of paying attention to what happens around you.

Early in his career, Red Skelton spent a year as an emcee alternating between appearances at Montreal's Princess Theater and Toronto's Shea Theater. Both theaters were managed by Harry Anger. The regular patrons got to know and like Red. One night Anger advised Red to get some new material. He said that while people still laughed, they didn't laugh as much because they knew all of his jokes. Red resented the advice, but in hindsight was grateful that being shaken out of his complacency made him receptive to new ideas.

Going to a coffee shop for a midnight snack, he became fascinated watching a man clumsily dunking doughnuts in a coffee cup. That inspired a Slice of Life routine where he demonstrated different types of doughnut dunkers: the careful dunker, sloppy dunker, fancy dunker, the one who allows the doughnut to dissolve, and finally the cowardly dunker who waits until he thinks nobody is looking before slipping the pastry into the cup. It took several sleepless nights and performances to perfect the routine. At first, he used actual doughnuts for reality. He ate 12 doughnut a show, three times a day. He gained 35 pounds in the first three weeks. So, he turned it into a pantomime piece. The doughnut routine propelled Red into big time vaudeville, and he created other demonstrations of how people did things.

Use experiences from your own life, especially mistakes that you made. When I was in grade school, my family went to Knott's Berry Farm. We saw a framed map of the park on a wall. There was a little red arrow pointing to one spot on the map. The words "You Are Here" were printed on the arrow. I walked away slowly, and then ran back quickly to see if I could return to the map before the arrow moved back to show that spot. In my mind, I pictured the arrow moving to keep track of me throughout the day.

As an adult, I created a magic routine with an atlas book. I talk about how hard it is to locate something because even if you know that it is at K7 that is still a good-sized square filled with small lettering. I tell the story of my experience with the map at Knott's Berry Farm. Then I say that maybe I can use magic so a red X will appear on the atlas page showing me my location. I snap my fingers, and now all of the pages have been transformed so they each have a large red X and the words "You Are Here. You Can't Get There."

I changed the presentation of that routine one year at Clown Camp. The staff members were invited to a dinner the evening before the educational program began. I rode in a car pool. The driver was using GPS to find the location. She kept making the wrong turns. When she did that, the GPS voice would say "recalculating." So, I began the routine by describing that experience. Then I said that I use the original form of GPS which is called a map. I pulled out the book, and showed how I could use it to find my location and directions to where I was going. Because everyone had experienced their GPS recalculating, they related to the story and the routine got a better than average response.

A variety artist named Chumleigh said, "When you incorporate your life, you increase your sincerity. When you are more sincere, your audience is more willing to suspend their disbelief."

My wife, Carole, would tell this story. "One day I decided to get some exercise by going for a walk. I put on some headphones and was listening to a John Denver recording. I was really getting into the music without paying attention to where I was going. You know when you are walking you don't think about how far you are going. You forget that you have to go that same distance to get back. I began to get really tired. I wasn't sure how I was going to get home. Then I noticed a pizza parlor. I went in and ordered a Hawaiian pizza to be delivered, and rode home with the guy."

The story isn't true. It is just a joke. However, the details are true. Walking is her favorite form of exercise. John Denver was her favorite recording artist. We both love Hawaiian pizza. Because the details are true, she tells the story convincingly, and people believe it. When she told her son, his response was, "Which pizza parlor was it? How far were you from home?"

Magician Kirk Charles said, "If you are going to incorporate your life, the first thing you have to do is get a life."

★　★　★

SLICE OF LIFE

☞ Without trying to be funny, write a one-page description of something that you have experienced. Then when you are finished, go back and look for ways to add humor. Try to add at least one joke. While looking for jokes to add, think back to details about the experience.

☞ Pick one of your favorite jokes or routines. Now add personal details to make it seem more believable.

☞ Write a true description of something you experienced that you think is funny. Is there some way that you can turn it into a routine that you can perform in your shows?

COMMENTS

This is an example of how to write humor for a speech or news-letter column. It is the message that is important. Know what you want to say. Write that first. Then tailor the humor to fit it. Don't start with a joke and try to contrive the message to make a place for it.

Here is an example from a column I wrote for The Klassic Klowns of Southern California Newsletter. The purpose of my column was to increase participation by emphasizing how much fun everyone had at club events. I wrote, "Who said clowning is a tankless job? After the last parade two of our female members were invited by soldiers to go for a ride on a tank. I hope they remembered to say, "Tank you, boys!"

During one period of his life, Victor Borge raised and sold Cornish Game Hens. It was a product that was still new to the public so Borge included a recipe pamphlet. He wanted to include some humor along with the actual instructions. So, he included these instructions for cooking a two-minute egg. "Push your piano into the kitchen and play the Minute Waltz twice."

I knew my high school physics teacher because he was also my advisor in a couple of Scout groups that I belonged to. I knew that he had a sense of humor. The instructions for an experiment we did on electrical charges said, "Assign names to the charges and describe how they interact." I knew that they meant for us to call one charge positive and the other negative. But I wrote, "One charge is named boy and the other is named girl. Boys repel each other. Girls repel each other. However, boys and girls attract each other." My instructor accepted it. He said it was okay to use humor because my facts were correct.

It is also how I approach a variety arts ministry. I almost always start with the lesson that I want to teach. Then I figure out what visual aids I can use to illustrate it and where I can add humor.

&XAGGERATION

N EPISODE OF the Burns and Allen radio program included this exaggerated line, "His allergy was so bad he sneezed from morning until night. He earned extra money standing in front of windmills on days without a breeze."

In *Fried Green Tomatoes at the Whistle Stop Café*, Fannie Flagg wrote, "I caught a catfish so big that I couldn't haul it out of the water. So, I took a photo of it. The picture alone weighed 40 pounds."

Johnny Thompson performed a comedy magic act with Pamela Hayes, his wife. It was titled The Great Thompsoni and Company. Pamela played an assistant who was bored with her role. At one point, Johnny is producing scarves from a top hat. He notices that Pamela is chewing gum. He silently, but obviously, tells her to get rid of the gum. She removes it from her mouth and looks around for a place to get rid of it. She puts the wad of gum into the top hat. Johnny reaches in to produce another scarf. He pulls his hand out with the gum stuck to his thumb. He gives her a disgusted look. Then he pulls back the lapel on his tuxedo disclosing a long line of chewing gum wads. He adds the new one to the bunch, and smooths his lapel back down.

Exaggeration is often used in clown wardrobe. When Patty Wooten created her Nancy Nurse character, she created her version of a carpenter's tool belt. She had a large pill bottle, two bed pans, an enema bag, cleaning bucket, hot water bottle rubber chicken, and an oversized stethoscope. She carried a giant hypodermic needle. She wore an oversized nurse's hat.

Clowns often use props that are an exaggerated size. One reason is to make sure that they can be seen and understood from a distance. However, it can be funny in itself. For example, during a circus walkaround, Lou Jacobs smoked a cigar that was so large a little person had to walk in front of him using a pole to support the end of the cigar.

The same approach can be used in other variety acts. I have seen many photos of comedy jugglers in vaudeville using clubs that were about four times the normal size. The contrast to what other jugglers used in their act is visually funny.

Exaggeration is often used in education. The wrong way to do something is demonstrated. One of the first classes that my wife taught on hospital clowning was at a regional Fellowship of Christian Magicians conference. She recruited me to be a hospital patient for a demonstration introducing the class. We turned a lawn chair into a hospital bed. We got an IV bottle which we set up with the tube held in place under my watch band. My wife did everything the wrong way. She flounced in and sat on the bed landing on my stomach. When she accidentally pulled my IV out, she couldn't figure out what to do with it. She ended up putting the end of the tube in my mouth. She decided to pour me a glass of water, and spilled most of it on me. She produced a box of chocolates from her bag. When she started to offer them to me, I announced that I was diabetic. Realizing that she couldn't give them to me, she began eating them in front of me. The students began suggesting other things she could do to torment me. Then she led a discussion of why the things she did were wrong. It turned out to be a very effective class.

★　★　★

EXAGGERATED DESCRIPTION

☞ Write a description of what happened when you caught an oversized fish.

☞ Choose your own activity. Write an exaggerated description of ten things that happened while you were involved in it.

☞ What would happen if you exaggerated the size of some of the props that you use?

UNDERSTATEMENT

THIS IS THE opposite of exaggeration. It is often associated with the "British sense of humor. " If deflates the seriousness and importance of an event. The response to a report somebody was stepped on by an elephant would be "that might hurt a bit."

A character would exit the stage, followed by a yell and extended crashing and thumping sounds, only to return with the report, "I fell down."

In "Safety Last", Harold Lloyd is climbing a building as part of a Human Fly publicity stunt. He has almost fallen several times by the time he reaches the tenth floor. An older woman leans out of an open window to look at him. She says, "Young man, if you fall you might hurt yourself."

In slapstick comedy, you don't react realistically to the inflicted pain. That is to prevent the audience from being concerned that you were really hurt. Often, the response to being hurt is understated. The person hit may wait a moment, and then quietly mutter "ow."

In one of my routines, I have a child use a magic wand to tap a bag that I am holding on my hand. They usually tap it very gently. I gesture for them to hit it harder. They often hit it very hard. When they do that, I inhale deeply, hold my breath. I look at them. I release my breath. I take my hand out from under the bag. I very gently kiss my finger tips to make them feel better. I make the okay sign so they know that I am alright. Then I have them tap the bag again, but first I make sure that my hand isn't under the bag. Finally, I open the bag to show that they made something happen by magic.

Exaggeration can include using an oversized prop. Understatement can be using an undersized prop. I got a miniature Change Bag from Ted "Suds" Sudbrack. The bag was just a little larger than my thumb. I am not sure if it was his original creation. A Change Bag is one with at least two compartments. By secretly switching compartments you can cause a magic transformation to occur. The miniature one that I got from Suds looked like the larger Change Bags that are commonly sold. However, it did not have an extra compartment. A different method was used to make it work. I have had a lot of fun performing with my tiny Change Bag. It looks funny to be performing magic with a bag that is that small. It is especially effective with audiences that have seen the larger versions.

☛ How might you use understatement? How would your character react to being injured? What would happen if you created a miniature version of one of the props that you perform?

★　★　★

Post Cards

☛ Now for a change of pace, write three post cards.

A. From a kid at summer camp to their parents.
B. From somebody on vacation to their neighbor.
C. From your own comic character to anyone you choose.

After you finish, read the comments.

COMMENTS

My brother Kenneth participated in the 1973 National Boy Scouts of America Jamboree. As part of the trip, they toured Yellowstone National Park. We received a postcard from him that said, "I fell into a hot spring trying to get away from the bear. I'm okay." Now that got my parent's interest. We laughed about it later.

Look at the postcards you wrote. Are they interesting? Do they appear to be written by a specific person, or could they have come from anyone?

The way the words are written on the card could express personality; A typed card would come from a different person than one written in crayon. Things that have happened to a card can be a clue to who has written it. A postcard smudged with chocolate probably wasn't written by an accountant to a business associate.

This exercise is sometimes used by authors and actors as part of their character development process. However, it can be used to create material for performance. Many entertainers incorporate unseen characters by reading something they have written.

Gracie Allen frequently received letters and cards from relatives on the Burns and Allen radio show. In one episode, Gracie was reading a letter from her mother when she suddenly began laughing. When George, asked her why she was laughing, she replied, "My mother said my sister did something funny."

"Well, what did she do?"

"I don't know, but if my mother says it was funny, believe me, it was funny."

Nat M. Wells, the Happy Tramp, would read telegrams that he discovered in a trash can. Here are some that he read to the audience during World War I.

> "Here's one from a war correspondent, SCANDAL
> IN PARIS—FRENCH OFFICER FOUND IN BED
> WITH GERMAN MEASLES.... Oh, here's one from

an arctic explorer to the geographic society, BUMPED INTO CLOTHESLINE IN THE DARK—EXPECT TO DISCOVER THE POLE SHORTLY. ... From a troop commander to Allied Headquarters, GERMAN TROOPS ISSUED LIMBURGER RATIONS. WE FIND THEIR TRENCHES UNAPPROACHABLE. ... From a foreign correspondent of a small newspaper. SAW THE CZAR ATTENDING THE OPERA IN MOSCOW. THE CZARDINE WAS IN THE BOX WITH HIM."

I have performed his telegram routine as part of my Tramp Tradition show. I usually get chuckles with the first lines. "CZARDINE WAS IN THE BOX" always gets a big laugh.

I have seen magicians do something similar with Torn and Restored Newspaper routines. After the paper has been torn, they pause to read items from some of the pieces. Then the newspaper is restored.

☛ Now write a letter, text, email, or news item that you could use as part of your performances.

CONTRAST

ONE THING EXAGGERATION and understatement have in common is their contrast to what is normal.

According to Freud, something is humorous only in contrast to normal.

We judge things by contrast. If you see a photograph of a rock, you have no idea how large it is. If a man is shown standing on top of it, you know it is larger than a grain of sand.

Contrast with the serious makes something seem even crazier. In the Walt Disney cartoon, "The Symphony Hour", the Disney stable of characters first play a symphony seriously at a radio audition. Then on their way to the broadcast studio, the instruments get dumped down an elevator shaft, and flattened by the descending elevator. The second half of the cartoon is a wild burlesque of the symphony with the altered instruments.

As I have mentioned earlier, the traditional role of the White-face clown in circuses was to demonstrate the correct method of doing something to contrast with the bumbling way the Auguste attempts it.

Not only is something humorous in its contrast to normalcy, but we find things that contrast greatly with each other funny. For example, a very tall man walking down the street with a tiny puppy, or a little child walking a Great Dane. Felix Adler wore padded costumes to give himself a large silhouette and then carried tiny umbrellas on tall, skinny handles. Frequently in comedy very small characters are given gigantic hats.

Contrast in size is often used in comedy duos. Stan Laurel was tall and thin while Oliver Hardy was stout. The Disney studios paired short, thin Gene Sheldon with tall heavy-set Henry Calvin in the Zorro television series, and in the films "Toby Tyler" and "Babe in Toyland." RONE and Gigi are the leaders of Open Sesame, Japan's Theatrical Clown Troup. RONE is naturally tall and thin. Gigi, who is shorter, wears padding to make herself appear fat.

During a Gospel Clown Ministry Workshop, I was coaching the participants preparing to present a clown skit during a worship service. One of the participants was over six feet tall. Another participant was very short. So, I paired them in one scene. They looked funny. The stage had more than one level with a single step in between each one. To increase the contrast, I had the tall clown stand on top of a step and the short clown below it. One of the biggest laughs in the skit came when the two approached each other and the contrast could be clearly seen.

Contrast contributed to Emmett Kelly's success. He noticed that other clowns performing in circuses tended to move very fast. In order to stand out, he consciously moved much slower than the others. Because of the contrast, he attracted the attention of audience members so that they watched him.

Alfred Hitchcock said that comedy and fright are heightened by contrast. He suggested having a character become anxious by sounds of something approaching. If the door swings open, and a kitten enters, the audience will laugh in relief. Then if a killer reaches out for the character, the audience will scream in terror.

I sometimes contrast humorous and serious content to make each stronger. I was performing at a clown conference on October 11, 2001. That was exactly a month after the terrorist attacks. I knew that I had to somehow acknowledge the tragedy. I wrote a tribute to the victims. I put that in the middle of my running order. I led up to it with my Mismade Flag routine. That includes comedy, but also served as a segue to the tribute. The contrast did increase the impact of the serious segment. Part of the tribute was describing how humor had helped people deal with the tragedy. I didn't want to leave the audience feeling the negative emotions associated with the tragedy. So, the next routine was one that I knew contained a lot of comedy. Due to the contrast with the tribute, that routine got the strongest response that it ever has in my career.

I use the same approach in my Gospel Clown Ministry presentations. I perform a comedy routine just before I do a serious routine teaching the lesson of that presentation.

☛ How can you use contrast?

☛ What contrast between characters or objects is funny? How can you increase that contrast?

☞ How can you contrast something with what is considered normal? How can you demonstrate the proper way to do something so the contrast helps the audience understand when a clown does it wrong?

☞ How can you use dramatic material in contrast to humorous material in order to increase the effectiveness of both of them?

★ ★ ★

ᴀ̲DVICE C̲OLUMN

H̲ᴜᴍᴏʀᴏᴜs ᴀᴅᴠɪᴄᴇ ᴄᴏʟᴜᴍɴs are popular. For example, Garfield, by Jim Davis, frequently has Dear Ask a Dog. Garfield reads the question from a laptop, and then Odie gives his answer.

Steve Bhaerman is a motivational speaker and humorist who uses the stage name Swami Beyondananda. An advice column is one of his formats. Here is an example that was printed in *Laughing Matters* Volume 5 No. 4 (1989)

Dear Swami,
What is the difference between wisdom and knowledge? Karen Ufer, Ann Arbor. Michigan.

Dear Karen,
Knowledge is knowing. Wisdom is knowing and not telling.

Here is an advice column joke by Bill Kelly:

Should women have children after thirty-five?
No, thirty-five children are enough.

Sometimes the reply is limited to one unimportant point, ignoring the main concern of the letter, as in this example.

Dear Clarence,
I've just been promoted in my company, and am now expected to attend important social events. I come from proud, but poor, parents, and never learned the social graces. My mother suggested that if there is more than one fork at a place setting, I watch the host, and use the same fork as he does. That doesn't apply to all situations. How can I keep from disgracing myself?

Yuppie

Dear Yuppie,
If you wait to use the same fork as the host, your food will be cold before he finishes with it.

Clarence

You will find a wide variety of advice columns in newspapers ranging from child care to gardening to business to health to the singles scene. Choose a letter from one of these and write a humorous reply.

☛ Then create ten letters from scratch asking for advice and write a humorous reply to each.

SLAPSTICK/ PHYSICAL COMEDY

SLAPSTICK COMEDY IS generally based on hits and falls. This comic violence is an illusion. Either there is no actual contact or safe props are used.

It is an ancient form of comedy. Court Jesters performed slapstick comedy. The bladder from a dead animal can be inflated like a balloon. Jesters would attach an inflated bladder to the end of a stick. Then they would hit each other with the bladder.

The term slapstick comes from a stick or paddle. It is a double layer with a hinged leaf. When the stick is swung, the leaves separate, and when the swing is stopped the leaves clap together creating a loud sound of a blow without any contact being made. Sometimes a spring hinge is used to attach the leaf. A slapstick was most frequently used to hit somebody in the seat of their pants.

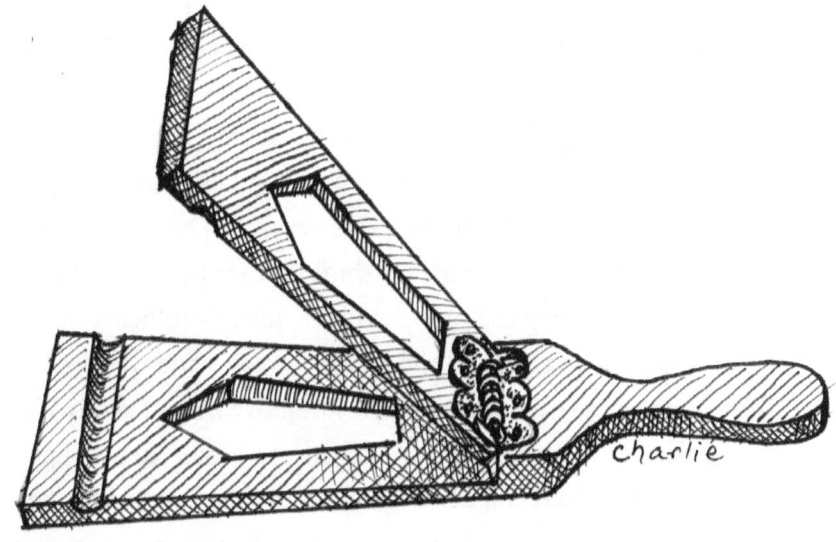

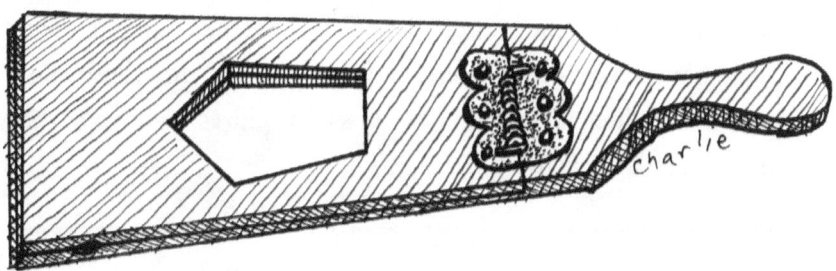

The most common hit used in slapstick comedy is a slap to the face. The person delivering the slap frequently touches their partner to judge their distance. For example, in an escalating fight they may give the other person a little shove in the chest before they decide to hit them. Then they extend their arm fully behind them. This makes sure everyone in the audience can see the hit. It also is a signal to their partner that the slap is coming. Then they swing their arm to the front. They stop the swing just before making any actual contact.

The person receiving the slap creates the sound of contact by clapping their hands together. It is timed so the sound occurs at the same time that their partner ends the swing. They then react to being hit. Their reaction may be exaggerated, understated, or a delayed reaction to the pain. However, it is never a realistic reaction of pain. If the audience thinks a performer is actually being hurt, they may feel sorry for them and it stops being funny.

In a clown Boxing act, the fighters wear wide flat boxing gloves. They are generally made of soft glove leather sandwiching a thick stiff piece of hide. When the gloves are slapped together, they make a much louder sound then simply clapping your hands. Often in a Boxing act, the referee comes between the fighters and gets hit themselves. When that happens, the person delivering the hit does it as normal. If the referee slapped their hands together it would obviously sound differently. So, the other fighter surreptitiously claps their gloves together at the time the referee is hit.

If you are going to be hit by an object, you frequently stop it with your hand which causes the sound of contact. For example, if you are going to hit yourself in the face with a serving tray, you hold the tray in your left hand. As you swing the tray upward, you raise your right hand so it is in front of your face. You stop moving the tray before it makes actual contact and then slap it with your right hand. You move your right hand away as you pause to let the audience imagine what has happened. Then you lower the tray and react to being hit.

Paul Jung used Little People and dummy parts for extreme slapstick. For example, in a baseball act the batter swung at the ball and hit the catcher's head instead. Their head went flying away. The catcher was a short person with built up shoulders supporting a dummy head which was knocked off. Jung's acts were sometimes described as living cartoons.

Sometimes you do make actual contact safely. I sold coloring books during the 1981 season of the Carson & Barnes Circus. I wanted to try to make it entertaining. So, I would hold up a coloring book with my right hand. I would walk along looking up into the seats for somebody to signal that they wanted to make a purchase. I would walk into one of the quarter poles holding up the circus tent. I used the fleshy part of my upper left arm to actually contact the pole. It would cause me to bounce back a little. I would look at the pole, and then admonish it for hitting me by shaking my finger at it. I would carefully step around the pole, and continue down the Hippodrome Track until I ran into the next pole. I knew that it got great response from the audience, but I later learned that some of the other performers would sneak along behind the bleachers so they could watch me perform it.

Some people dislike slapstick comedy because they equate it with the violence of the Three Stooges. I did perform a Boxing act and a few other slapstick routines during my circus career that were motivated by a character's aggression. However, there can be nonaggressive slapstick humor.

Here is an example, of accidental slapstick motivation. I produced a Clown Band act in 1977 for Circus Kirk. Playing a base drum, I led the other three clowns into the ring. When I stopped, Modine didn't notice that so she ran into the back of me. I fell forward. When the drum reached the ground, I pushed off with my feet and rode the drum as it rolled forward. I used my hands to stop my momentum just as my head reached the ground. I stopped with my feet sticking up into the air. Modine pulled me upright.

A solo entertainer can perform slapstick. In my golf routine, I swing the club missing the ball but hitting my left foot. My clown shoes are eighteen inches long so I can hit the toe of the shoe without coming into contact with my foot. I hop around on the right foot for a moment. I gingerly put my left foot back on the ground. Then I hit the head of the club on the ground in anger. The club bounces back and hits me in the head. (I stop the club just before it reaches me and jerk my head back as if contact had been made.) I rub my forehead and prepare to swing the club again. I stop because I remember what has just happened. I move my left foot back so it is out of the way. However, this puts me in an unstable stance. When I swing the club, I miss the ball. Since my foot isn't there to stop the swing, I continue the movement which spins me around and I fall to the ground. My hat comes off. I stand up and put the club over my shoulder. I bend over, and pick up my hat. When I put my hat on, I miss my head so the hat ends up on the end of the club. I then go into an audience interaction bit where I can't find my hat.

A traditional juggling slapstick routine is the Hard Head. The juggler displays three pool balls. He drops some of them or clicks them together so that the audience hears the solid clunk. When the juggler begins juggling, they throw one ball higher than normal. It comes down hitting him on the head with an audible thump. The juggler catches the ball that has bounced off their head. Then they reassure the audience by bouncing it on the floor proving that it is rubber. The juggler has two pool balls and one rubber ball. When the rubber ball hists their head, the juggler creates the sound of the collision by clicking the other two balls together. I introduce this gag by asking the audience if they would like to see me juggle with eight balls. Then I bring out two billiard balls that are eights, and a rubber ball painted black using India ink.

I have seen this gag done with two bowling balls and a four-square ball. I have also seen it done where the soft ball is bounced off another entertainer in the act. When the Passing Zone (Jon Weis and Owen Morse) appeared on "The Tonight Show", they hit Johnny Carson with the soft ball.

If you perform slapstick, make sure that you are doing it safely. In 2000, I had a herniated disc in my neck. My surgeon wanted to know what position I had played in football. He was surprised when I told him that I had never played that sport. He said that the damage the x-rays revealed to my neck was usually caused by prolonged participation in a contact sport. I finally realized that it was probably caused by the way I used to do forward falls. I would do a dive roll no matter what surface I was on. For example, I would trip over the ring curb which propelled me into a dive roll. I toured for several years with the Funs-A-Poppin' Circus. It was a small one-ring show that often set up on asphalt playgrounds because it was framed to be a PTA fundraiser. I had heard many people say pay attention to what your body tells you. They said stop doing something that causes pain. I thought that I was doing the dive rolls correctly because I did not feel any pain. After my diagnosis I asked a knowledgeable friend to watch my dive rolls. He confirmed that I landed wrong on my neck. So, while each fall did not do enough damage to cause pain, the cumulative effect was a lot of damage to my vertebra. I have reached a stage in my life and career where I have decided to no longer take falls during my performances.

For safety, slapstick routines should be choreographed and carefully rehearsed.

When some people use the term Physical Comedy, they mean Slapstick. However, Physical Comedy is anything using your body. It includes eccentric dance, mime, and other disciplines. I am not qualified to discuss those approaches, but there is a lot of material available covering them that is available to you.

Here is a low impact example of physical comedy that I saw Mike Course perform with several different partners in ice shows. Mike would step in front of his partner and strike a pose with his arms spread up and out asking for applause. (In the circus this pose is called a style.) His partner would grab him by his coat collar and seat of his pants. He lifted Mike slightly and moved him off to the side. This is known as a Bum's Rush. His partner would return to his position. Mike would step in front of him a second time and style. His partner gave him the Bum's Rush a second time. His partner returned to his position again. Mike stepped in front of him for the third time. Mike struck a style. Then he reached over his shoulder, grabbed his own collar, lifted himself up onto his toes, and gave himself the Bums Rush off to the side.

The secret in doing the Bum's Rush is that the person being moved is in charge of everything. Their partner puts their hand on their collar. Then they rise on onto their toes and tip toe away. Their partner simply keeps their hand in position on the collar and follows along. If they are going to throw the person at the end of the Bum's Rush, they step closer. Then the person being "thrown" jumps away. Their partner just keeps their hands in contact as long as possible and follows through as if they have used great effort in throwing the person.

Clown The Physical Comedian, by Joe Dieffenbacher, is an excellent book with games and exercises to help you learn to use your body expressively. It is particularly good for building ensemble work. However, it is also excellent for solo clowns. Joe points out that a solo entertainer really does not perform alone. They interact with their audience. In effect, the audience becomes their partner. So, a solo clown learning to work with others strengthens their ability to involve their audience.

Another excellent book is *Mime Spoken Here: The Performers Portable Workshop* by Tony Montanaro and Karen Hull Montanaro.

☛ How might you use slapstick? What would motivate the hits and falls? Would somebody hit you on purpose? Would it be the result of an accident? What would you be hit with? What would cause the sound of contact? What safety precautions do you need to take?

☛ What other types of physical comedy can you perform?

★ ★ ★

PHONE CALL

N AT M. WILLS, (1873–Dec. 14, 1917) was a vaudeville head-
liner appearing as the Happy Tramp. His most famous
routine was No News. Answering the phone, he would say,
"Hello. No Sir! There is no news except that you don't have to
bring home any more dog food—well, because the dog died—
trying to save the baby—from the fire—the one that your wife
started when she ran away with the chauffeur. Except for that,
there is no news.'

It was a widely copied routine. Flip Wilson performed his
version of it. I include it when I perform my Tramp Tradition
Show. It continues to entertain audiences.

According to Georgie Jessel, early in his career he was wondering why his vaudeville routines weren't going over as well
as he liked. Al White told him, "Your stuff is too smart. If
you could tell your gags as if they were things you had heard,

instead of things you made up, the audience would believe you and laugh. Why not come out on stage and call up your home on the telephone and tell these things to your mother?"

Jessel followed White's suggestion and was a big hit. Here is a sample of one phone call. "You're at Mrs. Barton's? What are you doing there? Mrs. Barton's little baby had an accident? It bumped its head against the ceiling. How could a little baby three months old bump its head against the ceiling? Mr. Barton was lying on the floor playing with the baby. Yes, go on. The baby was sitting on his stomach, and Mr. Barton sneezed. I get it."

Bob Newhart was famous for his telephone routines. You only heard his side of the conversation. They are preserved in several of his comedy LP's. His first LP was *The Button Down Mind of Bob Newhart* released in 1960. That recording included a phone call from a marketing consultant to Abraham Lincoln. The consultant said, "Hi yah, sweetheart. How's everything going? How was Gettysburg? Abe, listen, I got your note, what seems to be the problem? You're thinking of shaving it off? Abe, you're kidding, aren't you? Don't you see that that's part of the image? It's right, with a shawl, and a stovepipe hat..."

When Bob Gibbons was performing on stage in a shopping center, he would pretend to receive a phone call from the mall manager informing him that it was time to finish the show. That was Bob's way of informing the audience that he was starting his finale so they should be ready to applaud.

I have heard people complain that there aren't enough solo clown skits available. However, you can sometimes turn a duo skit into a solo skit by making one of the characters an unseen character. The solo performer can communicate with them through a phone call.

For example, I learned the Candy Store as a skit for two people. One clown plays a customer calling a candy store on the telephone. As it is normally performed, you hear both sides of the conversations.

One of my students knew the skit and wanted to perform it as a solo skit. I realized that the audience doesn't have to hear the customer. What the clerk says on the phone explains everything. So, we simply eliminated the role of the customer. It worked out very well.

I have helped other students create solo versions of standard skits by substituting a phone conversation for a character.

In the discussion of Revelation as a comedy technique, I talked about how Fibber would have a conversation with Mert, the phone operator, on the Fibber McGee and Molly radio program. Molly, his wife, and the audience, just heard Fibber's side of the conversation. It was written so it created one impression of what Mert was saying. At the end, it was revealed she meant something completely different.

When half of the call can be heard, both sides of the conversation should still be written. The key to timing and believability is for the performer to think the words the other person would be saying.

Hearing half of the conversation is just one option. Sometimes both sides of the conversation are heard.

The distant voice is a ventriloquism specialty. I have seen it demonstrated many times as part of a phone conversation. The performer speaks in a normal voice during their half of the conversation, and then the audience hears the distant voice as if it is coming out of the phone.

Of course, two or more characters on stage can perform a phone conversation.

When my mother was undergoing hospice care in a nursing home, I would visit her every day. One of the other residents would usually talk to me when she saw me. One day, the woman's son told me, "My mother would probably talk to a pillar if she didn't have anyone to talk to."

The next day I was surprised to see the woman standing outside the nursing home. She was facing a pillar. When I got out of my car, I could hear her talking. I thought her son was right, she didn't have anyone to talk to so she was speaking to the building. As I got closer, I realized that she had a cell phone in her hand carrying on a conversation with somebody who had called her.

More than once I have heard someone near me say hello. I turned towards them and returned their greeting. Sometimes I answered a question that they asked me. When they looked at me with a puzzled expression, I realized that they were speaking to me at all. They were talking to someone else on their cell phone.

☞ Write a comedy phone conversation. Who would be talking on the phone? What would be the topic? Would the audience hear one side or both sides of the conversation? If the audience just hears one side, what do you want them to think is being said by the other person? Would you use revelation as the punchline of the routine? If you aren't using revelation, what would be the finale of the conversation?

☛ Write a routine where you overhear someone speaking on a cell phone and mistakenly think they are speaking to you.

☛ Write ten more comedy phone conversations.

THRILL

ANGER IS OFTEN a component of comedy. That fits the theory that laughter can be the release of tension. The danger makes the audience feel anxious. That is released in laughter when the entertainer reaches safety.

Harold Lloyd was known for his comedies involving danger. For example, in "Safety Last", (1923) he played a character known simply as the Boy. He is working as a salesman at a department store. He has been sending his girlfriend back home little gifts purchased at a pawn shop trying to convince her that he is a success and will soon have enough money so they can marry and buy a house. She comes to visit and thinks that he is the store manager. When the store offers a bonus to anybody who has a great publicity stunt idea, he suggests a human fly climbing the store's exterior. He offers to split the bonus with Bill, his roommate, who is a human fly. A policeman wants to arrest Bill. When the policeman shows up for the publicity stunt, Bill can't begin the climb. He tells Harold to climb to the second floor and then then they can switch places through a window. Bill can't shake the cop, so he keeps urging Harold to climb just one more floor. Eventually Harold reaches the safety of a ledge and is standing in front of a window. Bill opens the window to talk to him. The window has a horizontal pivot so that it opens out and up. The window forces Harold off the ledge and lifts him upward. He grabs hold of the hands of a giant clock to prevent himself from falling when the window is closed. He dangles in safety for a moment, but then the clock face pivots outwards away from the wall of the building.

Lloyd suggested that each moment of apparent safety propel you into more danger. While hanging from the clock, he grabs a rope that Bill dangled out a window for him. However, the rope has not yet been secured so it starts slipping out the window. Bill and the cop grab the rope just before the end disappears. They begin hauling Harold up. However, he is below a ledge sticking out from the wall. As they try to pull him past the obstacle, he repeatedly bangs his head on the lower surface of the ledge. He lets go of the rope, and grabs the crevices of the wall on either side of a window. His foot gets stuck in a crevice. After he frees his foot, he manages to climb a couple more stories before he encounters his next obstacle.

In films, the actual danger is minimized. The climbing scenes in "Safety Last" were performed using a façade built on the roofs of buildings. As his character apparently climbed higher on the department store, the facades were placed on taller buildings. The camera angle was controlled so the audience saw only distant objects that were at a lower elevation. However, the facades were placed right at the edge of the roof. They were each three stories tall. As Harold worked closer to the top of a facade, platforms were placed below him. That minimized, but did not eliminate, the danger. In the long shots, Bill Stricken, who was an actual human fly, took Harold's place in climbing a real building.

The danger is real in some clown performances. One area where this is true is rodeo clowning. Clowns perform comedy skits during breaks in the action. Then they perform during the bull riding competition. They have a serious role, distracting the bull so a fallen rider can escape. They also keep the audience entertained by interjecting comedy. In contemporary rodeo, the barrel clown is responsible for most of the humor. The bullfighter clown has evolved into more of an athlete than a comedian.

Another venue where clowns mixed comedy and apparent danger was Auto Thrill Shows. Jackie LeClaire performed in this venue. He told me that one of the gags was to sit on the top of a ramp reading a newspaper while two cars approached him. They moved sideways just before reaching the ramp so the cars were pitched over onto two wheels. They continued driving with the car leaning sideways at an angle. One car would pass to his right and the other to his left.

Circus clowns perform thrill acts. One act that was exclusively performed by clowns was the Toppling Tower of Tables. In this act, several card table size tables are stacked on top of each other. Then the clown sits in a chair placed on top of the tables. The clown begins rocking the tables back and forth. The degree of lean gradually increases. The clown pretends to pull themselves back up using an invisible rope. The audience reacts when the rocking tower almost falls, but then leans in the other direction. Finally, the tower topples backwards. The clown rides the tower down, and does a backward summersault when it hits the ground. Harry Rittely was famous for performing this act. Directions for building the equipment and learning to perform the act safely are included in *Basic Circus Skills* by Jack Wiley.

Clowns have performed wire acts, both slack wire, tight wire, and high wire. Pio Nock increased the danger of his act by walking the wire above an arena filled with lions or tigers.

During the classic circus period, many clowns performed aerial acts, including horizontal bars, rotating ladders, and flying trapeze. A clown performing in a flying trapeze act appears in the 1934 film "Circus Clown", starring Joe E. Brown.

I wrote a comedy single trapeze act when I toured with the Carson & Barnes Circus in 1981. It incorporated tricks used in regular trapeze acts. The comedy was based on my reaction to what happened and my motivation for the next trick. For example, I was hanging by my knees from the bar, I slipped my hands through my suspenders when I reached up to grab the bar. When I dropped down to hang from the bar, my pants slipped down to my ankles. To get the pants back into position, I swung my legs up and hooked my feet on the trapeze ropes. I let go of the bar so I was hanging upside down again. My pants slid back into place and I could put my arms back through the suspenders. Fernando Bautista was teaching me how to do the tricks. I practiced the routine for several months, and purchased a trapeze. Unfortunately, I never did perform the act. I toured with a small open air show the next season so I didn't have a way to rig my trapeze. Then two years later I began working outdoors at an amusement park.

In 1987, an aerial thrill clown act was created by Keith Anderson at the Ringling Bros and Barnum & Bailey Circus Clown College. It was based on an act that had been performed on a South African ice show. In the act, three tourists are ascending in an aerial cable car. A bomb goes off causing the body of the car to fall away. The three passengers cling to the framework trying to reach safety. After swinging around, one of the passengers falls off. His arms stretch out very long. In the RBB&B Clown College version, he landed on a crash pad. When the act was performed on the RBB&B Circus, he fell and began bouncing up and down. He had inserted his wrists into hand loops at the bottom end of bungy cords which were attached to the apparatus. The bungy cords were hidden in fabric tubes that matched the sleeves of his costume. Then the cable car framework descended safely to the ground.

Kevin Kraft, Jeff Schott, and Steve Lough performed the act at the RBB&B Clown College. A clip of it was included in the Clown College Twentieth Anniversary television special. All three received contracts to tour with the RBB&B Circus Blue Unit in 1988. The act really was dangerous. When one of them broke his arm during rehearsals, the other two decided that they weren't interested in continuing with the act. James Roberson, Kenny Ahern, and Chris Hudert were the first team to perform it in the circus. Eventually a second team was trained that alternated with them in Blue Unit performances. Another team performed the act at Disneyland as part of the 1988 Circus Fantasy special production. After the Disney event, they performed it in Japan with the Ringling Bros. and Barnum & Bailey Circus Gold Unit.

☞ How can you add apparent danger to a routine? What safety measures do you need to take for your protection? What problems would you encounter in trying to reach safety? How would you end the routine?

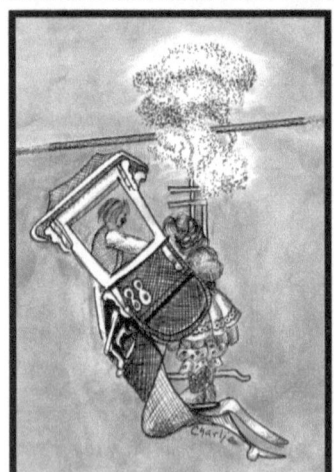

EXERCISE

SUPER HERO OR VILLAIN

NGEL CONTRERAS IS a talented artist and clown. One time when he was visiting my home, he spent some time with one of my young grandson's. The two of them had a lot of fun designing their own comic book hero. They named him Captain Slick. His super power was shooting out banana peels that made the villains slip and fall. After they discussed what his costume should look like, Angel drew a picture of it that he left with my grandson.

Magician Rudy Colby's stage character is a super hero. He actually created a comic book describing the background of that character. Many of his magic routines resemble something that would have been seen in comics.

One of my friends wanted to perform magic as a super hero character. Rope Sand-sational is a rope routine developed by George Sands. It is sometimes referred to as the no cut—cut and restored routine because you don't have to actually cut the rope. George would make a scissor action in the air with his first two fingers, and the rope would fall into two pieces. My friend performed that trick as if his x-ray eyes cut the rope apart. The two pieces of rope are different lengths, and you magically make them the same length. He acted like he stretched the short rope with his super strength. Finally, he restored the rope by welding it back together with his heat-ray vision.

I had a magic effect called X-ray Box from a toy magic kit. An audience member would put a die in a box, remember the number on top, and put a lid on the box. When the box is handed to the magician, they can immediately identify the number without removing the lid. I gave that to my friend so he could further demonstrate his x-ray vision. We came up with several other magic effects that apparently demonstrated his super vision.

Tweedy the Clown was featured in the 139th edition of the Ringling Bros. and Barnum & Bailey Circus (2009–2010.) He was cast as Mr. Gravity, an accident-prone villain. Three of the shows other clowns were cast as his comedy henchmen. In the plot of the show, the other acts had to defy gravity in order to accomplish their feats.

☞ Design your own comic book super hero or villain. What is your name? What does your costume look like? What is your secret identity? What is your special power? How would you demonstrate that power? What are your weaknesses?

HISTORY

YOU ARE NOT limited to performing things that are new and original. We have had thousands of comedy writers and performers preparing material that we can adapt and use.

My first circus experience was touring with Circus Kirk in 1976. In the middle of the show, Planters Dry Roasted Peanuts were promoted. Baby Lisa, a five-year old elephant, and somebody wearing a Mr. Peanut costume were introduced. Then it was announced that dry roasted peanuts were available for sale for the first time during that performance. The vendors entered the tent, and then fanned out going through the stands selling peanuts. Next the clowns entered to perform walkaround routines to entertain the audience while the sales continued.

One day a man gave me a peanut. I had read Emmett Kelly's autobiography just before the season began. In his book, Emmett described a routine where he tried to crack open a peanut with a sledge hammer. The peanut was smashed completely when he hit it. So, I decided to attempt performing my own version of Emmett's routine. I spotted a sledge hammer nearby. I pretended to try cracking open the peanut with my hands without success. Then I got the hammer, and placed the peanut on an elephant tub. I smashed the peanut, and then searched through the remnants trying to find any bits of the kernel. The man started laughed heartily. He encouraged children around him to offer me peanuts. I tried to gently crack each one open with the hammer, but didn't succeed. I could hear the laughter swelling around me. What I didn't realize until after the performance was that Doc Boas, the show's founder and director, had also been laughing at my antics. Since by circumstance, the man had been seated by the center ring so the entire audience could see me, Doc waved the other clowns to leave and ordered the Ringmaster to delay whistling me out. He let my routine continue as long as the audience was entertained. Then he had me signaled to leave. I was surprised to look up and not see any other clowns still in the tent.

Knowledge of Emmett Kelly's career provided me with the solution to another performance problem. I was one of the entertainers hired to perform in a clown review that was part of the Auburn Good Ole Days Festival. Two of the entertainers had toured as backup singers prior to becoming clowns. They wanted to open the show with everyone participating in a song and dance number. I am definitely not a singer and don't consider myself to be a dancer. I got permission to recreate a routine Emmett Kelly had done when he was cast in "Keep Off the Grass", a 1940 Broadway musical. I entered first in the role of a janitor cleaning up the stage. When the others began singing, I sat down on the side of the apron. I pulled a newsprint packet out of my coat's pocket. I opened it out revealing a sandwich. While the others sang and danced, I started munching on the sandwich. When they reached the final verse, I wrapped up the rest of the sandwich. Just as the song finished, I pulled the stub of a toothbrush out of my pocket and began cleaning my teeth. That little routine got a nice response.

Nasir Ed Din was an Arab Court Jester. One of the stories associated with him tells of the time a King suddenly saw himself in a mirror. The King was shocked by how old he looked, and began crying. The other members of the court decided that if the King was crying, they had better start crying. The King thought the sight of everyone crying was funny so he stopped crying. When he stopped, all the other courtiers stopped crying with the exception of Nasir Ed Din. When the King asked the Jester why he was crying, Nasir Ed Din replied, "Sire, you looked at yourself for a moment and you started crying. I have to look at you all of the time."

I was hired by Disneyland as a backup Royal Court Jester in 1992–1993. Most of the time I appeared as a Jester at Medieval themed banquets for conventions at the Disneyland Hotel. I performed magic and juggling. I also told the Nasir Ed Din story in the first person as if it had happened to me.

When I created my balloon swan routine, I incorporated the Nasir Ed Din story. That routine is described in the section on Storytelling.

Another way to use historical material is in performing tribute shows. I debuted my Tramp Tradition Show at Clown Camp in 1990. During the show, I recreate routines that had been performed by famous or significant Tramp clowns beginning with

McIntyre and Heath in 1874. During the one-hour performance, the audience is entertained while also being educated about the rich history of the Tramp clown. I have repeated the show at special events during the past 30 years.

I have had other opportunities to do tributes. One year a nursing home hired me to perform on Emmett Kelly Sr's birthday. Most of the show was my own original routines. However, I included some associated with Emmett. Emmett was a chalk talk artist, so I concluded my performance by doing some chalk talk drawings. Afterwards some of the residents told me about when they had seen Emmett actually perform those routines.

★   ★   ★

EXERCISE

BLOOPERS

A BLOOPER IS ANOTHER word for a mistake.

I was a member of the youth group at Our Savior's Lutheran Church in Long Beach, CA. Another church in town was First Lutheran Church. The two youth groups sometimes joined in hosting events. I remember one event where the program listed presentations by two pastors. According to the program, we would hear from:

* Pastor Landis, First
* Pastor Boer, Our Savior

The members of our youth group thought that was hilarious and we kidded our pastor about his new job title for a long time after that event.

Books of television bloopers have been published. They are humorous reading.

Because I sometimes perform as part of church humor celebrations, I collect church bloopers, especially from bulletins and newsletters. Then I perform some of them as if I am making the announcements for the day. Here are a couple of samples:

* After the service, visit the basement where the church women have cast off clothing of all kinds.
* For those who have children and don't know it we have nursery service available.

☛ What types of events do you participate in? Begin to collect bloopers related to it. How might you incorporate bloopers into your performances?

☛ Many of the bloopers that I have collected are supposed to be actual unintentional mistakes. However, you can write your own original bloopers.

☛ Write at least ten mistaken lines that might have appeared in a newsletter or program published by a group with which you are associated.

ENJOYMENT

IN HIS AUTOBIOGRAPHY, Joe E. Brown describes being on the road performing a trampoline act in vaudeville theaters. He got a phone call just before a show informing him that his wife had just given birth to a child. He said that he had never felt so much joy while performing the act, and the audience response was greater than normal. His conclusion was that the audience enjoys watching you doing something that you enjoy performing.

Another way to express it is that when you perform, your emotions are contagious. If you are bored with performing something, your audience will be bored observing it. If you are having fun while you perform, your audience will have fun.

During the height of Jack Benny's radio program, he had four writers. Two of them were Jewish. For one script, Milt Josefsberg wrote "I think when I get to the TV store, I may buy a new phonograph record. The gang keeps complaining that they're tired of dancing to 'Cohen on the Telephone.'"

The writers debated including that line in the broadcast. The two who were not Jewish had never heard of "Cohen on the Telephone." It was an early comedy record that was popular with Jewish Americans. The record was a monologue of a man speaking with a heavy Yiddish accent trying to complain about something to his landlord. The two Jewish writers thought the line was worth keeping in the script. The other two thought it should either be eliminated or rewritten to explain more about the original recording.

Jack Benny, who was Jewish, decided to keep the line in the script. He said the title sounded funny even if people weren't aware of the original recording. His final argument for keeping it was, "If we can't devote fifteen seconds in a half-hour program for our own amusement, we are in the wrong business."

When Jack performed it, he got a nice laugh from the studio audience. He also got a phone call from Cole Porter, who was Jewish, explaining how funny he thought it was.

When I toured with the Family Showcase Theater, Tim Balster performed an illusion act. One of his illusions was a guillotine where he put an audience volunteer in the stocks under the blade. Tim would point to a red dowel rod. It was two-and-a-half inches long and three-quarters-of-an-inch in diameter. The dowel rod was inserted in a hole in the guillotine's frame. He would explain that it was the safety catch and nothing would happen as long as it was in place. He pulled it out of the hole, shrugged, and said, "Oh, well, I guess we don't need that." Then he tossed it over the backdrop curtain stretched behind our performing area.

One day Dan Reynolds yelled ouch when Tim tossed the safety catch over the curtain. After the show, Tim said that he thought that was funny. So, the next show, Dan yelled ouch and dropped a couple of folding chairs. Tim liked that as well. Dan and I decided that we were going to find a new response to the safety catch being thrown at each show.

During one show, I entered the stage with a safety catch sticking out of my mouth. I pulled the safety catch out, and handed it to Tim. Then I began spitting out teeth. The teeth were actually lima beans. Wally Boag was famous for performing his teeth spitting routine during the Golden Horseshoe Review shows at Disneyland. I loved watching him perform it many times while I was growing up. It was a great thrill being able to perform my version of that routine one time.

Another time, when the safety catch was thrown, I fell out through the performer's entrance in the curtain. I remained laying on the floor. Tim knew he had to respond so he started towards me. Just before he reached me, Dan reached out under the curtain, grabbed my ankles, and pulled me off the stage. I particularly enjoyed doing that because I knew being pulled off the stage that way was something that Red Skelton had performed frequently on his television show.

I enjoyed creating and performing two new safety catch routines each day that we were on tour. Tim also enjoyed being surprised by what I might come up with. That enjoyment carried over into our other acts. At the end of the tour, Tim signed a safety catch for me. He wrote, "To Charlie, My safety catch catcher. Thank you for all of your help."

I never want to throw off one of my performing partners. However, if I know they can handle improvisation, I will sometimes surprise them. I was appearing with an emcee during a stage show one season at Raging Waters. He would respond verbally to my routines. When I did my Clay Ball gag he began saying, "Charlie, I think you need to get something with more bounce." After hearing him repeat that several days in a row, I decided to surprise him. When he said that I needed something with more bounce, I reached into my treasure chest and pulled out a box of Bounce fabric softener sheets. Then I juggled the box and two balls. Afterwards the emcee told me he knew that I was planning a surprise because I seemed to be more joyful during the first part of my show.

Your source of enjoyment does not have to be something that the audience is aware of. When my father turned 80, he decided that he didn't want to just watch TV in the evening. He wanted a new hobby. He decided to learn to perform magic. He bought several magic props and had fun developing his own routines with them. When he passed away, I gave many of his magic props away. However, I kept his drawer box. I am reminded of him every time that I use that prop in one of my shows.

I needed a book for a routine that I performed at Clown Camp in 2019. It just needed to be a large book that looked old. The audience didn't care what the book was titled. Most of them would not be able to read the title. I had just retired from my positions as Cub Scout Roundtable Commissioner and Cub Scout Pack Commissioner. Boy Scouts was founded by Lord Baden Powell. He was a friend of Rudyard Kipling. Many of the terms used in Cub Scouts came from Kipling's *The Jungle Book*. When

I went to a thrift store to purchase a book, I was delighted to find an appropriately worn copy of *The Jungle Book*. Using a book that meant something to me meant that I handled it with more respect during my performance. I had fun using the book with a secret meaning.

I like western clothing. When I found out that the theme for the 1981 Carson & Barnes Circus Spec was going to be cowboys and Indians, I got permission to make my own cowboy costume. That way it would belong to me and I could use it after the season ended. I was very pleased with how it turned out, and had a lot of fun wearing it. I used it many more times over the years. Most of it has worn out and had to be replaced. I do still have some of the original pieces. I have a lot of fun every time that I find an excuse to wear it.

I also get great joy when I perform something that I have created. It gives me great satisfaction to hear the audience laugh at something that I wrote. I feel great pride when the audience reacts to a prop that I have built.

☛ What do you enjoy? How can you incorporate that into your performances?

EXERCISE

YES, AND...

YES, AND... IS a group improvisation game that I have often seen taught in clown classes.

The participants form two lines. The first person in each line moves into the performance area. The person who had been in the line on the left makes a ridiculous statement. The person who had been in the line on the right responds, "Yes, and..." They then make another ridiculous statement related to the first one.

For example, the first person says, "The sky is a beautiful shade of green today."

The second person says, "Yes, and the grass is a wonderful shade of orange."

Then they go the end of the opposite line.

TIPS

If you are the second person, be sure that you always start your response by saying, "Yes, and..."

Don't think too hard. The first person has time to think of something while standing in line. However, the second person has to react quickly. Don't worry about your idea making sense or being funny. If you stop to evaluate the quality of your idea, you shut off the flow of ideas.

APPLICATIONS

Often participants have difficulty with this game because it doesn't make sense. However, it teaches something valuable.

When you are improvising with somebody else, you can't contradict them. Doing so ends the flow of ideas.

It is also a valuable viewpoint to have when working on other material. Chuck Jones said that a new idea is fragile. Somebody saying no can crush it before it has a chance to grow into its potential. The writers and directors at the Warner Bros. Cartoon Studios held "Yes" sessions. One writing and directing team would describe their idea for a cartoon to the other writers and directors. The others could say anything they wanted as long as it was positive. According to Chuck Jones, they soon knew an idea was no good by the silence of the others failing to find anything good to comment on.

☛ How can you use the "Yes, And" concept in your performances?

★ ★ ★

Personalize & Localize

BILL COSBY GOT a tremendous ovation when he entered for a performance at the University of Wisconsin – La Crosse. The students responded because they immediately recognized that he was wearing a UW – LC sweatshirt.

In 1977, when I was the producing clown for Circus Kirk, one of my duties each day was to find out the name of the local high school marching band. I would give that information to the Ringmaster. During the show, he would announce that the high school band was appearing as a special guest. When he did that, I could hear a rustle of excitement in the tent. Then our clown band marched in. The Ringmaster would stop us and insist that the high school band was supposed to be there. Then one of the clowns would announce that they couldn't make it so we were there instead. The fact that the Ringmaster used the actual name of the local band made our opening much more effective.

471

Faye Reynolds was the matriarch of the Reynolds family. I met the family when we all toured with the Carson and Barnes Circus in 1980 and 1981. Lucy Loyal, a highly skilled equestrian was also touring with the show then.

The Reynolds family eventually founded their own shows, the Family Showcase Theater and the Reynolds Family Circus. I toured with the Family Showcase Theater in 1985. We had a day off in Faye's hometown. The Carson & Barnes Circus was performing in town that day. So, the cast of our show went to see the other circus perform.

The 1985 Carson and Barnes Circus show included a big equestrian act with children who had grown up on the show performing pyramids on the backs of two horses circling the ring. The Ringmaster announced that they were auditioning new members for the equestrian act. A woman wearing a loose sweater and baggy skirt came down out of the stands to accept the challenge. When the Ringmaster asked her name, she replied, "Faye Reynolds."

Our group whooped and hollered as we looked at Faye seated with us. The woman auditioning was actually Lucy Loyal. After the Ringmaster attached a safety harness around her waist, Lucy performed a hilarious routine impersonating a person doing everything wrong while trying to ride a horse. As we were leaving the tent, Faye's friends would stop her and laughingly tell her they were impressed by her attempt to ride the horse.

Each day, the Carson & Barnes Circus performed for a local sponsoring organization. In exchange for handling ticket pre-sales, the organization received a percentage of the ticket price. Lucy always learned the name of a well-known woman in the sponsoring organization to use when she performed the act. On this particular day, she decided to honor Faye instead.

Audience members appreciate it when you take the time to learn a little about them and incorporate that into your performances. They are flattered that you made the effort. That connection with the audience increases the amount of laughter that you receive overall.

When I entertain at a birthday party, I proudly display a printed greeting for the guest of honor. Some of the words are upside down. There is an extra zero on their age. For example, if they are eight, the greeting wishes them a happy eightieth bathday. (It is usually the parents who notice that I spelled birthday wrong.) I rip up the greeting trying to correct it. Finally, I magically restore the greeting so that not only is it a single piece of paper once again, but all the errors have been corrected. I give that to the guest of honor.

I would also give the guest of honor a Happy Birthday greeting card that I made using my computer. Their name would be printed on the front. I selected a different elephant joke each year so that the cards received by repeat customers would be different. For example, one year the cover said, "How do you hide an elephant?" The inside said, "Paint his toe nails red and put him in a cherry tree. Have you ever seen an elephant in a cherry tree? See it works." The next year, the cover said, "What time is it when an elephant sits on your fence?" The inside said, "Time to get a new fence." Each year I put an origami elephant in the card. Years later I heard from families that told me how much those cards meant to them.

When I perform a show for a corporate client, I perform a card trick. When I apparently can't find the selected card, I hand somebody an envelope that has been on display since before the show began. When they open the envelope, they discover a notecard with the company name and logo on the front. Inside the card is a picture of the selected card captioned, "Thank you for picking this card." That always gets a big laugh. I know that those cards are kept as souvenirs of my performance. I put my contact information on the back of the card. Years later I have gotten a call from somebody at that company asking if I am available for a repeat performance.

I very seldom do a performance without at least one routine that is personalized for that client.

Sometimes you can rely on somebody else to help you personalize a routine. I was on staff for a Clown Camp program in Japan in 2005. Tomoko was a translator from Japan who was hired to help us prepare. She taught each of us on staff how to write our clown name in Japanese. When we were in Japan, we did two days of strolling entertainment at the World Expo in Nagoya. Many of the children had autograph books. At first when they asked me to write in their book, I signed my name as Charlie. They would peer at my signature and thank me. When I started signing my name in Japanese, they would look at the page, smile broadly, and say, "Oh, Charlie! Thank you, Charlie!" Later children passing me would greet me by name. Other American clowns were amazed that the kids knew my name.

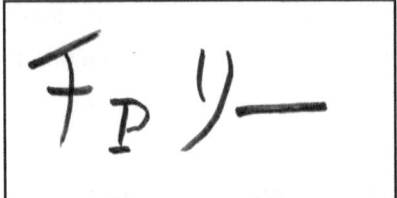

I wanted to use my Juggle with Four gag during the two shows that I performed in the World Expo amphitheater. I asked Tomoko to translate the sign for me. I attached her sign to the back of the one that I normally used. During the show, I held up my sign that said, "Do you want me to juggle with 4?" Naturally the audience didn't respond to it. I looked at the audience and then at the sign. Then I slapped myself on the forehead. I turned the sign around so the same question could be seen in Japanese. That got great response from the audience. Then I juggled with two balls and a large cut out number four.

Years later I was preparing a show for a World Clown Association Convention. I knew that there would be a large contingent of clowns from Japan. I also knew that there would be many clowns from Latin countries. So, I asked my friend Aurora Krause to transplant my juggle four sign into Spanish. I made a sign with a flap on the front. I held up the sign showing the question in English. When I noticed where the clowns from Japan clowns were seated, I flipped the sign over to display the question in Japanese. I let the flap on the other side fall covering up the English version and uncovering the Spanish version. When I noticed the Latin clowns, I turned the sign around and displayed the question in their language. That got great response from the entire audience.

The participants taking classes at Clown Camp in Japan were about evenly divided between clowns from America who spoke only English and Clowns from Japan who spoke Japanese and perhaps knew a few words in English. Tomoko told me, "As a joke you can introduce yourself by saying, 'Watashiwa bulu-su sensei des.' Your Japanese students will laugh."

The joke that Tomoko recommended translates as "my name is Bruce the teacher." She explained that it is funny because Japanese instructors are modest and would never introduce themselves that way. Even though I did not completely understand the humor of the joke, I used it as the opening for two of my classes in Nagoya. Both times it got a lot of laughter from the Japanese students. Then for the benefit of the students who spoke English, I explained, "That is the only joke I know in Japanese. Tomoko taught it to me." I think using a joke in Japanese helped with the rapport that I was able to develop with the students who spoke only Japanese. An interpreter joined me in all of my classes to translate my words into Japanese. I had to keep stopping to allow them to repeat what I had said. I felt that distanced me a little from the participants so I was glad that I was able to connect with the Japanese students without having to rely on the interpreter.

One year, I was hired to do a holiday show at a center for people with hearing impairment. Since most of my routines are silent ones, I didn't worry about the audience being able to understand what I was doing. However, I wanted to personalize it. So, I asked Vicky Miller, a clown who was studying American Sign Language, to teach me how to sign Merry Christmas and Happy New Year. At the end of my show, I signed that greeting to them. I realized that I had made a mistake half way through so I stopped and started over. I received a thank you letter from my contact person at the center. She said the residents had not stopped talking about the clown who tried to say something using American Sign Language. She said that they had many entertainers there over the years, but I was the only one that made the effort to do something in their language. They were excited that I had done that even though it wasn't perfect.

During the Clown Camp program in Japan, I taught a class on Trick Cartoons, also known as Chalk Talks. I demonstrated how to print words in English and then with a few extra lines turn it into a related drawing. One of the Japanese participants asked if that could be done with Japanese words. I had just demonstrated how to turn the word "dog" into a drawing of a dog. I asked them to write dog in Japanese. I discovered that I could quickly turn that into a drawing of the face of a dog. I got great response when I used that while strolling at the World Expo in Nagoya. That is the only trick cartoon that I have learned in Japanese. There are enough Japanese immigrants living in my community that the public library has story time in Japanese once a month. So, if I think somebody in my audience might be Japanese, I draw the Japanese dog. They are always surprised and delighted. I have started to develop at least one trick cartoon in as many languages as possible to personalize my performance no matter the nationality of an audience member.

I do a sleight of hand routine with half dollars that includes changing one coin into another. I originally learned to do it by changing an American half dollar into an old English penny. For the trip to Japan, I purchased a half dollar size Edo coin to use in the routine. While doing strolling entertainment at the World Expo, I got great response when audience members realized that I was performing with an old-style Japanese coin. (Edo coins are no longer used as currency, but are still sold in souvenir shops.) I have started collecting half dollar size memorial coins so that I can choose one appropriate to a specific audience when performing my coin routine.

☞ How can you localize a performance? How can you personalize the routines that you perform? What opportunity do you have to use information that you learn about your clients? Is there something you can easily customize so that it has a client's name or logo? When you perform for an audience that speaks a different language, what do you need to have translated so it can be understood? Who can help you with your translation? How can you perform something in their language? How can you localize a routine?

★   ★   ★

BOOKS NOT WRITTEN

T HIS IS A formula joke that is often included in the joke pages at the back of each issue of *Boys Life* magazine published by the Boy Scouts of America. The magazine refers to them as "books not written."

The joke consists of funny names of authors for imaginary books. For example, *The History of Aviation* by Emma Byrd, and *Law for Beginners* by Dewey, Cheatem, and Howe.

I have used this exercise in creating books that are props for some of my routines. Often, I don't call attention to the author's name. However, they are details that provides further entertainment for those who notice them. Such details create a texture to your entertainment. They also encourage people to pay more attention because they know that if they don't, they may miss something funny.

A good place to study this is the que area for Mr. Toad's Wild Ride at Disneyland. The loading area for the attraction is the library in Mr. Toad's home. All of the books on the library shelves have either a title or an author's name that is a pun.

☞ Write at least ten "books not written" jokes.

STORYTELLING

INSTEAD OF TELLING a series of jokes, you tell a story that includes humorous elements.

Storygami is a combination of storytelling and origami. With each origami fold the paper forms a new shape that represents something in the story. Several storigami books by Christine Petrell Kallevig have been published.

Storigami inspired a routine with balloon sculpture that I call the Fairest in the Land.

(Inflate a white 260 balloon the proper amount for making a balloon swan. Sometimes I use a Sharpie to color the end of the balloon black. Hold up the straight balloon.)

You say, "There once was a young woman who was tall and slender. She had hair of ebony black and her smooth skin was white as the snow. She was the fairest in the land. You may have heard of her. Her name was Snow White. After she married Prince Charming, she became the queen.

(Form a loop with about half of the balloon so that it is shaped like a hand mirror.)

"Her favorite possession was her hand mirror. She loved to sit and look at herself for hours. But as she got older (Move balloon mirror a little away from you.) she found that she had to hold her mirror further and further away from her to be able to see herself clearly. Then one day her arm was not quite long enough. She reluctantly decided that she had to get glasses. But she didn't want glasses that she had to wear all of the time because people would think she was getting old. She wanted fashionable glasses on a handle.

(Divide large loop into two smaller loops.)

"That way she could use her glasses to point when she gave orders. (Point with balloon glasses.) You go over there, and you go there. Then when she thought nobody was looking, she could hold up her glasses and take a peek. (Hold up balloon glasses in front of your face.) She eagerly looked in her mirror so she could see herself clearly once more. She gasped. Her hair was no

longer solid ebony. It had threads of silver running
through it. He skin was no longer smooth. There were
fine lines all over her face. She began to cry. 'Boo
Hoo Hoo!'

"The members of the court saw her crying. They
didn't know why, but they decided to join her, So, they
all began crying, 'Boo Hoo Hoo!' The court jester
saw everyone crying so he joined in, 'Boo Hoo Hoo!'

"The jester looked so funny, that the Queen stopped
crying. The members of the court saw that she had
stopped crying, so they stopped crying too. But the
jester kept crying, 'Boo Hoo Hoo!'

"When the Queen asked him why he was still crying,
he replied, 'Your majesty, you saw yourself in the
mirror briefly and you began to cry. I have to look at
you all the time.'

"He continued, 'You cried because you thought you
are losing your beauty, but you misunderstood. You
have to look inside. (Insert one loop into the other to
form the swan's body.) It was your kindness and com-
passion for others that made you beautiful. (Curve
straight section of the balloon to form the swan's neck,
and tuck the base into the joint of the loops. Display
completed swan.) When you change the direction of
your thoughts you will see that you can still be the
fairest in the land."

Sometimes I would tell the story, and then perform a magic effect where I caused the balloon swan to float in midair.

When I performed at an educational event for clowns, I would follow up the story by saying, "I think that sometimes clowns judge each other too much based on their makeup and costuming. However, your appearance is not the most important part of your performance. The most important part is the love that you share with your audience. (I remove two round balloons from my prop trunk. I hold them by their nozzle with string hanging down.) Being a clown is like a balloon. It doesn't matter what you look like on the outside. It is what is on the inside that makes you go up." (I release both balloons. One falls to the floor and the other floats up to the ceiling. Obviously, one is inflated with atmospheric air and the other is filled with helium. I tie a thin monofilament line known as invisible thread to the helium balloon. The audience doesn't see the line, but it allows me to retrieve the balloon after the show. I have known of several times problems were caused by helium balloons left on the ceiling.)

Telling a story can make a magic effect more entertaining. My wife and I did a series of story-telling hours as Santa and Mrs. Claus for the King County Library system. I had a magic effect where I could use a prop called a Dove Pan to produce a Christmas Tree that had been carved out of foam rubber. I used it as the finale of a story that was a switch on the classic Rock Soup folktale. I cut food shapes out of felt and painted them. I started the story by saying the people living in a castle saw a court jester coming through the woods. They were worried that he was going to beg them for something to eat. So, they decided to hide all of their food.

I displayed each of the food props. When I held up the flat depiction of a roasted chicken, I asked if anybody knew what kind of a chicken it was. When nobody had a guess, I told them it was a "fat free chicken." That was the first joke in the story. We passed out the food props to children in the audience and told them to hide them.

Continuing the story, I said that the Jester saw the lights of the castle. He knew that the people who lived there were stingy. So, he broke off the end of a pine tree branch. When he knocked on the door, the people told him that they didn't have any food so they could not share with him. He told them that was okay because he simply wanted a pot and some water so he could make some Christmas Tree Soup. I put the pine tree branch cutout into the bottom of the Dove Pan.

Then I explained that when it had simmered a little while, the Jester tasted it and he said, "Yum, yum, mighty good Christmas Tree Soup. It is almost good enough to share, but it is missing something. What can it be? I know, a potato. If only somebody had a potato it would be good enough to share. I wish that somebody had a potato."

The child with the cut-out potato would usually announce that they had one. I would have them come up and put it in the bottom of the Dove Pan. I thanked them for sharing. Then I tasted the soup again, and repeated, "Yum, yum, mighty good Christmas Tree Soup. It is almost good enough to share, but it is missing something. What can it be? I know…" I announced another ingredient that was needed. I improvised an interaction with each child that brought their ingredient up. I always concluded by saying, "Thank you for sharing."

When all of the ingredients had been put in the bottom of the pan, I put the cover on it to let it cook just a little longer. I had all of the kids point their index finger at the pan and wiggle their finger up and down. I thanked them for helping cook the Christmas Tree Soup by microwave. That was the final joke in the routine. I uncovered the pan letting the foam rubber Christmas Tree expand. I concluded by saying, "The Jester shared his Christmas Tree Soup with everyone. They all agreed that it was the best soup they had ever tasted because it was flavored with love. They all told the Jester, 'Thank you for sharing.'"

Professor's Nightmare is a magic effect where you display three pieces of rope that are different lengths. You magically make them all the same length. At the end, they become different sizes again.

Richard Snowberg always told a story when he performed Professor's Nightmare. He changed the story to fit each audience. One of his stories was about three worms. One of the worms was dissatisfied because he was shorter than the other worms so they didn't always let him play games with them. The others made fun of him and called him names like Short Stub. He always wished that he could be longer. Another worm was dissatisfied because he was longer than all the other worms and didn't feel like he fit in. The others made fun of him and called him names like Stretch. He always wished that he could be shorter. One day their wishes became true. The worms all became the same size. At first, they were happy, but since they were all the same, nobody could tell them apart. One day they needed something that was on the top shelf, but nobody was long enough to reach it. Stretch wished that he was tall again. Then another day, they needed to fit through a hole but nobody was small enough to get into it. Short Stub wished that he was short again. They got their wish. Stretch was longer than anyone else. Short Stub was shorter than everyone else. They realized that their differences were what made them special, and that made them the happiest of all.

When I perform my Gospel Ministry presentations, I tell the story of David and Goliath while performing the Professor's Nightmare magic effect. The medium rope represents King Saul that the Bible describes as 'an impressive young man without equal among the Israelites—a head taller than any of the others.' (1 Samuel 9:2) The short rope represents David, a shepherd boy who was the youngest, and smallest, of Jesse's sons. The longest rope represents Goliath who was over nine feet tall. After telling the story of the battle, I make all three ropes the same size. Then I say, "The heroes of the Bible were really all average people. They all had their faults and committed sins. They all had their doubts and at times their faith was weak. The only reason they were able to accomplish wonderful things is that they relied on God. They didn't succeed because they were strong, but because God is strong. You can be one of God's heroes as well. It just requires that you rely on God and listen for His commands."

While entertaining in the out-patient clinics at Children's hospital, Carole used a small drawer box that would vanish and reproduce small objects. She put a small cat toy that looked like a mouse in the drawer. She told the kids a story about the mouse being a very fast runner. When she vanished the mouse, she described it running all around the clinic. Then it ran back into the drawer. She opened the drawer showing that the mouse had returned. She kept describing the mouse running faster and faster. Finally, she opened the drawer showing the mouse gone, closed it, and immediately opened it showing the mouse again because it had run around the room extremely fast.

Many of the illusions performed by David Copperfield are used to tell stories. In one of his routines, a man is busy typing on an apartment balcony. His son has a baseball and bat. He tries to get his father to play with him, but the man is too busy working. David encounters the boy, and decides to help him. David covers the boy with a sheet and causes him to float. That gets the father's attention. However, the sheet slips off revealing that the boy really isn't floating. He is holding a pair of dummy legs in front of him. (That is a traditional clown act.) The father dismisses the boy's prank and returns to work. David covers the boy with the sheet again. This time the boy really does rise up into the air. Now the boy has his father's undivided attention. David grabs a corner of the sheet and pulls it down. The boy has vanished. The father waited too long and the boy is gone.

I have seen many other magicians perform levitations, and have forgotten most of them. I remember David's performance because of the story.

You can tell stories without magic. When I was a Cubmaster, I would tell stories from the Northwest First People nations. For example, "When the sky was raised, the songs of the birds were trapped above it. The Hawk said, 'I will fly up above the sky to get our songs and bring them back.' (I direct everyone to

stand and flap their arms like a hawk. I tell them to act out the
story as I tell it.) Hawk flew as high as he could, but be began
to get tired. He flapped his wings slower and slower. Finally, he
had no more energy. So, he stretched out his wings and glided
back to the ground.

"Then Eagle said, 'I am the mightiest of all birds. I will fly
above the sky and bring back our songs.' Eagle flew as high
as he could. He also began to get tired. He flapped his wings
slower and slower. When he was out of energy, he stretched out
his wings and glided back to the ground.

"Then little Goldfinch said, 'I will get our songs and bring
them back to everyone.'

"Hawk and Eagle made fun of Goldfinch. If mighty birds
such as they could not reach their songs, there was no way such
a little insignificant bird could succeed.

"Goldfinch hopped on the back of Kingfisher. 'Please take me
as high as you can,' Goldfinch asked Kingfisher. So, Kingfisher
flew as high as he could. Then he began to get tired. When he
ran out of energy, Goldfinch said, 'Thank you for your help my
friend.' Then Goldfinch hopped off his back. Goldfinch beat his
little wings as fast as he could. Suddenly he burst through the
sky. He collected all of the bird songs and brought them back
with him. He distributed a beautiful song to each bird. But
because Hawk and Eagle had made fun of him, he didn't give
them a song. That is why to this day, Hawk and Eagle can only
say 'awk, awk.'"

The story does not have any obvious jokes, but it always generated a lot of laughter because audience members look silly
flapping their arms.

Another story that I told when doing library shows as Santa was *Why Christmas Trees Aren't Perfect* by Richard H. Schneider. I didn't read the story word by word from the book. Instead, I use the plot as the basis for my story which is about a little tree called Small Pine. The characters in the story are Small Pine, a Queen, a woodsman, a rabbit, a bird, and a deer. I cast audience members as each character and give them an appropriate hat. In addition, I ask the rest of the audience to provide the sound of the howling wind and the barking of a pack of dogs. Then my volunteer cast acts out the story as I tell it. I interact with each cast member and change the words based on their actions. There are no specific jokes, but there is a lot of humor. Something that happens in each chapter is "Small Pine's heart shuddered." I usually cast an adult as Small Pine, and their way of demonstrating that their heart shuddered are frequently funny. The story was so popular that I heard from families that purchased their own copy of the book and made acting it out part of their annual Christmas tradition.

Stories can make your performance memorable and give them a meaning that they would not otherwise have.

★ ★ ★

EXERCISE

STORY

CHOOSE A ROUTINE that you currently perform. Write a story that explains what is happening in the routine.

☛ What other stories can you adapt to your performances? How would you present them?

PREMISE

A PREMISE IS A basic idea that motivates a routine.

The premise for the Burns and Allen radio program in 1940 was that Gracie was running for president of the United States. That led to material for their program. For example, Gracie's campaign song was composed and sung on many episodes. Her campaign slogan was "Grace the White House with Gracie." On some of the episodes, she discussed who would have positions in her cabinet. The mayor of San Francisco was a guest star when Gracie returned to her hometown to hold a campaign rally. Gracie was running as the Surprise Party candidate. A party convention was actually held in Omaha, NE.

That premise led to guest appearances on other radio programs as Gracie campaigned door to door. When Fibber McGee and Molly answered a knock on the door on their March 5, 1940 episode, they discovered Gracie asking for their support. She said, "I think it is time we had a woman in the White House."

Molly asked, "What about Eleanor Roosevelt?"

"She's never in the White House," responded Gracie. (Eleanor was known for her charitable work and Good Will tours which kept her busy outside of the White House.)

A premise on "The Burns and Allen Show" on television was that if George turned on the TV in his den, "The Burns and Allen Show" was on the air. That allowed George to see what the other characters were doing in different locations. He could thwart their plans or surprise them by revealing that he knew what they had said in a recent conversation.

Two of Victor Borge's most famous routines were built upon premises. In "Inflationary Language" he explained that everything has gone up except for our words. So, to keep up with inflation, every word that includes a number will be increased by one. "That means that wonderful becomes twoderful, and so fifth." Then he read the story of Don Juan which has been inflated to Don Two.

In his other routine, he explains that punctuation marks aid us in understanding written messages. Sometimes it is hard to understand what people say because there is no punctuation. He proposes adopting verbal punctuation which is a sound and hand movement representing each punctuation mark. Then he demonstrates their use while reading a romance story.

Sometimes changing the premise can improve a routine by strengthening the motivation. Vanishing Water is a clown act. As it is frequently performed, a clown magician and their assistant enter. The magician pours some water into a glass. They step forward to announce that they are going to make the water disappear. The assistant picks up the glass and drinks the water. The magician steps back, sees the empty glass, and is upset that the water is gone. They refill the glass, and then step forward to address the audience. The assistant drinks the water again. The magician is even more upset that the water has vanished. They refill the glass. This is repeated several more times. The last time, the assistant does not swallow the water. The magician accuses the assistant of taking the water and demands that they give it back. The assistant then spits out the water in a fine mist that hits the magician. The magician becomes enraged and chases the assistant off the stage.

I didn't care for that version of the routine. First, I think that if you announce that you are going to make the water disappear, and it vanishes, you would simply declare success. Second, the routine serves as weak motivation for one character to spray water on another. There is no reason for the assistant to drink the water.

Mary Beth Martin and Ann Lieske changed the premise. Mary Beth played a cooking instructor, and Ann was her assistant. Mary Beth announced that she was going to make some instant potatoes. She poured some of the dry flakes into a bowl. Then she poured the proper amount of water into a glass measuring cup. Mary Beth began commenting to the audience about how dry the potato flakes were before you mix them with water. That made Ann thirsty which motivated her drinking the water in the cup.

When Mary Beth discovered the cup empty, she measured out more water. Then she explained to the audience that it is important to have enough water because otherwise the potatoes are just too dry. Her explanation made Ann thirsty again, so she drank the water. Mary Beth measured water the third time. She started talking to the audience, but looked back at Ann just in time to see her drinking the water. Mary Beth demanded that Ann return the water, and Ann sprayed it on her.

Six Card Repeat is a magic effect where you count six cards and then discard three. You count the cards again and still have six. You discard three more, and when you count the cards there are still six. The premise that is frequently used is that you saw a magician count six cards, discard three, and still have six cards left. You try to find somebody who knows how to do it. Each time that you describe the trick, you demonstrate what happened. Finally, the magician goes into a magic store and asks the owner if they know the trick. The owner replies that they know the trick, but it is out of stock so they can't sell it to the magician.

Again, I think that the motivation is very weak.

Aldo Columbini greatly improved it by changing the premise. Holding a packet of cards, he announced that he was going to perform a trick that required five cards. When he counted the cards, he discovered that he had eight. So, he discarded three. Announcing that he was now ready to perform a trick with five cards, he counted the cards. There were still too many so he discarded some. He repeated this a couple more times. Then instead of purposely discarding cards, he began dropping them accidentally as he tried to count them. More than three cards would fall at a time, but he still always ended up with eight. Finally, he announced that he was sorry but he couldn't do the trick that required five cards.

★　★　★

ᴀNOTHER ᴄAPTIONS

W E WILL WORK with photo captions again in this exercise. In an earlier exercise, you used unusual photos to inspire comic captions. This time you will use a phrase to inspire a caption, and then describe the photo that would go with it.

In performing this type of humor, I use clip art to create a picture. After displaying the photo, I then read.the caption.

Here are some examples based on the phrase, "Rites of Spring."

- ★ The caption under a photo of books on spring gardening says, "the Writes of Spring."
- ★ A caption under a photo of Orville & Wilbur with their original airplane says, "the Wrights of Wing."

☛ When I have used this as an exercise in class, participants have been able to come up with many more comedy caption puns based on "Rites of Spring." How many puns can you create based on that phrase?

☛ Now choose ten more phrases. They can come from either Appendix A or phrases that you know. See how many comedic captions you can create based on each of those phrases.

SKILL

YOU SHOULD GIVE the audience moments when they can feel superior, but you need to stay at least their equal overall.

A dumb character should have some skill that they excel at which the audience can admire. Frank Fontaine playing Crazy Guggenheim on "The Jackie Gleason Show", aka "The American Scene Magazine", is an excellent example. Fontaine appeared in 106 episodes between 1962 and 1966. Crazy would visit with Joe the Bartender. Crazy wasn't too bright, getting things wrong, and telling dumb jokes. At the end of each sketch, Joe would say Mr. Donoghue, put a dime in number seven. Then Fontaine would perform an exquisite rendition of a song in his wonderful singing voice. The audience could feel superior to Crazy's stupidity, but Fontaine was not an inferior entertainer. He won the audience's respect with his singing.

George Carl was known for playing a bumbling character who had trouble getting a microphone into a stand and properly positioned. I have seen many performers imitating his routine, but they fail to get the same audience response. The reason is that they don't include an important element from his act. In the midst of all his difficulty, Carl performs an amazing hat manipulation sequence. He wins the respect of the audience with that skill.

Earning respect is especially important for family entertainers. Children between the ages of eight and thirteen are often antagonistic towards clowns. That is because they are trying to demonstrate that they are too mature for childish activities. If you start off with a comedy bit, they may identify you as being only for children. Once they have made that determination, they may heckle you throughout the performance or may even become physically abusive. However, if you win their respect by demonstrating skill you are no longer just for children. Once they have made that determination, they will relax and enjoy all of your comedy bits. So, I always start my family shows with either a juggling or magic routine that appears to require skill.

It takes more skill to do a comedy act than a straight one. Rachel Schiffer, a wire walker and aerialist, is quoted in *Circus Smirkus: 25 Years of Running Home to the Circus*, as saying, "I've said for a long time that a good clown is the most talented person in the show... When an aerialist doesn't succeed, she gets to try it again and the audience will go wild when she does succeed. But a clown doesn't have that option. There's no second try. You can't redo a gag."

In my juggling act, I would hold a spinning plate in my right hand at the height of my waist. I extended my left arm straight up over my head. Then I flipped the plate up and caught it in my left hand. Then I would pick up a stick, place it under the plate, and start the plate spinning. If I missed the plate the first time that I flipped it, I could try it again.

I decided to turn it into a comedy bit. I did a few tricks with the plate first. Then I bent my left elbow and held my arm so that it was parallel to the floor. I placed my plate on the crook of my elbow. I would tip my hat. Then I tipped my left arm down so my elbow was pointed towards the floor The plate slid off my arm. I would straighten out my left arm and bend forward at the waist catch the falling plate just before it hit the floor. I put my hat back on my head. I would then repeat the trick with my right arm. As I bent down to catch the plate, I lifted my left arm high above my head.

When I straightened up after catching the plate, I kept my left arm straight up in the air. I raised my right hand holding the plate up to the level of my waist. I looked towards somebody in the audience. Then without looking at the plate, I flipped it up to my left hand. When I looked back at my right hand, I was surprised that the plate was gone. I looked around for it on the ground. When the kids began shouting instructions for where the plate was, I misunderstood what they were telling me. Eventually, I discovered where the plate was. I tried to grab it with my right hand, but I couldn't reach it. Inspired by Mike Course, I would jump into the air trying to reach it. So, then I got the stick to be able to reach the plate. I put the stick under the plate and then started it spinning.

Turning that juggling trick into a comedy bit required more skill. When it was a juggling trick, I watched the flight of the plate. If I didn't throw the plate high enough, I could lower my hand a little to catch it. If I threw it a little too hard, I could wait for it to descend to the proper height and then catch it.

Doing the trick without looking meant that I could not adjust the catch if my throw was off. I had to flip the plate so it hit the palm of my hand properly rotated. When I felt the plate, I would close my hand to hold it. I had to develop the muscle memory to consistently throw the plate the same way every time. If I hesitate because I am nervous, the plate does not go high enough. If I am excited, the adrenaline makes the plate fly too high. I have to be able to do the trick without thinking about it. So, in preparing for a show, I practice performing the flip until I succeed fifty times in a row with my eyes closed.

If I didn't catch the flip, I could not do it over again and pretend that I did not know where the plate was going. If the audience knows I purposely flipped the plate up to my hand, they won't believe that I don't know its location. So, when I miss, I have to forget about the comedy and just perform it as a juggling trick.

Although a comedy act generally requires more skill than a straight act, you don't have to wait to develop that level of expertise to begin using a skill to entertain your audiences. John Wooden said, "Don't let what you cannot do interfere with what you can do."

I taught myself how to do the basic three ball cascade. At first, I didn't know any other juggling tricks. I had difficulty ending without dropping a ball. When I tried catching a ball in a hand that was already holding a ball, the descending ball frequently hit the ball I was holding and then careen away. I didn't let that stop me from performing juggling in shows put on by the amateur clown club that I had joined. My sister was also a member of the club. When my juggling act was introduced, I began juggling. My sister snuck up behind me with a butterfly net. She used the net to catch one of the balls. That meant I only had to catch two balls, one in each hand. I could do that easily. Then I acted as if I was mad because she disrupted my juggling act. I ended the act by chasing her off the stage. The entire act lasted about thirty seconds, but the audience always applauded. I think they might have been surprised that any of the young clowns in the club could actually do something.

Before too long, I figured out how to successfully catch all three balls. I began performing other simple juggling gags that were incorporated into longer routines with other props. Eventually, I developed the skill to perform an entire juggling act.

Every time I have started to learn a new skill, I have tried to begin using it as soon as possible. For example, when I learned to draw trick cartoons, I perfected one of them. When doing strolling performing at Raging Waters, I would draw that one cartoon and give it to somebody as a souvenir. Then I left that group and found another audience before I repeated that cartoon. It was well received because the audience didn't know that was the only cartoon that I could draw. Once I had built up my confidence with that cartoon, I learned a second one that I added to my performances. Gradually my repertoire grew until now I can draw many cartoons. I can often choose one that connects with a specific audience member.

☛ What type of skill does your character possess? What can you do to earn the respect of your audience?

☛ When you begin to learn a new skill, how can you use it to entertain others? How can you compensate for what you have not yet learned? How can you incorporate that new skill into a joke? As you increase your ability, what new routines can you perform using that skill?

☛ How can you develop the skill to consistently do something without thinking about it? How can you do something without having to look at your props while you are doing it? If something is supposed to happen accidentally, how can you make that happen automatically?

EXERCISE

PATTER PUNS

I HEARD MANY MAGICIANS claim that card tricks don't work with young children. I saw a famous magician with a charming, gentle performance style invite a young girl up on stage with him. She related with him very well. He had her pick a card from a poker deck. Then he said, "It is important that you remember the name of your card!"

Her expression immediately indicated her panic. I realized that she didn't know the name of the suits. Her mother got up from the audience, stood at the foot of the stage, and motioned to her daughter. Her mother whispered the name of the card to her. Then the girl relaxed and the rest of the act went very well.

I realized that it is not that card tricks don't work with young children. It is tricks with poker decks don't work with young children because they don't have experience with them.

So, I started using decks that children are familiar with. These decks include Old Maid, Animal Rummy, and Go Fish. Not only do children understand these decks, but the decks can inspire comedy.

As an example, I'll use a Go Fish deck which has pictures of fish on the cards.

Start off by making a list of everything you can think of associated with fish. That can be parts of fish, types of fish, and things in the fish environment. A list might look like this:

Tail, Fin, Gills, Scales, Eye, Tuna, Shark, Halibut, Flounder, Porpoise, Salmon, Barracuda, Flying Fish, Catfish, Worm, Anchor, Reef, Seaweed, Clam, Lobster, Starfish, Octopus, "One Fish Two Fish Red Fish Blue Fish," School, Sushi, Chowder, Fish and Chips, Fishing Season, "The One That Got Away," "Why do women say that they go shopping?—For the same reason men say they go fishing."

Then write as many lines as possible using items on your list. Here are some that I use in my routine.

> After my guess of the chosen card is wrong, I say, "I picked the wrong one on Porpoise because I knew that you like to see me Flounder."
>
> "I perform this trick just for the Halibut."
>
> "Do you know why fish have scales? It's so they can weigh anchors."
>
> "Did you know that you can tune a piano but you can't Tuna fish."
>
> Sing, "Oh, if you knew Sushi like I know Sushi, oh, oh, oh, what a Gill."

Sometimes I use a Go Fish deck to perform a Card on the Ceiling effect. After a card is selected, I ask, "Do you know what kind of fish these are? They are flying fish. Look up." When the audience members look upward, they see the selected card stuck to the ceiling.

I use fish puns while performing magic with a Go Fish deck. That is not their only application. The first time that I created a list of fish jokes was when a friend was working on a routine where she juggled Gold Fish crackers. Some of the jokes were related to juggling. For example, "Look, they are flying fish." The jokes weren't all successful. The line "Don't they scale nicely" didn't work because too few audience members knew that one definition of "scale" is "throw."

☛ Choose something that you use in your performances. Can you change it so that it is another object that your audience has experience with so they will relate to it?

Now create a list of as many things you can think of related to that object. Next, use that list to inspire as many puns as possible.

☛ Try out your new routine with an audience. What jokes get the best audience response? What jokes need to be edited out?

MUSIC

USIC IS A skill that is used by many variety artists. It can help create comedy.

Prerecorded music can help set a mood. You can also choreograph your actions to it.

In my spotlight routine, all the lights in the theater are turned off except for a spotlight. I get ready to juggle three balls, but the spotlight moves to a different part of the stage. I move to where it is, but it shifts back to where I was originally standing. Every time that I am ready to juggle, the light moves. So, I drive a nail into the front edge of the pool light to keep it in place. Now when I am ready to juggle, the spotlight goes out entirely. The three balls now light up. Music begins to play. It is "Kid-Toons," a royalty free song that I purchased from Richard Wayne. The song has several tempo changes and funny segments. I do a comedy juggling routine with the moves choreographed to the music. When the song ends, I put the balls away. The spotlight comes back on. Now "Someday," a gentle Richard Wayne composition, starts to play. I begin to exit, but the light does not follow me. I remember that it is nailed in place. I pull the nail, and begin to exit with the light following me. I spot a broom. I use the broom to sweep the spotlight into a smaller pool. I drop my hat onto the pool of light. The hat covers the pool, but light can be seen shining out the holes in my beaten-up hat. I scoop my hand under the hat, and pick it up. I turn my hat over. I remove my hand from covering the brim of my hat. Light is visible shining up from my hat onto my face. Just as the song ends, I blow out the light. The theater is in darkness momentarily. In the dark, I return to center stage. All the stage lights come up, and I take my bow. (This routine combines ideas performed by Gene Sheldon, Emmett Kelly, and the duo of George Percelly & Steve Pedley.)

I recommend using royalty free music. That means that when you purchase the music you also pay for the rights to use it in your performances. Royalty free music used to be very expensive, but in the past thirty years variety artists who are also musicians have been creating and selling royalty free music that is more affordable. The entertainers creating royalty free music understand what is needed for variety acts. Their tracks fit our needs.

Legally, you should use royalty free music. Also, it opens up opportunities. Early in my career I missed out on some great situations because I did not have the rights to the music that I was using.

There has been a long history of variety artists performing music.

Joseph Grimaldi (1778–1837), the Father of Modern Clowning, was a singer. One of his hits was Hot Codlins. It was the story of a woman selling hot codlins (taffy apples) in the winter. The first verse explains that she even though what she sold was hot, she herself felt cold. The verse concludes

"So, to keep herself warm, she thought it no sin
To fetch for herself, a quartern of..."

Grimaldi would pause. The entire audience would shout "Gin."

Grimaldi would exclaim, "Oh, for shame!"

He would leave off the last word of each verse, but the audience could easily guess what rhyming word would finish it. They would shout it out, and he responded "Oh, for shame!"

The song was so popular that for years after Grimaldi's death British theatrical clowns were expected to include it in their repertoire.

In America, prior to the inventions of the phonograph and radio, popular songs were spread through performances by nineteenth century singing clowns performing in circuses. After the performance, Songsters, pamphlets with the song lyrics, would be sold by the clown to increase their income. The Songsters might also include a collection of jokes associated with the clown. William Burke was the last clown given permission to sell his own Songster. Sometimes a Songster was published with the name of the show in the title. Clowns who sold those received a commission.

Sheri Lewis was a singing ventriloquist. In her "Kooky Classics" 1984 home video production, Sheri sang a musical argument with Hushpuppy over whether a piece of music was the overture to Rossini's "William Tell" opera or the theme song to "The Lone Ranger." Some of today's most successful ventriloquists include singing in their act.

Many clown acts, especially in Europe, are built around playing instrumental music. The Rastelli's are one famous musical clown act.

Dimitri built one of his stage acts around trying to play his mandolin. He kept losing his pick inside the instrument. So, he tried using other objects that wouldn't fit between the strings. He started using a ping pong ball as a pick. Then he turned his instrument horizontally, and played by bouncing the ball on the strings. Suddenly the ball bounced into his mouth, and he swallowed it. He pulled a rolling pin out of his big trunk. He lay down on the floor, and rolled the pin over his stomach. That caused the ball to shoot up out of his mouth. When it came down it landed in his mouth again. That gave him an idea. He got out some more ping pong balls and juggled three of them by spitting them up into the air and catching them again. He finished by juggling five ping pong balls with his mouth. He put the balls into his trunk and moved it out of the way. However, he accidentally set it down on the rolling pin. His trunk began wobbling back and forth. He climbed upon the trunk trying to steady it and performed a rola bola routine. He finally got down and put the rolling pin away. He pulled out a dinner plate to use as a pick. That led to a plate spinning routine. Everything in the act was carefully motivated and related in some way to playing the mandolin.

Sometimes a clown would play an instrument in an unusual way. I have seen clowns play a bugle while it is balanced on their lips. Dimitri concluded his train porter act by playing four saxophones at the same time. He played the melody and harmony on the two outer instruments and produced the rhythm on the two inner ones.

Sometimes clowns make a mistake in how they play. Larry Pisoni would begin playing a flute, but the sound was very discordant. He looked at the flute and realized that he was holding it the wrong way with the end pointing to his left. He turned it around so that the end pointed to his right, and played a beautiful song.

Clowns also play unusual instruments. Hokum W. Jeebs played a car muffler as if it was a bugle. When he finished the song, he would pause before announcing, "Excuse me. I'm feeling a little exhausted."

Sometimes music is used as a set up. For example, a Whiteface clown or other straightman character trying to play music, but they are constantly interrupted.

During the first 25 years of his career, Arthur Pedlar was a tramp clown. He had learned how to ride a unicycle in school and wanted to build his act around that skill. In the first version of the act, Arthur woke up and began inspecting the contents of a trash bin. He found two pieces of a broken bicycle. One piece was the front wheel, fork, and handlebars. The other piece was a unicycle. He got the pieces lined up properly. When he tried to ride it, the front wheel went forward and the back wheel went backward dumping him onto the ground. Arthur told me that he didn't get the laughter he anticipated because many audience members thought that it was a real accident and were concerned that he might be hurt.

He decided to set up the unicycle with some musical comedy accompanied by a pianist. According to Arthur, "I place the violin case on the piano, take a white cloth out of my pocket which I tuck into my collar. I open the violin case, and take out my nine-inch violin and bow. I bow to the pianist who starts the introduction of "Speak To Me Of Love."

> "I play the first bar and my bow collapses on me. By the time I've got the bow sorted out, which I treat like a bow and arrow and it twangs back straight, I start to put the violin back under my chin but suddenly realize it's not there. The violin has disappeared. Eventually I find it stuck in my pocket underneath the white cloth, and retrieve it. I tap the piano to get the pianist's attention, bow, and she plays the introduction again.

> "I put the violin under my chin, do the first upstroke of the tune, and the bow goes right through a hole in

the rim of my hat and jams in there. I take my hat off and yank the violin bow out of the hat. Then I play through the tune "Speak To Me Of Love."

Arthur told me that the violin routine taught the audience things are going to go wrong. So, when he tries to ride the wreck of the bicycle, they aren't surprised that it collapses and he falls. They know that it is part of the act and not an accident. That means they aren't concerned that he might have been hurt so they relax and laugh at his misadventures.

Music is often used to earn the audience's respect. Bobo Barnett would enter driving a tiny automobile. Seeing such a large man exiting the small car looked funny. In addition to Bobo, the car contained dogs and a descented skunk. Bobo would perform a dog act with lots of comedy. At the end, Bobo would get a trumpet out of the car. He would sit down on the ring curb. All of the lights would go out in the arena except for one spotlight shining on Bobo. Then he played a soulful version of "Peg of My Heart". Jackie LeClaire told me that often there wasn't a dry eye in the audience when he concluded. Nobody had any doubt that they had just been entertained by a talented performer.

☛ How might you use music in your performance? What effect would it have?

★　★　★

EXERCISE

WORD PUNS

O NE YEAR I mailed a bunch of my friends an empty envelope.
There was a label attached to the back. The label said,

- ★ "This envelope contains Nothing.
- ★ "Nothing is as important as your health.
- ★ "Nothing works like magic.
- ★ "Nothing is sacred.
- ★ "Nothing lasts forever.
- ★ "Nothing makes sense.
- ★ "Nothing is too good for you, but you're getting it anyway."

That was inspired by Steve "Swami Beyondananda" Berman who would distribute boxes of nothing. Most of my friends thought that was very funny. However, one of my friends called me to say, "I don't understand it. You sent me an envelope and there is nothing in it."

I responded, "Exactly."

She didn't understand and I soon felt like we were doing a real live version of a switch on Abbott and Costello's Who's On First. I realized that she had not read the label on the back of the envelope. When I told her to do that, she started laughing.

That inspired this bit that I sometimes have used in magic performances. Holding a bag, I ask an audience volunteer to look into the bag and tell everyone that there is nothing in the bag. They look into the bag. Then, they often look at me doubtfully because they can see that there is something in the bag, but can't identify it. I tell them, "Go ahead, tell everyone that there is nothing in the bag." They usually follow my directions, but the audience can tell that they are doing it reluctantly. Then I tell the audience, "They really are telling you the truth." I reach into the bag and pull out the word "NOTHING" that has been cut out of felt. Then I turn the bag inside out demonstrating that it is now empty.

I used that same cut out word one time in another short bit. The emcee said, "Charlie, I don't trust you. I think you are up to something. What do you have on your mind?"

Then I held up the word "NOTHING" and put it on top of my head.

One of my friends did a short bit with a cut out of the word "TIME." When his partner was slow to do something, he held the cut out and said, "Don't hurry. I have plenty of time on my hands."

Another friend used the cut-out word in a doctor act. When the patient complained that they had hurt their hand, the doctor handed him the word TIME. Then the doctor said, "Here, time heals all wounds."

We used words cut out of felt or fun foam. There are other possibilities. The words could be on a sign, speech bubble cut out, painted on a scarf, or presented some other way.

☛ Can you think of other phrases that include the word TIME? How would you act them out?

☛ How could you use the word "SOMETHING?" Write as many phrases as possible containing "SOMETHING." How would you act out each phrase?

Now, choose another word and do the same thing with it.

☛ Instead of actual words, what else could you use to represent the idea?

SOUND EFFECTS

S OUND EFFECTS CAN enhance a comedy performance.
There are three types of sound effects, recorded, live,
and vocal.

RECORDED SOUND

RONE and Gigi, the founders and directors of Open Sesame,
Japan's Theatrical Clown Troupe, incorporated many comic
sounds in their performances. They frequently traveled with
another member of their group who handled prerecorded sound
cues. RONE and Gigi told me that they were greatly influenced
by Tom and Jerry cartoons when they first began clowning.

To understand the effectiveness of sound effects in comedy,
watch a classic cartoon with the sound muted. Then watch it
again with the sound turned up.

Daniel Sylvester Battagline performed as Sylvester the Jester.
His magic act has been described as an animated cartoon come

to life. Specifically, he was a living Tex Avery cartoon. He also incorporated prerecorded sounds into his act. He wore a special vest that contained push button contacts. When he pushed on one of the contacts, a specific sound could be heard over the sound system. I don't know the technical details of how his system worked. However, it allowed him to precisely control the timing of sounds emphasizing his magic effects. For example, I saw him perform on the Parlor stage at the Hollywood Magic Castle. At one point, a cartoon style safe fell from the ceiling onto the stage. There was the sound of a loud crash as it hit the floor.

Carole, my wife, wore a distinctive headband with a flower. A toy goldfinch was perched on the flower. In her pocket, she kept an Electronic Music Button, manufactured by Darice Inc., that produced a bird song. When she noticed someone looking at her headband, she would push on the button. When the recorded sound of the bird chirping began, she would exclaim, "Listen! My bird is talking to you. He must like you."

Another source for small push button sound boxes is Build A Bear Workshop. The little boxes are intended to be placed into stuffed animals made at the store. They are sold separately and are small enough to be easily hidden in your hand or a pocket.

When Carole visited adult patients in a hospital she would sometimes explain that she was bringing brunch. She would pull an egg carton out of her cart of props. She would remove an egg carved from foam rubber out of the carton, squeeze it, and identify it as a soft-boiled egg. She would remove an imitation fried egg, stretch it, and comment that it seemed a little rubbery. She asked the patient if they had ever cooked one like that. Finally, when she reached into the carton, cheeping could be heard. She pulled out a toy baby chick and announced that it had been in there a little too long. The toy had two contact points on the bottom. If she touched both contacts, the toy would play recorded cheeps. The sound was an important part of the routine because it indicated that the chick was alive. A motionless, silent chick might be perceived as being dead because it had been there too long.

Aurora Krause uses electronic sound effects that she finds in gift shops. They are part of greeting cards that make a noise when they are opened. Aurora removes them from the greeting card. That provides a small source of sound that plays when you pull on a strip sticking out of the device.

A classic sound used in comedy is "boing!" It is used for many different things including a character suddenly understanding something. It can be difficult to produce as a live sound effect, but there are many toy devices that will produce an electronic version.

LIVE SOUND

Wally Boag starred in Disneyland's Golden Horseshoe Review. When he entered for his Pecos Bill act, he was wearing a gun belt with two holsters. Each holster contained a gun. He stopped center stage and struck a pose with his elbows bent, his arms out towards the side. He announced, "I'm the fastest quick draw in the land! Want to see it?" He didn't move, but a gun shot was heard. (A pistol with a blank was fired off stage.) Then he asked, "Want to see it again?"

Early in my career, I developed a series of comedy handshakes. In one of them, a clacketing sound was heard when I shook a child's hand. I pulled a small oil can from my pocket and greased up their elbow. Now when we shook hands there wasn't any noise. I used a prop called a watch winder that was sold in magic stores. It was a small ratchet that you hid in your hand. Secretly turning the wheel on the prop caused the sound. I secretly held it in my left hand when I started shaking the child's hand. I dropped it in my pocket while I got out the oil can. The can that I used had contained oil for lubricating sewing machines. It was empty, but squeezing the sides made a little noise.

Most of my personal experience has been as a Foley Artist performing live sound effects. Radio Enthusiasts of Puget Sound (REPS) is an organization for fans of classic radio drama and comedy. I provide live sound effects when their group of actors do a live on-stage recreation of a classic radio program. I do sound effects for both drama and comedy shows. I have also started providing live sound effects for Midweek Mystery Theater, a group that performs new comedy programs in the style of classic radio comedy. The MMT shows are written and directed by John Ruoff.

I have learned that producing live sound effects is a visual as well as audio artform. Audience members are intrigued by how the sounds are created. Usually when I am performing with an in-person audience, my equipment is set up on a table in front of the stage. During the Covid-19 pandemic, I performed the sound effects as part of a ZOOM performance. The camera of my laptop would be directed at the equipment on my table so the audience could see what I was doing. All the audience saw of me was my hands.

There are two ways to create footsteps. One way is to wear shoes with a leather sole and actually step on a board or boxes on the floor. The other way is to hold the shoes in your hand and tap them against a board on a table. Some directors prefer that I wear the shoes because that produces more realistic sounds. Other directors prefer that I hold the shoes so the audience can see me producing the sounds. That can be particularly effective when switching between male and female footsteps. Seeing me holding a pair of high heels aids the audience in identifying the sound.

During an Open Mike session at Clown Camp in 2019, I provided live sound effects for Diana McCurtain and Aurora Krause while they performed a clown act titled "Stagecoach". When they walked on stage, I used a pair of shoes on a table to create the sound of footsteps. I held a small toy tambourine in my hand so it sounded like they were wearing spurs. I used a slapstick to create the sound of a whip when Diana acted like she was cracking one. She shouted "Giddy up!" I didn't do anything. She cracked a whip a second time, and I performed the corresponding sound. She shouted "Giddy Up!" a second time. She looked over to where my table was set up at the side of the stage. I had my arms crossed. She cracked the whip a third time, and politely said, "Giddy up, please." Then I began using a pair of coconut shells to provide the sound of horses pulling the stagecoach.

When I appeared in circuses with a live band, the drummer would sometimes provide sound effects timed to my actions. For example, at the start of the bucket chase in the Scotty's Garden act, I picked up the bucket and took one step towards Scotty and paused. The drummer hit the base drum when my foot hit the ground. Scotty took one step backwards. I took another step forward, and the drummer hit the base drum again. Scotty took another step backwards. As I began to speed up my steps, the sound of the base drum also came faster. That sound effect helped build up the tension of starting the chase.

VOCAL SOUND

A famous gag in radio was the sound of Jack Benny's Maxwell automobile being started. The Maxwell sputtering as Rochester tried to start the car was a vocal sound effect originally created by Pinto Colvig and continued to be performed by Mel Blanc.

That inspired a deflation of authority skit that was performed frequently when I was in Boy Scouts. One of the boys would get on their hands and knees. The Patrol Leader explained that was their lawnmower. Each member of the Patrol took turns pretending to pull on the starter rope. The lawnmower would sputter and cough before falling silent. Finally, the Patrol Leader would ask Mr. Stevenson, our Scout Master, to try. When he pretended to pull on the rope, the lawnmower would roar a couple of times and then continue with a rumbling sound. The Patrol Leader would announce, "I guess all it too was a big jerk."

Often the sounds of animals are created as a vocal effect. In one Jack Benny radio program, the script called for Blanc to perform the sound of a British horse. His solution was to whinny, and then add "uh huh" in a British accent.

Tom Keith was known for doing brilliant vocal sound effects on the Prairie Home Companion NPR radio program.

A type of forbidden subject humor is sounds associated with body functions. Those sounds are considered rude. Young kids think they are hilarious. I have seen many ventriloquists have their figure make one of these sounds. They are also sometimes used in animation.

Sometimes the Sound Effects Man would be referred to on a show or be a character. In the last episode of Jack Benny's radio show, Jack got into a dispute with the sound effects man played by Mel Blanc. Blanc refused to do any more work. Benny, and the rest of the cast, tried to perform a skit without any sound effects. The silence where you would expect to hear a sound was funny. Realizing how vital the sound effects were, Benny apologized to Blanc. For the rest of the skit, greatly exaggerated sound effects were performed by the joyful Sound Effects Man.

☛ What sound would enhance your performances? How would they be produced?

★　★　★

Forced Relationship

A Forced Relationship is often used to jump start creativity. That means that you generate a list of possible items. Then you choose several of the items at random and try to fit them together. It is often used as an exercise during clown classes.

HERE IS AN EXAMPLE:

PEOPLE
2. Mail Carrier 3. Priest 4. Dancer 5. Police Officer 6. Chef 7. Janitor 8. Society Matron 9. Small Child 10. School Teacher 11. Hobo 12. Soccer Player

PLACE

2. Airport 3. Church 4. Park 5. Grocery Store 6. Beach 7. School 8. Hair Salon 9. Bus 10. Circus 11. Gas Station 12. Cruise Ship

ACTIVITY

2. Take a photo 3. Eat a meal 4. Read a book 5. Wash clothes 6. Paint a picture 7. Make a phone call 8. Perform a card trick 9. Take a nap 10. Sing 11. Perform a dance 12. Meet an old friend

OBJECT

2. Box 3. Chair 4. Ladder 5. Rope 6. Table 7. Piece of Paper 8. Loaf of Bread 9. Ball 10. Shoe 11. Umbrella 12. Glass

Roll a pair of dice to make your selections. Choose two people and one place. You can choose one or two activities. Sometimes humorous conflict comes from characters with different goals having to interact. Choose one or more objects. Then try to write a routine that includes those items. You can add additional items if your routine requires them.

It is important that your choices be made at random. Otherwise, you will tend to pick items that you think you can easily combine.

Another way to make random choices it is to write possibilities on slips of paper. Then you draw the slips at random to decide what you will use.

Another variation used often in clown classes is to put a bunch of items in a box. The participants try to come up with a way to use as many of them as possible in a skit.

☞ Create five different possible routines based on forced relationships. You can use the list provided in this exercise or you can create your own lists. How would you choose items at random?

HAPPY ACCIDENT

A HAPPY ACCIDENT IS something that you didn't plan, but you can take advantage of it.

Perhaps the most famous joke on the Jack Benny radio program was created by accident. John Tackaberry and Milt Josefsberg were working on a script for the March 28, 1948 episode. Ronald Colman had just won the Best Actor Academy Award for the film "A Double Life". On the radio program, Colman lived next door to Jack Benny. (Colman really was not his neighbor.) In this script, Jack borrowed Ronald Colman's Oscar statue and a thief stole the Oscar while Jack was walking home. That set up a premise for a running gag. The next week Jack would borrow an Oscar from another Academy Award winner, and gave that to Colman as if he was returning the first one. Each week Jack had to borrow another Oscar to give to the person he had borrowed one from the previous week.

Tackaberry and Josefsberg agreed to use the cliché of having the thief demand "your money or your life?" Josefsberg kept suggesting possible responses while Tackaberry was lying on a couch in their office. His final suggestion was "You mean that I have a choice."

Josefsberg said that Tackaberry ignored that suggestion. Josefsberg was mad that his partner didn't appear to be making effort to help complete the script. He demanded that his partner suggest a possible line. Tackaberry angrily retorted, "I'm thinking it over."

Tackaberry's comment was in response to Josefsberg's demand that he contribute a joke. It was not meant as a possible joke. However, both men immediately realized that it was the perfect punchline for the routine.

Victor Borge was a popular and successful actor in Denmark prior to the Nazi invasion. During a rehearsal for a play, many of the cast members had a cold. They frequently coughed, sneezed, and wheezed. They often finished their lines with a gasp or sigh. It disrupted the rehearsal. However, Borge realized that the sounds seemed to be punctuating what people were saying. That inspired his Phonetic Punctuation routine that he performed the rest of his life.

Grock was performing his musical clown act in a circus. The ground was muddy. When he sat down on his piano bench, the legs sank into the ground and he could not move it. He realized that the bench was too far from the piano. The feet of the piano had been placed on boards so he could move it. Moving the piano closer to the bench got a great laugh, so he made that a permanent part of his act.

Don Weed said, "The difference between an amateur and a professional is that happy accidents happen to both, but the professional figures out how to make it happen again."

Early in my career, I created a routine where I couldn't figure out how to put my hat on properly. I tried to follow instructions from audience members. However, I never managed to get it correct. So, I would give my hat to a small child and bend over to let them put it on me. One day I didn't bend over quite far enough and a little girl couldn't quite reach. Her efforts to get my hat on my head were hilarious.

I wanted to recreate that situation. I quickly learned that if I leaned over too far, they didn't have any trouble. However, if I didn't lean over far enough, they wouldn't attempt it because they knew it was impossible. I needed a way to measure how far to lean over. I would close my eyes, but peek out through my eyelashes when I leaned over. I discovered that if I lined up the tip of my nose with the top of their head, I was at the proper height for that child.

According to circus legend, Otto Griebling was running down the Cole Bros. Circus hippodrome track. He tripped and fell into a water trough that was used by a seal act. When he climbed

out, his disgusted expression as he stood there dripping water drew great laughter. The show's director demanded that Otto fall into the water trough during every show for the rest of the season. Otto's challenge was to make it look like an accident at each performance. The audience would not laugh if they thought he dove into the water on purpose.

☛ When an accident happens during a performance, are you able to take advantage of it? How can you turn a mistake into a potential new trick? How can you make something that was originally an accident happen again? When you recreate something that happened accidentally, how can you make it seem like it is happening for the first time?

★ ★ ★

DEFINITION REVIEW

☞ Using the table of contents as a list of techniques, write your own definition of each one.

★ ★ ★

CONCLUSION

THIS ISN'T AN end. It is just a new beginning.

Gene Perret said, "Allow your career and your talents to grow slowly. As Arnold Glascow said, 'the key to everything is patience. You get the chicken by hatching the egg... not by smashing it.'"

Be patient with yourself. Give yourself permission to continue learning and growing. I am still studying comedy, attempting to create new material, and struggling when it doesn't meet my expectations.

A friend once asked me if writing got easier the more that I do it. Not really. As I work at it, I experience moments when it seems to go right. That demonstrates what is possible to me. That means my standards of excellence keep changing. What I once thought was great, I may now think is just acceptable.

Continue studying comedy. Go see other people perform. Sometimes I see wonderful entertainers who inspire me to want to do better. I don't always know how they achieve their results. Sometimes I see entertainers that make obvious mistakes. I instantly know what I want to avoid. Most people are a mixture of good and bad. I know that I certainly am. I have seen people with very little experience perform a brief moment that is brilliant. I have seen experienced people that I greatly respect do a little thing in a performance that makes me cringe.

Continue to do the work of writing comedy. I have tried to create my own exercises, or at least my own version. They are all ones that I have used in developing my ability to write comedy. They are ones that I have used in teaching comedy writing and found to be effective. You can repeat these exercises many times and come up with different results.

However, if you would like more writing exercises, I recommend Gene Perret's *Comedy Writing Workbook*. It contains 87 writing exercises. His book is devoted mainly to verbal comedy. Another book with lots of exercises is *Clown: The Physical Comedian* by Joe Dieffenbacher. As the title indicates most of the exercises are physical and are done as a member of a group.

Go back over the material that you have written as a result of these exercises. Try to improve that, even if you change just one word. Mark Twain said, "The difference between the right word and the almost right word is the same as the difference between lightning and lightning bug."

Don't try to develop your comedy in isolation. Connect with your peers. Let them inspire you. Find out what they are working on and support them. Generate some ideas that you think they might be able to use.

Find places to try out your comedy. It doesn't have to be a large audience. I started playing Pickleball once a week with a small group of people. During the games I make humorous comments which keeps the atmosphere light. Sometimes we are having so much fun that nobody can remember the score of that game and we have to start over.

A friend was going through a difficult time. I tried supporting him by sending him frequent humorous emails. His wife said that she could tell that he had received an email from me when she heard him laughing.

Every time that I attempt to create humor, the audience, no matter how large or small, teaches me something new.

Above all, thank you for joining me on this journey of discovery. Thank you for bringing more joy and laughter into the world. Never doubt for a moment that what you do is worthwhile.

APPENDIX A

Proverbs, cliches, and popular phrases are a good jumping off point for comedy writing. They can be taken literally, placed in a new setting, be given a new ending, or be turned into puns and malaprops.

They are invaluable, but when you need them, they tend to take flight and go right out of your head or perch tantalizingly on the tip of your tongue.

By making a list of them you tie them down to where you can find them. Looking over the list often will keep the phrases flitting through your brain so they are there to come winging out when you need them. Here is a list to get you started, and to use in the comedy creation exercises.

- ★ The show must go on.
- ★ Don't look a gift horse in the mouth.

* An apple a day keeps the doctor away.
* Early to bed and early to rise makes you healthy, wealthy, and wise.
* Laugh and the world laughs with you. Cry, and you cry alone.
* My eyes were too big for my tummy.
* Don't count your chickens before they hatch.
* Don't bite the hand that feeds you.
* Don't judge a book by its cover.
* Don't put off until tomorrow what you can do today.
* People who live in glass houses shouldn't throw stones.
* If it ain't broke, don't fix it.
* When the going gets tough, the tough get going.
* It's not what you do, but how you do it.
* He's such a know-it-all.
* You can 't burn the candle at both ends.
* He sleeps like a log.
* A stitch in time saves nine.
* Be it ever so humble, there is no place like home.
* Did you ever have one of those days?
* I've got some good news and some bad news.
* Two heads are better than one.
* The grass is always greener on the other side.
* All's well that ends well.
* All that glitters is not gold.
* You can't have your cake and eat it too.
* You can lead a horse to water, but you can't make him drink.

- ★ Don't bite off more than you can chew.
- ★ All's fair in love and war.
- ★ A rolling stone gathers no moss.
- ★ Curiosity killed the cat.
- ★ Money doesn't grow on trees.
- ★ It takes two to tangle.
- ★ Don't blow your own trumpet.
- ★ Half a loaf is better than none.
- ★ Out of sight, out of mind.
- ★ While the cat's away, the mice will play.
- ★ Rome wasn't built in a day.
- ★ You can't teach an old dog new tricks.
- ★ In the nick of time.
- ★ Absence makes the heart grow fonder.
- ★ All good things must come to an end.
- ★ A picture is worth a thousand words.
- ★ Time heals all wounds.
- ★ A watched pot never boils.
- ★ Too many cooks spoil the broth.
- ★ Many are called but few are chosen.
- ★ A little bird told me.
- ★ He took the words right out of my mouth.
- ★ He fell head over heels in love.
- ★ Where there's a will there's a way
- ★ Beggars can't be choosers.
- ★ A mind is a terrible thing to waste.
- ★ I don't know much about art, but I know what I like.
- ★ You'll catch your death of cold.
- ★ That was before my time.

- ★ Here today, gone tomorrow.
- ★ We have ways to make you talk.
- ★ Beauty is in the eye of the beholder.
- ★ Cleanliness is next to godliness.
- ★ May the Force be with you.
- ★ He's got a chip on his shoulder.
- ★ Are you a man or a mouse?
- ★ Give me five
- ★ Home Sweet Home
- ★ Stop horsing around.
- ★ Contact Free
- ★ Breaking News
- ★ Google It
- ★ The New Normal
- ★ Keep Calm and Carry On
- ★ Do you want fries with that?
- ★ When life hands you lemons, make lemonade.
- ★ I only have two hands.
- ★ I'm afraid not.

This list is just a beginning, a drop in the bucket, the tip of the iceberg, It is just a small part of the list I have for my own use. It should be a small part of the list that you use. Add to your list, put down everything you can think of, and when you hear somebody use an interesting phrase, add it to your list. No list is too long as long as you use it.

$\star$ $\star$ $\star$

APPENDIX B
DOCTOR GAG FILE

Here is a short doctor gag file.

DOCTOR: Come in, take a chair.
PATIENT: Thank you, I'll take it on the way out.

DOCTOR: What is your complaint?
PATIENT: I've been having nightmares. Last night I dreamed that I was a teepee. The night before that I dreamed that I was a wigwam. What does it mean?
DOCTOR: You're two tents.

PATIENT: Doctor, did you ever make a serious mistake in diagnosis?
DOCTOR: Yes, I once treated a patient for indigestion when she could have afforded an appendectomy.

DOCTOR: Has this ever happened before?
PATIENT: Yes.
DOCTOR: Well, it has happened again.

PATIENT: Doctor, you've got to help me. I think that I'm losing my mind. I can't remember anything.
DOCTOR: When did you first become aware of this problem?
PATIENT: What problem?

DOCTOR: I know your problem. You've got snu in your blood.
PATIENT: Snu? What's snu?
DOCTOR: Nothing much, what's snu with you?

DOCTOR: I'm going to have to operate and remove your henweigh?
PATIENT: What's a henweigh?
DOCTOR: About eight pounds.

PATIENT: My insomnia is so bad I can't even sleep when it is time to get up.

PATIENT: I've heard of cases where a doctor treated a patient for pneumonia, and he ended up dying of typhoid fever.
DOCTOR: Don't worry, when I treat somebody for pneumonia, they die of pneumonia.

DOCTOR: The best thing you could do is to give up drinking and smoking, get up early every morning, get lots of exercise, and go to bed early every night.
PATIENT: What's the second best?

DOCTOR: What's wrong with you?
PATIENT: (Raises arm to shoulder height.) I can only raise my arm this high.
DOCTOR: How high could you raise it before?
PATIENT: (Raises arm straight over head) This high.

PATIENT: is it true that sleeping outside will cure insomnia?
DOCTOR: Yes, but sleeping inside will do the same thing.

DOCTOR: What's wrong?
PATIENT: See this? (Turns head to the right) That I can do. See this? (Turns head to the left) That I can't do.

DOCTOR: Do you get much exercise?
PATIENT: Well—Sometimes my mind wanders.

PATIENT: Doctor, I fell off a twelve-foot ladder.
DOCTOR: Where does it hurt?
PATIENT: Nowhere, I was only on the first step.

DOCTOR: You're fine.
PATIENT: I want a second opinion.

DOCTOR: Okay, you're real fine.
PATIENT: From a SECOND DOCTOR!

WOMAN: My husband thinks he's a chicken.
DOCTOR: Well, then I'll refer him to a psychiatrist.
WOMAN: Don't do that. We need the eggs.

MOTHER: Don't you think, doctor, that you have over-charged me for attending Johnny when he had the measles.
DOCTOR: You must remember that my bill includes 13 office visits.
MOTHER: Yes, but you forget that he infected the entire school.

PATIENT: Do you think my face will break out if I eat too much candy, doctor?
DOCTOR: I don't know. I try not to make rash decisions.

DOCTOR: My advice to you is to give up drinking and smoking, get up early every morning, get lots of exercise, and go to bed early every night.
PATIENT: Thanks, Doc. Good bye.
DOCTOR: Hold it! You haven't paid me.
PATIENT: I know. I'm not taking your advice.

DOCTOR: Do you have a headache?
PATIENT: No!

DOCTOR: (Hits the patient on the head with a mallet) Now you do!

DOCTOR: What's wrong with you?
PATIENT: I don't know doctor. I just feel kind of funny.
DOCTOR: (Puts his hand on the patient's forehead and starts laughing) You're right.

DOCTOR: We'll have to give you a huge, painful cortisone shot in your shoulder.
PATIENT: On second thought Doc, no thanks! (starts to exit) That's a great doctor. I feel better already.

DOCTOR: You're suffering from dipsopopsiladiladiladihoo.
PATIENT: What's that?
DOCTOR: The fear of yodeling.

DOCTOR: Let me hear you cough!
PATIENT: Cough.
DOCTOR: Again!
PATIENT: Cough.
DOCTOR: Again!
PATIENT: Cough.
DOCTOR: You've got to do something about that persistent cough.

PATIENT: What is the difference between ammonia and pneumonia?

DOCTOR: Ammonia comes in bottles; pneumonia comes in chests.

DOCTOR: The trouble with most people today is that they let themselves get too run down.
PATIENT: Would you say that I look run down?
DOCTOR: You look run over.

PATIENT: Doctor, would you say I look run down?
DOCTOR: Okay, I look run down.

Here are some endings that have been used for doctor acts in circus performances.

DOCTOR: I am going to have to pump your stomach. (Then he gets out something that looks like an oversized bicycle pump or balloon pump. After using it, he opens one end of the pump releasing a live dog.) It looks like you had a hot dog for lunch.

DOCTOR: I am afraid that you have an ingrown hair. (Reaching inside a pocket of the patient's clothing he pulls out a live rabbit or a bunny puppet.)

DOCTOR: I think you have a corn on your foot. (Reaching inside the cuff of the patient's pants, he pulls out an ear of corn.)

A stretcher is carried in by a nurse and is laid down on the ground. The patient is placed on the stretcher. The nurse and doctor pick up the poles of the stretcher. The fabric breaks away leaving the patient lying on the ground. The patient notices that they are leaving without him. The patient grabs the fabric and chases them out.

★ ★ ★

SELECTED
BIBLIOGRAPHY

Allan, Barbara *Antiques Ravin': A Trash 'n' Treasures Mystery* (Kensington Books New York, NY) 2019

Allen, Steve with Wollman, Jane *How To Be Funny: Discovering the Comic You* (McGraw-Hill) 1998

Allen, Steve *Make 'Em Laugh* (Prometheus Books, Buffalo, New York) 1993

Allen, Steve *More Funny People* (Stein and Day/Publishers, New York) 1982

Allen, Steve *Steve Allen's Private Joke File"* An Encyclopedia of his Favorite Gags, Anecdotes, Essays, and Monologues* (Three Rivers Press, New York, NY) 2000

Andrews, Bart *The "I Love Lucy" Book* ((Doubleday & Company, Inc., Garden City, New York) 1985

Benny, Jack and his daughter Joan *Sunday Nights at Seven: The Jack Benny Story* (Warner Books New York, NY) 1990

Berle, Milton *Milton Berle's Private Joke File: Over 10,00 of his Best Gags, Anecdotes and One-Liners*, Edited by Milt Rosen (Crown Trade Paperbacks, New York, NY) 1989

Berman, Garry, editor *Between The Laughs: Our Greatest Comedians Talk Seriously About Comedy and Each Other* (BearManor Media, Albany, Georgia) 2012

Bjorklsn, Harry C. *Chalk "Talkies" "A New Kind of Fun* ( ) 1929

Blythe, Cheryl and Sackett, Susan *Say Goodnight, Gracie! The Story of Burns & Allen* (E. P. Dutton, New York) 1986

Boz (Charles Dickens) editor *Memoirs of Joseph Grimaldi* (George Routledge and Sons, London) 1838

Brandon, James R. *Theatre in Southeast Asia* (Harvard University Press, Cambridge, Massachusetts) 1967

Brown, Joe E. and Hancock, Ralph *Laughter is a Wonderful Thing* (A. S. Barnes and Company, New York) 1956

Buehl, Lorle "Busy Bee – A Variation" *Clowning Around* (World Clown Association) November 1991

Burns, George *Gracie: A Love Story* (G. P. Putnam's Sons, New York) 1988

Cahn, William *Harold Lloyd's World of Comedy* (Duell, Sloan and Pearce, New York) 1964

Coco the Clown *Behind My Greasepaint* (Hutchinson & Co. Ltd. London) 1950

Corrigan, Robert W., editor *Comedy: A Critical Anthology* (Houghton Mifflin Company, Boston) 1971

Dardis, Tom *Keaton: The Man Who Wouldn't Lie Down* (Charles Scribner's Sons, New York) 1979

Davis, Lon & Debra, editors *Chase! A Tribute to the Keystone Cops* (Bear Manor Media, Orlando, FL) 2020

Dickson, Rick, Coordinator *The Best of Clowning Around* (World Clown Association, Pekin, IL) 1994

Dieffenbacher, Joe *Clown: The Physical Comedian* (Methuen Drama, London) 2021

Downer, Alan S., editor *The Memoir of John Durang American Actor 1785–1816* (The Historical Society of York County, York, PA) 1966

Epstein, Lawrence J. *Mixed Nuts: America's Love Affair with Comedy Teams from Burns and Allen to Belushi and Aykroyd* (Public Affairs, New York) 2004

Faith, William Robert *Bob Hope: A Life in Comedy* (G. P. Putnam's Sons, New York) 1982

Fein, Irving A. *Jack Benny: An Intimate Biography* (G. P. Putnam's Sons, New York) 1976

Findlater, Richard *Grimaldi King of Clowns* (Maggibbon & Kee, London) 1955

Franklin, Joe *Joe Franklin's Encyclopedia of Comedians* (The Citadel Press, Secaucus, N.J.) 1979

Frow, Gerald *"Oh, Yes It Is" A History of Pantomime* (British Broadcasting Corporation, London) 1985

Fry, William F and Allen, Melanie *Creating Humor: Life Studies of Comedy Writers* (Transaction Publishers, New Brunswick) 1994

Gilbert, Douglas *American Vaudeville: Its Life and Times* (Dover Publications, Inc. New York) 1940

Grock *Grock: King of Clowns* (Methuen and Co Ltd, London) 1957

Grock *Grock: Life's a Lark* (William Heinemann Ltd, London) 1951

Hall, Rich & Friends *More Sniglets* (Collier Books – Macmillan Publishing Company, New York) 1985

Harmon, Jim *The Great Radio Comedians* (Doubleday & Company, Inc. Garden City, New York) 1970

Harris, Ed *Chalk-Talkers Comic Trickartoons* (Ed Harris) 1977.

Hart, Christopher *Drawing on the Funny Side of the Brain: How to Come Up with Jokes for Cartoonists and Comic Strips* (Watson-Guptill Publications, New York) 1998

Helitzer, Mel *Comedy Techniques of Writers & Performers* (Lawhead Press, Athens, Ohio) 1984

Helitzer, Mel with Shatz, Mark *Comedy Writing Secrets 2nd Edition* (Writer's Digest Books, Cincinnati, Ohio) 2006

Hugill, Beryl *Bring On the Clowns* (Chartwell Books Inc.) (Seacaucus. New Jersey) 1980

Jessel, George *"Hello, Momma": Jessel's World-Famous Phone Conversations with His Momma, Plus Other Hilarious Essays, Jokes, and Skits* (The World Publishing Company, Cleveland and New York) 1946

Jones, Chuck *Chuck Amuck: The Life and Times of an Animated Cartoonist* (Avon Books, New York) 1989

Jones, Chuck *Chuck Reducks: Drawing from the Fun Side of Life* (Warner Books New York, NY) 1996

Josefsberg, Milt *Comedy Writing for Television & Hollywood* (Harper & Row, Publishers, New York) 1987

Josefsberg, Milt *The Jack Benny Show: The Live and Times of America's Best Loved Entertainer*, (Arlington House Publishers, New Rochelle, New York) 1977

Kachuba, John B., editor *How to Write Funny: Add Humor to Every Kind of Writing* (Writer's Digest Books, Cincinnati, Ohio) 2001

Kellevig, Christine Petrell *Bible Folding Stories: Old Testament Stories and Paperfolding Together as One* (Storytime Ink Inc., Broadview Heights, Ohio) 1993

Keaton, Buster and Samuels, Charles *My Wonderful World of Slapstick* (A Da Capo Paperback New York, NY) 1960

Keeshan, Bob *Good Morning Captain: 50 Wonderful Years with Bob Keeshan, TV's Captain Kangaroo* (Fairview Press, Minneapolis, Minnesota) 1996

Keeshan, Bob *Growing Up Happy* (Berkley Books, New York) 1989

Keane, Bil *The Family Circus Album: A 25th Anniversary Celebration* (Fawcett Columbine, New York) 1984

Kelly, Emmett with Kelley, F. Beverly *Clown: My Life in Tatters and Smiles* (Prentice-Hall, Inc. New York) 1954

Lahue, Kalton C. *Mack Sennett's Keystone: The Man, The Myth, and the Comedies* (A. S. Barnes and Co. Inc. Cranbury, New Jersey) 1971

Leeflang, Thomas *The World of Comedy* (Windward, Leicester, England) 1988

Linkletter, Art *Kids Say the Darndest Things!* (Prentice Hall, Inc., Englewood Cliffs, N.J.) 1957

Marx, Arthur *Red Sketton: An Unauthorized Biography* (E. P. Dutton, New York) 1979

Maltin, Leonard *The Great Movie Comedians: From Charlie Chaplin to Woody Allen* (Harmony Books, New York) 1982

Montanaro, Tony and Montanaro, Karen Hull *Mime Spoken Here" The Performers Portable Workshop* (Tony and Karen Montanaro) 1995

McCabe, John *Charlie Chaplin* (Doubleday & Company, Inc. Garden City, New York) 1978

McCabe, John, text, Kilgore, Al, compilation, Bann, Richard W., filmography *Laurel & Hardy* (Bonanza Books, NY) 1983

McNamara, Brooks *Step Right Up* (University Press of Mississippi, Jackson) 1996

Mermin, Rob and Curwitt, Rob *Circus Smirkus: 25 Years of Running Home to the Circus!* (The Circus Barn inc. Greensboro, Vt) 2012

Miller, Vicky "Tongue Twisters" *Clowning Around* (World Clown Association) September 1991

Mitchell, Glenn *The Chaplin Encyclopedia,* (B.T. Batsford Ltd., London) 1997

Moody, Jr., Raymond A. *Laugh After Laugh: The Healing Power of Humor* (Headwaters Press, Jacksonville, FL) 1978

Oppenheimer, Jess with Oppenheimer, Greg *Laughs, Luck... and Lucy: How I Came to Create the Most Popular Sitcom of All Time* (Syracuse University Press) 1996

O'Sullivan, Judith *The Great American Comic Strip: One Hundred Years of Cartoon Art* (A Bulfinch Press Book) 1990

Otto, Beatrice K. *Fools Are Everywhere: The Court Jester Around the World* (The University of Chicago Press, Chicago) 2001

Perret, Gene *Comedy Writing Workbook* (Sterling Publishing Co., Inc. New York) 1990

Perret, Gene *Damn! That's Funny! Writing Humor You Can Sell!* (Quill Driver Books, Sanger, CA.) 2005

Perret, Gene *The New Comedy Writing Step by Step* (Quill Driver Books/Word Dancer Press, Inc., Sanger, CA.) 2007

Popov, Oleg *Russian Clown* (Macdonals, London) 1970

Reilly, Adam *Harold Lloyd "The King of Daredevil Comedy"* (Collier Books, New York) 1977

Remy, Tristan *Clown Scenes* (Ivan R. Dee, Chicago) 1962

Rosenbloom, Joseph *Daffy Definitions* (Sterlling Publishing Co, Inc., New York) 1983

Saks, Sol *The Craft of Comedy Writing* (Writer's Digest Books, Cincinnati, Ohio) 1985

Schneider, Richard H. *Why Christmas Trees Aren't Perfect* (Abingdon Press, Nashville) 1988

Schulz, Clair *Fibber McGee and Molly On the Air 1935–1959 Revised and Enlarged Edition* (Bear Manor Media, Albany, Georgia) 2015

Shalit, Gene *Laughing Matters: A Celebration of American Humor* (Doubleday & Company, Inc. Garden City, New York) 1987

Sklar, Marty *Dream It! Do it! My Half-Century Creating Disney's Magic Kingdoms* (Disney Editions Deluxe) 2013

Skretvedt, Randy *Laurel and Hardy: The Magic Behind the Movies* (Moonstone Press, Beverly Hills, CA) 1987

Snowberg, Richard *The Caring Clowns: How Humor, Smiles, and Laugher Overcome Pain, Suffering, and Loneliness* (Visual Magic, La Crosse, WI) 1992

Snowberg, Richard *Clowning for Children* (Visual Magic, La Crosse, WI) 1982

Snowberg, Richard *The Clown In You: A Basic Textbook* (Visual Magic, La Crosse, WI) 1985

Speaight, George *The Book of Clowns,*(MacMillan Publishing Co. Inc, New York) 1980

Stumpf, Charles and Price, Tom *Heavenly Days! The Story of Fibber McGee and Molly* (The World of Yesterday, Waynesville, NC) 1987

Tarbell, Harlan *Chalk Talks for Sunday Schools* (T.S. Denison & Co., Chicago) 1928

Tarbell, Harlan *Chalk Talks for Stunts* (T.S. Denison & Co., Chicago) 1926

Tarbell, Harlan *The Tarbell Course in Magic Volume* 8 (D. Robbins & Co. Inc. Brooklyn, NY) 1993

Thomas, Bob *Walt Disney The Art of Animation: The Story of the Disney Studio Contribution to a New Art* (Golden Press, Inc., New York) 1958

Towsen, John H. *Clowns* (Hawthorn Books, Inc.) 1976

Treadwell, Bill *50 Years of American Comedy* (Exposition Press, New York) 1951

Vorhaus, John *The Comic Toolbox: How to Be Funny Even If You're Not* (Silman-James Press, Los Angeles) 1994

Walker, Mort *Backstage at the Strips* (A & W Visual Library) 1975

Wertheim, Arthur Frank *Radio Comedy* (Oxford University Press, Oxford) 197

Whiting, Percy H. *How to Speak and Write with Humor* (McGrawoHill Book Company, In. New York) 1959

Wilde, Larry *The Great Comedians Talk About Comedy* (The Citadel Press, New York) 1968

Wiley, Jack *Basic Circus Skills* (Stackpole Books, Harrisburg, PA) 1974

Wilson, A. E. *The Story of Pantomime* (Home and Van Thal, London) 1949

Woerner, Gail Hughbanks *Fearless Funnymen: History of the Rodeo Clown* (Eakin Press, Austin, Texas) 1993

Wooten, Patty *Compassionate Laughter: Jest for Your Health* (Commune-A-Key Publishing, Salt Lake City, UT) 1996

Wright, Barton *Clowns of the Hopi: Tradition Keepers and Delight Makers* (Northland Publishing, Flagstaff, AZ) 1994

Young, Jordan R. *The Laugh Crafters: Comedy Writing in Radio and TV's Golden Age* (Past Times Publishing Co., Beverly Hills, CA) 1999

Youngman, Henny *Henny Youngman's 10,000 One-liners: An Encyclopedia of One-Liners from "The King of One-Liners* Edited by Ed Shanaphy (Ballynote Books, Katonah, NY) 1989

Super Circus DVD (Alpha Home Entertainment, Narberth, PA) 2008

★ ★ ★

ACKNOWLEDGEMENTS

M Y PARENTS, BRUCE L. Johnson and Irene R. Johnson were very supportive of my career. At least my mother was after she got over the shock of me changing my major in college from pre-med to technical theater. My father was an industrial arts teacher and helped me build some of my props. He was also my most important critic.

The support of my wife, Carole, has been invaluable. She was also a clown so she understood what I was doing. We worked in different venues so we could encourage each other without being competitive. I have made important changes in my material based on her thoughtful guidance.

Sally "Hobo Kelly" Baker and Bev "Rebo" Bergeron were clowns that I watched on TV while growing up. They both greatly influenced my concept of clowning. I particularly appreciated their gentle approach.

Helen Cure was my high school American Literature Teacher. She was the person who discovered my writing ability and encouraged me to pursue it. In recent years, I have taken some wonderful writing classes taught by Beth Jusino who helped me learn how to navigate the modern publishing world.

Pastor Tom Lange was serving at the church where I was a member when I began clowning. He was the person who got me involved in Gospel Clown Ministry. He loved to use visual aids in his sermons. He had heard of clowns performing routines that taught spiritual lessons. Neither of us had seen any of them perform. So, we developed our own style. He would write the lesson that he wanted to present, and I would make some suggestions for how my routines could be adapted to those topics. Together we worked on creating the final script. Our concept was that I was preaching the sermon without saying a word. Tom worked as my straightman and asked questions about what I was doing. By the time he understood, everyone in the congregation understood all of our symbolism. We did an annual sermon together for nearly two decades.

Herb Camburn taught many of my university technical theater classes. He helped me develop my work ethic and taught me that education and developing your talent is a lifetime effort. He also taught me how to critique my own work and that of others.

Charles "Doc" Boas, the founder and director of Circus Kirk, and D.R. Miller, the owner and producer of the Carson & Barnes Circus, provided me with opportunities that allowed me to break into the entertainment business.

Randy Pryor is a magician and juggler. I took his juggling classes for about ten years early in my career. I learned a lot about juggling from him. More importantly, I learned a lot about being an entertainer from him.

Cathy Gibbons was the editor the Laugh-Makers Variety Arts Magazine, She invited me to write a column for her publication. I learned a lot about writing by comparing my original text to her edited version. I also created my first original illustrations for that magazine. Being part of the talented staff of that magazine opened up many opportunities for me. Cathy was Co-Director first Laugh-Makers Variety Arts Conference. She, asked me to teach a comedy techniques class at the Conference and suggested that I write a companion book. A few years later, she invited me to teach a weekend intensive class on Comedy Techniques.

Richard Snowberg founded Clown Camp. He started his own independent publishing company to produce books that he wrote. He published my book *Comedy Techniques for Entertainers*. He also got me involved in the World Clown Association. Richard provided me with opportunities to teach and perform outside of the United States. He also gave me helpful feedback on my writing. I have worked with him frequently since 1986. There were very few years that we did not work together at least once. In some years we were in contact at least once a month.

Lee Mullally also begin writing for variety arts publications in the early 1980's. We began corresponding with comments on each other's articles and trading ideas. He and I served together on the World Clown Association Board and committees. He eventually became the Assistant Director of Clown Camp where I have worked closely with him. He is very creative and I have learned a lot from being around him.

Both Richard and Lee are Doctors of Education. They each retired from teaching in university education departments. They worked hard to develop the teaching ability of the Clown Camp Core Staff. At the end of each week that I served on staff; I received a thank you note from Lee providing positive feedback on things that he would like to see me continue to do.

The philosophy at Clown Camp is that everyone is a student and everyone has something to teach. Staff members are frequently seen taking classes led by other Staff members. Over the years, participants have shared many great ideas with me. Many staff members and participants have become lifelong friends. I am grateful for all that they have contributed to my life and career.

I met Patty Wooten at Clown Camp, and was fortunate to become her friend. I heard her speak many times in different settings about the benefits of humor. I heard her speak to medical professionals, hospital volunteers, members of the Association for Applied Therapeutic Humor, and groups of clowns. We also had many private conversations. I wrote some comedy material for her and had the pleasure of seeing her perform it. The sections with information provided by her did not come from any single source. They are a compilation of notes that I took each time I heard her speak.

Many of the drawings that I have done of my own performance are based on photographs taken by Merilyn Barret, Roger Grant, and Bruce L. Johnson.

Jim Howle and Angel Contreras are talented entertainers and talented visual artists. Both of them have provided me great encouragement and suggestions that have improved my illustrations.

David Persson taught me to perform live sound effects. I have continued to learn more about that art by working with the talented directors and voice artists associated with REPS (Radio Enthusiasts of Puget Sound). The REPS membership includes many radio historians. I appreciate learning from them. Also, through REPS, I have heard children of famous comedians talk about their parents.

I have enjoyed working with Colleen Sheehan at Ampersand Bookery. She guided me through the final steps of getting this book ready to be published. I appreciate her knowledge and advice. She did the internal layout design. She also designed the cover.

Merilyn Barrett is one of my favorite photographers as well as being a wonderful friend. She has taken many of the photos that I have used for publicity over the past dozen years. She took the author photo that I am using on this book.

INDEX

★ ★ ★